For this very reason, make every effort to add to your faith goodness; and to goodness, knowledge; and to knowledge, self-control; and to self-control, perseverance; and to perseverance, godliness; and to godliness, brotherly kindness; and to brotherly kindness, love. For if you possess these qualities in increasing measure, they will keep you from being ineffective and unproductive in your knowledge of our Lord Jesus Christ. But if anyone does not have them, he is nearsighted and blind, and has forgotten that he has been cleansed from his past sins.

Therefore, my brothers, be all the more eager to make your calling and election sure. For if you do these things, you will never fall, and you will receive a rich welcome into the eternal kingdom of our Lord and Savior Jesus Christ. (2 Peter 1:5-11)

Maximum Impact

The Power of Virtue

by
Steve Beier

Bloomington, IN  Milton Keynes, UK

AuthorHouse™
1663 Liberty Drive, Suite 200
Bloomington, IN 47403
www.authorhouse.com
Phone: 1-800-839-8640

AuthorHouse™ *UK Ltd.*
500 Avebury Boulevard
Central Milton Keynes, MK9 2BE
www.authorhouse.co.uk
Phone: 08001974150

© 2006 Steve Beier. All rights reserved.

No part of this book may be reproduced, stored in a retrieval system, or transmitted by any means without the written permission of the author.

First published by AuthorHouse 12/7/2006

ISBN: 978-1-4259-6359-0 (sc)

Printed in the United States of America
Bloomington, Indiana

This book is printed on acid-free paper.

Contents

TO THE READER	vii
INTRODUCTION *The Life that Reflects Christ*	1
THE STANDARD: *Reaching your Potential*	5
THE SPIRIT: *Where we live our Life*	19
THE HUMAN SYSTEM: *The Dynamics of Our Body*	36
THE PROBLEM: *The Battle for our Spirit*	48
THE TRUTH: *The Power to Unite*	71
THE MIND: *Where Choices are Formed*	84
THE EMOTIONS: *The Destructiveness of Impulse*	100
THE WILL: *The Purpose behind our Actions*	113
THE LIFE OF VIRTUE: *The Fuel for our System*	130
THE CORE VIRTUES: *The Means to Achieve Maximum Impact*	146

THE VIRTUOUS LIFE:
The Power to Live Right   168

THE GLORY:
The Passion of God for His Glory   187

THE TRAINING:
The Process of Maximum Impact   205

CONCLUSION
Jesus Most Precious   223

BIBLIOGRAPHY   227

ENDNOTES   231

To the Reader

This book is about how to achieve Maximum Impact for Christ in your life, and in the lives of others.

In these pages, and through God's Word, you'll learn how to take Biblical principles and apply them to every part of your life. Jesus Christ is Lord of salvation, human life, nonhuman life, creation and everything in between. He is King of kings and Lord of lords (Rev 19:16). He makes all the laws and administers them as well. The Bible pursues this even further:

> "For by him all things were created: things in heaven and on earth, visible and invisible, whether thrones or powers, or rulers or authorities; all things were created by him and for him. He is before all things, and in him all things hold together." (Col 1:16-17)

Once this is understood we will come to see that God is the Maker of all things and the Sustainer of them. Thus to study His creation and understand specifics about it is to learn of God. Studying the Bible will help us to understand this world and all that is in it. By knowing God more and more we can live life as He has ordered it. We will understand the laws that apply to material and nonmaterial things.

As a tennis enthusiast I have learned that sports are a microcosm of life and that sports can train us for life more than life can train us for a sport. The apostle Paul spoke numerous times about races, most likely track and field, in his letters (Acts 20:24, 1 Cor 9:24, Gal 2:2, Gal 5:7, 2 Tim 4:7 and Heb 12:1). By comparing our life as a believer in Christ to running, he shows, by way of a sports analogy, that how we train for a sport can help us prepare for life.

Today we play a sport to win instead of playing a sport to grow in virtue and character. Winning must not be the primary or even secondary reason for competing in a sport. Personal growth in our moral fiber and growth in godliness is our goal. When Christ dominates your life, the world of sports becomes a training ground for Biblical principles, which in turn become the ground rules for living.

When Jesus dominates all you are and do, you bring glory to Him by using your abilities to the fullest of your potential. As Christians, we bear His name, and we must not dishonor it by giving less than our best. Our highest charge and greatest joy is to maximize the use of His gifts in our lives.

As an athlete and coach in the game of tennis, I have come to find more knowledge of the game of tennis in the Bible than I have in the latest magazines and tennis books. I have learned how, just as in life, Biblical truths apply to sports. As a result, I've improved both my life, and my game.

This point is made brilliantly in the movie hit of the 1980's *"Chariots of Fire."* Eric Liddel was a runner who ran for God and broadcast to the world God's talents in him. Under no circumstances would he surrender his core Christ-centered beliefs to win or compete in a race. At one point in the movie when he is explaining to his sister why he runs and competes as he does he says this,

> "God made me fast and when I run I feel His pleasure."

Another scene in the movie shows Liddel refusing to run a race on Sunday, because it is the Lord's Day. The top officials can't understand why he won't give in on this principle. One official comments to the other something like this,

> "His running is so much a part of who he is, that you can't separate one from the other."

In other words, his godliness and Christ-centered life are interwoven with his love of running. So, Eric Liddel competed as a runner in the world made by God with his body given to him by God. He ran to reflect the Glory of God. Anything else would have been blasphemy.

God made each one of us and only when we know Him as our Maker, Savior and Mediator do we come to understand all other areas of life. Once we do, we will come to appreciate our specific gifts and talents and use them for the Glory of God, just as Eric Liddel did. We will become more like Him and ultimately reflect more of Him in our lives. If we don't know Him as Savior and Lord none of this will matter.

May you find in these pages the power to deliver Maximum Impact for Christ in your life.

Steve Beier
August 2006

Introduction

The Life that Reflects Christ

"The supreme purpose of the Christian religion is to make men like God in order that they may act like God."

A. W. Tozer

We all have impact in life, the question is, is it a lot or a little? Is it for good or for bad? Is it temporal impact or eternal impact? As Christians, our reason for existence is to have a maximum impact, for the ultimate good, which is Christ, for eternity. We have one lifetime to do this and that is all. The question is how do we do this?

How we live must reflect what we believe. This being said, the life of a Christian must reflect who Christ is and what He taught. This is often the exception rather than the rule in Christianity today. God never planned it to be this way.

A man once had his hat and coat stolen. The thief then went on and robbed a bank in this stolen hat and coat. The thief then escaped discarding the hat and coat on the way out. The coat had the original owners name and address in it so the police went to his house and arrested him for robbing the bank. He of course was innocent but the police said your hat and coat were identified as those worn by the thief.

Today many Christians are like the thief — walking around in Christ's coat but not acting like Christ — they are acting like themselves. Simply because you wear someone else's coat does not make you act like that person. How you act will reflect your personality, not theirs. The other part of this is that the owner's character is the one that gets scarred.

In our society many people are wearing Christ's jacket but acting like themselves. It is the name of Jesus that gets covered in mud. We as Christians must become more and more like Jesus, not continue on as we always have. A.W. Tozer notes this about the regeneration that must take place in Christians,

> "True religion leads to moral action. The only true Christian is the practicing Christian…God always acts like Himself wherever He may be and whatever He may be doing. When God became flesh and dwelt among us He did not cease to act as He had been acting from eternity…In whatsoever He did He was holy, harmless and separate from sinners and higher than the highest heaven…He (God) enters a human nature at regeneration as He once entered human nature at the incarnation and acts as becomes God, using the nature as a medium of expression for His moral perfections."[1]

God dwells, makes His abode, in regenerated people. Therefore followers of Christ should act like Christ.

Jesus Christ lived a holy and righteous life; so should Christians. Jesus obeyed the commands of God; so should Christians. Jesus lived a life of virtue; so should Christians. The problem is, so few Christians reflect Christ. To a watching world, Christians are hypocrites, "holier than thou." They talk a good life but often don't live it. Gandhi said, "I like their Christ, but I don't like their Christians."

How we live is who we are, and who we are is how we live. Let that thought sink in because what we do with our life is critical. The Bible calls us to live a righteous, holy and godly life — a life that is obedient to the commands of God. One that bears fruit for the Kingdom of God (John 15:5-8) and one that loves God with all our heart, soul, mind and strength (Mark 12:29-30). This is the life God created us to live.

Tozer again noted,

> "Rightly understood, faith is not a substitute for moral conduct but a means toward it. The tree does not serve in lieu of fruit but as an agent by which fruit is secured.

Fruit, not trees, is the end God has in mind...so Christ-like conduct is the end of Christian faith."[2]

God gives us the ability and power to become like Him. It is through Him, with Him and in Him that we can become so. This is who God has created us to become. *Because of who He is we can become all we were created to be.*

This is the life of virtue, the life of Christ. In virtue we have power. In virtue we have perfect goodness. Virtue has tremendous power to bring out the best in us. It must be desired more than pure gold and then we must train to acquire it as an athlete trains for a competition.

Virtue allows us to impact the world around us. To become like Christ gives our life maximum impact. This then is the life well lived and rightly lived. Virtue, as Saint Thomas Aquinas said, is that which makes its subject good, absolutely. Aquinas said this of virtue,

> "...virtue is that which makes its possessor good, and his work good likewise...they make the work to be actually good, and the subject good absolutely."[3]

Jesus Christ is the greatest model and measure of virtue. He constantly taught about it and lived it out. He made the best use of His allotted time on earth. He utilized every minute to its fullest extent.

There are a lot of men and women who lived very impressive lives. They range from past presidents to saints of old; from Godly men and women who changed history to great sports figures...but none can compare to the impact Jesus Christ had on the world, two thousand years ago and today. He impacted our world more than any man ever has or will. He did more for mankind in His thirty-three years on earth than any society ever has or will. He lived a life of virtue.

We must become holy, as He is holy. The better we get to know Him the more we will love Him. The more we love Him the greater our desire is to serve Him. The greater our desire to serve Him the more we will reflect Him. We will then bear fruit for His Kingdom.

The problem for most of us is we just go on sinning and hope God will lower His standards. NO, God wants us to raise ours. He wants us to be righteous and holy. This is the life that Jesus demands of His followers. It is the life we must aspire to. It is also the life so few reach. The standard for our life is not man made but God ordained. It is the life He has called us to live, a life of virtue. When we grow in virtue, we grow in power, ability and opportunity and reach the pinnacle of human life, unity with God.

This book is dedicated to helping you grow in virtue and thus grow in holiness. My desire is that you not only become more like our LORD but also grow in love for Him and unity with Him in the process.

The Standard:

Reaching your Potential

...it is a wretched taste to be grateful with mediocrity when the excellent lies before us.

Isaac D'Israeli, 1834

We are called to be great! We may not lead a country out of slavery, or encourage a "war-beaten" nation to keep fighting, or be martyred for the cause of the righteous, but in our own world we were formed for greatness. Hand-picked and empowered by God to be His instrument in a broken-down world.

God not only tells us we can be great, He tells us we can become like Christ. He tells us that Christ must be formed in us.

> "My dear children, for whom I am again in the pains of childbirth until Christ is formed in you..." (Gal 4:19)

God uses ordinary men and makes them extraordinary. He takes tragedy and turns it into triumph. He often uses trials and suffering as His classroom. He doesn't work by man's methods either, but by His own ways in His own time. He does this out of love and because He has great plans for those who love Him (Jer 29:11). Look at a sample of His work:

- He took a murderer, Moses, and used him to lead the Israelites out of Egypt.

- He used a Shepard boy to slay a giant and then formed a nation out of him in King David.
- He took Job's great loss of a house, his children, his servants and his health. By this refining process God taught him things he could never have learned in prosperity.
- He took Joseph, let him be sold into slavery and spend years in jail. Through all of this he learned much and eventually became the Pharaoh's right hand man.

Think of what God has planned for you if you will let Him. He has plans of greatness but we must align our plans with His. The standard we are striving for is Christ and we must seek this through knowing who He is and how He lived. Jesus was holy, righteous, loving, truthful, graceful and so much more. This is the life, the prize we are reaching for (Phil 3:12-14). It is the standard of measurement that God has designed for you to reach (1 Thes 4:1-8).

As Christ followers, all are called to this same achievement level. We are called to live out the Sermon on the Mount (Matthew 5-7), exhibit the fruits of the Spirit (Galatians 5: 22-26), and love as Paul talked about in 1 Corinthians 13. To be able to do this we must go past our normal daily living and be Christ to a watching world. Not by acting the part as an actor in a play but by loving as He loved, thinking as He thought, and serving as He served.

To do this we must have increased abilities and capabilities (Matt 19:26). As Christians we do because we have God living in us. We have God in us working through us to enable us to be like Christ (John 14:26). The Apostle Paul said: "…for it is God who works in you to will and to act according to His good purpose." (Phil 2:13) God will grow us in virtue if we allow Him. This is seen in the fruits of the Spirit which are:

- Love
- Joy
- Peace
- Patience
- Kindness
- Goodness
- Gentleness
- Self-control
- Faithfulness

This is who we are called to be as Paul describes in (Gal 5:22-23). These characteristics are to be the descriptions of all Christians: joyful, loving, kind, patient, and so on. We must exhibit godliness and holiness, for that is what God commands. In fact we can do it with a heart of praise and a mind filled with genuine love to our fellow man.

As we grow and build virtue in our lives as believers in Christ, we grow in our relationship with the Holy Spirit. This is true because we are now working for Him and not against Him. We have new hearts and renewed minds in touch with the Living God. The Apostle Paul said, "That is because it isn't you but rather God in you conforming you to His Son." (Col 3:10-11) This new standard, Christ, will raise the bar of the expectations you have for your life. It is no longer man as the measure of all things but Christ.

The Problem

There are several problems with this concept. The first is that if you try harder to be your best you seldom accomplish this. We try to do it on our own and can't. We are born with a sinful nature and toward sin we are pulled. It is only when we come to Christ as Savior that we become born anew (John 3). You can't become better by trying to be better. You can only get there by admitting you can't do it on your own. God must remake you from the inside out.

The more you think about it and try to accomplish it alone, the less you are able to do it. It is not a question of total understanding but ability. We don't have the power to defeat our sinful nature, only God does. It is Superman saying "Hey I can't fly on planet Krypton, so I can't fly here on earth." He can't fly because he understands the concept of gravity and air speed velocity. He can fly because he is not from here. As Christians we are born as new creations in Christ and therefore live new lives here on earth. We died to our old nature and are born to a new nature, that being to serve God in righteousness (Rom 6: 1-23). God does this in us.

The second problem is once we exhibit godliness we think we have it down. *Yesterday's triumphs are today's defeats.* In other words, we can't live off what we did yesterday. We must win those same battles today. We must do this each and every day and never think we have this mastered. We will never have sin mastered. Each day brings new trials and challenges.

The last problem is, we experience this righteous living so infrequently that we have given up on this standard of holiness. We get in a critical situation and blow it. *Instead of demanding more of ourselves we hope for less in the situation.* We hope for easy days where no trials or difficulties arise. This way it will be much easier to not sin. Everyone is at their best when things are going their way. It is when things aren't going their way that they need to become better. This is what made Superman become who he was. When the test came, it was only then he became Superman, for only then were his extra abilities required.

Most of us are usually at our worst in the most demanding situations, thus we sin and sin often in them. The reality is we need to be at our best when the situation demands the most from us in order to be righteous. When we are weak we must become stronger. This is exactly what the Apostle Paul says about weaknesses. God strengthens us in them and makes us stronger through them (2 Cor 12:9-10).

We must also understand that God uses these difficulties to form us and shape us. The Apostle Peter tells us the worst of situations will help mold us to be who God created us to be. It is the gold refined in the fire; the fire gets rid of the impurities (1 Peter 1:3-9). The apostle Paul was like this. Notice a short glimpse of his life:

> "…been in prison more frequently, been flogged more severely, and been exposed to death again and again. Five times I received from the Jews the forty lashes minus one. Three times I was beaten with rods, once I was stoned, three times I was shipwrecked, I spent a night and a day in the open sea, I have been constantly on the move, I have been in danger from rivers…If I must boast I will boast of the things that show my weakness." (2 Cor 11:23-26, 30)

Paul isn't complaining about all the bad experiences he has lived through, instead he tells of how all of this has strengthened him. As if to say I became the man of God because of all of this. He trusted God so much that no matter what situation he was in, he knew God would use it to mold him into Christ's image. God would be with him through it all and draw him closer. This would also result in the recognition of his need for Him more and more.

These tough times are when most of us are at our worst. We must be our best in tough situations and stop hoping for these to all go away. We must realize these help us attain the ability to be more like Christ (Phil 2:1-12).

We run from these tests and storms. We determine to not allow them to happen to us as best as we can. We hope all the breaks go our way, that we get all the "good bounces" so to speak. When life doesn't turn out this way and a test or storm arrives, we panic. We have little or no expectation of being our very best in the very worst of situations. We don't see the learning and growth that can come from these tests. We usually only hope to avoid them. The reality is these storms are what Christ is training us for.

The Inner and the Outer Self

One of the main reasons people seldom reach the godly standard Jesus has called them to is that they focus on the physical aspect of their life and don't understand the spiritual aspect. They don't understand that there are two parts to the human system. There is the physical aspect, which is our body, the part we can see. There is also the spiritual aspect, the part we can't see, such as our emotions, thoughts, and desires.

The focus is on the physical body because we can actually see it and the results of it. This is the observable world we live in. Our body seems easier to direct and therefore easier to get instant feedback from. Take for example the game of golf. If I miss a shot I can practice my stroke more. Maybe the reason I missed the shot was because of a lack of focus or I tried the wrong club. It is easier to change my swing mechanics than it is to change my thinking on the course.

We can't see our spiritual side therefore it is harder to prove that it exists. In fact many doubt we even have a spiritual side. To help get a better handle on our spiritual side we must first define the term spiritual. The definition we will use is "the vital principle or animating force within living human beings, the essential and activating principle of a person."

As an example of the reality of our spiritual side let's consider how you would explain your personality, your thoughts or your emotions to someone. If I asked you to show me where they are in your body, like where is your stomach or your lungs, where would I go to find them? If I can't see them, does that mean they don't exist? Of course not.

We can't see our spiritual side, but yet we still have thoughts, ideas, feelings, desires, reasoning, logic, a will and so on. The hidden world of the self is our spirit. The emotions of love, anger, fear, doubt, hope are all real but we can't see them, yet we feel them or experience them in our inner being. This is the inner part of who we are. It gives us our consciousness and the sense that we are alive. This is all attributed to our spirit.

Dallas Willard says, "We are constantly aware of our spiritual side. We know immediately that it is what really matters. We pay more attention to it, in ourselves and in others, than to anything else. *For the spiritual is simply life.*"[4] In fact the spiritual side is the key to controlling the physical part of us. How we live and how we operate happens inside us.

The spiritual side is the key to getting us to become more like Christ. This is true because it is the inner workings of our human self.

The three key ingredients to our spirit are: our thoughts, our emotions and our will.

Our thoughts can lead us to fear or to trust. Fear is often bad because it paralyzes you and prevents you from acting. Trust on the other hand gives you confidence and enables you to act.

Our emotions are the feelings that are inside us that cause us to be angry with the person who "cuts us off" in traffic, or patient with them. Anger drains our ability to perform whereas patience gives us staying power to hang in there.

Our will, or our inner desires and motives, are the deep hidden drives that determine how we should act. It directly leads us to get divorced or stay in an unhappy marriage. It as well empowers us or destroys us.

The better we understand who we are and how we operate, the easier it will be to direct our outward actions.

It's About the Process not the Outcome

Many people try to focus on results instead of focusing on the process. God is more concerned about the process than He is about the outcome. Here's what I mean. An athlete will try to win the match or game, and this becomes their driving force. "Winning is everything and losing is nothing." A businessman can focus on just making more money. The "bottom line" is all they care about. Our social life can focus on pleasure and how can we maximize our happiness by sex, drugs, alcohol, recreational sports and the like. In the process anything that deters from winning, money or pleasure must be taken out of our life.

The dilemma of focusing on the outcome instead of focusing on the process ignores the most critical aspect of growing in godliness. It discounts the methods, motives and means that drive these outcomes. When we are outcome-focused the ends outweigh the means. That is, the person isn't concerned as much with performance, but rather with winning, making more money or maximizing our pleasure. For instance the athlete can cheat, intimidate an opponent or use gamesmanship to help him win. This becomes OK as long as he wins. He might have a terrible performance, but if winning is the main concern, he will seek it out at all costs. The businessman can embezzle, steal, lie, deceive, or intimidate to make more money. This often will help him make more money. The social scene becomes one of illegitimate pleasures of adultery, illegal drugs, alcohol abuse, and other harmful desires to feed our pleasures. These improper motives, methods and means are called sin.

Clearly when we set winning, money, or pleasure as our goal we can accomplish them in many wrong ways. God works on our spirit in the process whereas sin often results as we focus on the outcome. When we seek to reach the standard of Christ, the central issue is the process. The process is where we think, we deal with our emotions and our motives are revealed. Godliness and righteousness become the key issues for the man of God. He seeks to develop them in the process of everyday living. He then leaves the outcome up to God.

One process God uses to form holiness in us is by how we deal with different circumstances that occur to us. God desires to have us act in these situations in controlled and righteous ways, not react in spontaneous, malicious ways. When we **act** we are in control of our behavior and when we **react** the situation is in control of our behavior. God demands us to be in full command of ourselves at all times and in all situations.

These knee-jerk reactions often reveal the inner personalities we have. If you want to see who a person really is, watch how they react when they are angry or irritated. This is where it is much more difficult to hide the real "you." These reactions happen in our everyday lives quite often. We react to life instead of acting in life. *We must be in total control of ourselves at all times in our life. What happens to us is less important than how we react to it.* Anytime we are not "in control" we will not behave as we should.

We must be in full control of ourselves at all times of our life. We can't control other people but we *can* control our reactions to them and the situations we find ourselves in. Life isn't so much what happens to us but how we deal with what happens to us.

Trying or tempting situations become the fertilizer to grow our inner sinful natures. We are called to grow in the Spirit of Christ by suppressing our inner sinful natures. Virtue is the result when we act in godly ways and vice results when we react in sinful, malicious ways. Achieving virtue consistently without Christ is impossible, for only He can give us the power to overcome our sinful nature.

We must also understand what we can and cannot control. We can control ourselves but we cannot totally control other people and situations. I cannot control another driver cutting me off in traffic but I can control how I respond to him. I cannot control what my neighbor will say to me, but I can control what I say back to him. If we focus on what we can control in life and not worry as much about what we can't control, we will have an actionable focus that is more likely to lead to a positive outcome. Therefore the focus must be on the controllable not the uncontrollable. Much of life is out of your hands so stop trying to act like you can control it all. Rather, focus on what is in your control and give it your whole attention.

The key is to control ourselves. We must control our thoughts, emotions, desires, words, and actions ... this is what we must be responsible for. *We must **act** in the best way (with virtue) to get the maximum results. We **can** control ourselves 100% of the time.* When this becomes the focus we will have much less anxiety because it is what we **can't control** that usually causes the stress in us. Stress comes in when we try to control the uncontrollable. The effort spent on things you can control becomes the best use of your time.

It is all about Choices

We make thousands of choices every day of our lives. Some of them are good, and some of them are bad. Reaching the standard God has set for us in Christ requires us to make only the best choices and no "just OK" or bad choices. We often don't realize all of the choices we make. This includes the obvious ones from the clothes we wear to the thoughts we think. This barely scratches the surface of all the decisions we make. We choose the words we speak, the aspirations we seek, the use of our time, how we spend our money, what food we eat...

Once a person understands how many decisions they are making, they need to seek to better control these choices. There is a lot involved in these decisions. Each is made up of many little decisions. They form links in a chain, and each individual link determines the overall strength of the chain as a whole. They interact with each other as well and help improve or degrade the information to be used in other decisions.

The little decisions are made from the information, attitudes, research, worldviews and abilities we have at the time of each choice. These resources then become the groundwork for the choices we make. They become the foundation that our lives will be built on. This foundation can be made of sand or rock. If we build our lives on sand our lives can be swept away in the first storm. If we build our lives on rock we will be able to withstand the toughest of conditions (Matt 7:24-27). That is why only "best choices" are acceptable.

We need to understand all that we control when we make choices. Each of the alternatives from which we choose will be of vital importance to future choices and options available to us. Every choice, big or small, has consequences. Learning more about becoming better decision makers should challenge us to pick the best sources from which to gather information. The sources available are numerous and must be sorted out thoroughly. All sources are not good sources. In fact, many are inaccurate or unreliable. We must be very meticulous in evaluating all information.

The choices we make will have immediate impact on the outcome. They will have impact on our behaviors and attitudes as well.

Once you understand how many choices you are making, you must understand that only the best ones will help you perform better. The more you understand the power behind your choices, to help or hurt your performance, the more you will seek to better educate yourself on what these best choices are. *Each choice has the potential for infinite good or catastrophic bad.*

Another problem is that many decisions are made in split seconds. Since we have so little time to choose, we must seek to have these decisions made ahead of time. In other words the more choices you have to make in a short amount of time the easier it will be to make wrong choices. There becomes an information overload. If we can narrow the choices down to one — the best one — choosing the right one is automatic. There is only one choice, and you can't make the wrong choice because there is only one option.

To succeed at this we must have guidelines in place ahead of time, before we start reacting to situations. Deciding ahead of time to be truthful, honest, merciful, kind, generous and the like are guidelines that make these choices easier at the time we need to make them. Think of driving a car; the solid yellow lines on curves and hills, the traffic lights at intersections, the speed limit signs and knowing which side of the road to drive on are all guidelines put in place ahead of time, limiting our choices to the safe and lawful.

In dealing with life's situations, we must use the standard of Christ in all the decisions we will make. This will severely limit the choices we have to make, especially in short time spans where we have only seconds to decide. For instance in our daily life we must decide to always tell the truth or be kind in all situations. If we get cut off in traffic, kindness will be our guide to how we must respond. Once we do this we have drastically narrowed down our choices. Better choices lead to better performance, and better performance leads to better outcomes.

This is what makes top athletes so good. They have few choices to make, especially in split-second situations. They understand what they can and can't do — what they do or don't want to do — based on guidelines established in their training. These are determined ahead of time before the play is ever run. So too, we must decide ahead of time how we must act as Christ-Followers.

Investing our Time not Spending our Time

In most major sports a good rule-of-thumb is: the ball is only in play one-third of the time. Say, for instance, a football game ... the average length of a pro or college game is about three hours, but the ball is only in play about sixty minutes, or roughly one-third of that time. This is true for basketball, hockey, tennis and even golf. In most sports, the ball is only in play one-third of the time. So two-thirds of the time — the majority of the game — is non-playing time. When used properly, all that non-playing time makes the time actually spent playing much more effective and productive. Used improperly, or not at all, it can hinder your ability to perform at your best. The question is how well do you use this time? This is another key to improved performance.

This is even more vital in life as well. Most of our free time determines our worldview and outlook in life. This then affects the choices we will make. If we watch TV eighteen hours per week, as the average American does, we will develop a Hollywood mindset and not even know it. Contrast this to time spent in Bible study, time spent reading books by the world's best thinkers, time spent with another person accounting for how you live your life, quality personal time spent with your family, and so on. How well you use your free time will determine how well you do when key decisions must be made quickly.

This becomes the equivalent to studying for a test. The key to doing well on a test is not the taking of the test, but the studying for the test. The more we study, the better our chances to do well on it. This is even more critical on final exams. How well you study will determine how well you will perform. This same concept is true for life choices. If we want to do well in the "tests" and "trials" of life we must better use our "study" times. The better prepared we are, the better we will do come time for the test. This is true in all areas of our life.

One way people misuse their free time is by living in the past and not in the present. They spend great quantities of time thinking about past regrets, which they can't change anyway, instead of focusing on the present. You can only live in, and have an impact on, the present, the "right now." By living in the past the "could-haves," the "should-haves" and the "would-haves" control most of the thinking time. Living in the past brings regret and anger. Living in the present brings opportunity.

Another way this time is misused is by focusing on what we can't do instead of what we can do. We become negative in our thinking and therefore limit the opportunities we have. We must believe in our abilities and make the most of opportunities. *We must make our own breaks and not waste them.*

When you come to understand the importance of using this "free time" and how it is the key contributor to your future "performance time," you will regard it with the greatest value. We must invest our God given time not spend it frivolously. What we do or don't do with our time greatly affects the choices we make.

Training for Success

Training isn't supposed to be fun; it is supposed to improve your performance! Training is designed to get more out of you, and to get more out of yourself, you need to know yourself better. The human system is made up of 4 key elements. These elements are physical, mental, emotional and spiritual (your will). Jim Loehr said,

> "Human beings are complex energy systems …not simply one-dimensional. The energy that pulses through us is physical, emotional, mental, and spiritual (will). All four dynamics are critical, none is sufficient by itself and each profoundly influences the others. To perform at our best,

we must skillfully manage each of these interconnected dimensions of energy. Subtract any one from the equation and your capacity to fully ignite your talent and skill is diminished."[5]

Future chapters will deal with these four key areas in greater detail. Suffice for now to know these are 4 key areas in which we must train ourselves to perform better. Good training is not just physical. It should also be mental, emotional, and involve your inner will. When all 4 areas are incorporated, deeper and better training occurs.

Training must **enable** you to achieve higher levels of performance on a more regular basis, not **disable** you so your performance suffers because of it. We become disabled when behaviors are practiced that will be detrimental to us and corrupt our performance. Habits that are reinforced by poor training —such as gossip, dishonesty, lying, impatience, and anger — will disable us. These vices become programmed into us and become a way of life for us. Through repeated poor training habits, we will actually develop and acquire these vices in greater depth because we continue to repeat these wrong behaviors. It then becomes easier for us to react in anger when something doesn't go our way in an anxious moment. This will bring down your ability to perform under stress.

Many people don't even know they are practicing bad habits. They complain, "I keep trying harder but don't see the results." Advancement occurs when we practice skills internally, mentally and emotionally, as well as externally, physically. Just because you put time in training doesn't mean it is helping.

Take the example of studying for a test in school. You can read the textbook, but have little productivity. This is seen when kids watch TV or talk on the phone while studying. They are trying to study, but they are not very productive at it because mentally and emotionally they are not focused on the material. Spencer Johnson in his bestseller "Who Moved my Cheese?" noted,

"There is a big difference between activity and productivity."[6]

So it is with much in life, we must have our spirit and our body engaged at the same time. It is *quality and quantity* in training that makes it beneficial. Your training must change how you think, and reach your mind and emotions as well. It must affect your inner will, and when this occurs you will learn. This leads to changed behavior.

Training must **enable** you to reach new limits and force you to draw upon internal reserves from things such as Virtue and Truth. To do this will require you to give all you have, internally and externally. This will most assuredly be unpleasant, and even painful. It might not be fun, but that is not the purpose of training. Training is designed to improve you, not entertain you.

<u>The Well-Built House</u>

Ravi Zacharias tells the following story in his book "I Isaac Take Thee Rebekah"

> "There is a parable about a rich man who was going away on a long journey. Before he had left he hired a builder and said to him, "I will be gone for many months and I would like you to build me a house with the specifications I leave with you. I do not want you to substitute anything cheap for the genuine quality that I want. I am willing to pay the price for the best. And when I return I will pay you for it. But be sure to build it well."
>
> "When the rich man was gone the builder decided to cut corners and skimp here and there on things that wouldn't be noticed and would be hidden from the naked eye. The owner wouldn't notice these things. The months went by and the builder continued his sly ways that resulted in a house of poor quality while it looked expensive and solid."
>
> "Finally the day came when the rich man returned and inspected the house. After reviewing everything he said to the builder, "I have a surprise for you. Yes, I will pay for the house, but I want to present this house to you, for you and your family to live in. This is my gift to you."[7]

This parable illustrates how important the choices are that we make in our lives, for they become the house we will live in. Mr. Zacharias then makes this comment about the story,

> "You may be absolutely sure that as you build your life, so you will dwell. The single greatest lack of our time, perhaps of all time, is men and women of character, those whose lives are honest and whose transparency is real."[8]

We must seek to live in such a way as not to collect more trophies but to develop more virtue. This book is about the power of virtue formed in a human being and how it then becomes the fuel to run that individual. It is a daily process, not a one-time event.

The effect of the process is reaching the potential we have been called to in Christ. It is the well-built house God desires for each one of His children. Absolute virtue is the standard for each one of us. To achieve this we must train in such a way that enables us to reach the highest level on a regular basis. We must understand what we are training for. We must understand the keys to training that will make this possible. Finally we must know it is Christ in us who is managing the process, if we are believers in Him (Heb 12:2, Phil 1:6).

The Apostle Paul said,

> "Do you not know that in a race all runners run, but only one gets the prize? Run in such a way as to get the prize."
> (1 Cor 9:24).

The prize is Christ-likeness and we must seek this prize with all of our being. This is the race marked out for us. It is the race of life God has set us to run. We must train and run to get the prize. We will accept nothing less than our best performance everyday and in the toughest situations. This is a life that is well lived.

To achieve this, we must understand the makeup of the human system. We are spiritual beings. It is to this we now turn.

The Spirit:

Where we live our Life

Two artists of the ancient times competed to see who could paint the visible world most faithfully. "Now I shall prove to you that I am the best," said the first, showing the other a curtain which he had painted. "Well draw back the curtain," said the adversary, "and let's see the picture." "The curtain is the picture," replied the first with a laugh.

Nikos Kazanizakis

In our country today 84 percent of all Americans profess to be Christian[9]. They believe existence is more than just a physical life, detected only by the 5 senses. They believe in a spiritual existence that transcends physical death. It is this belief in a spiritual existence that forms the foundation of most of the world's religions, including Christianity. Does our sense of sight, smell, sound, touch, and taste reveal all there is, or is there more?

When you mention the term spiritual, people think of different things. Some think of spirits or ghosts, some of moral character, others of God and religion.

For Christians, spiritual has a special meaning as it relates to helping us achieve Christ-likeness. The spiritual part of our existence is inside each of us, existing apart from our physical bodies. It is the place where our inner will resides, directing our thoughts and molding our emotions. It is our moral center, our conscience, our guidance system. We can't see it, but still, it is there. It is what separates us from animals, which don't have such complex natures. Animals live only in the physical world around them and can live only a physical existence.

Human beings on the other hand have a much higher level of existence. Hank Hanegraff comments, "To say 'hominids' (prehistoric man) like Peking man and his partners are closely related to humans because both can walk is like saying that a humming bird and a helicopter are closely related because both can fly. The distance between an ape who cannot read or write and a descendant of Adam (human being) who can compose a musical masterpiece or send someone to the moon is the distance of infinity."[10]

What separates man is our spirit. The spirit is the inner being through which we think, we feel, we desire, and by way of which we heed our conscience (or don't!). It is the key that controls how we act in our external, physical body.

Most people live life with little if any understanding of how their own spirit works. They talk about "spirituality" but have little idea of how to grow spiritually. They act in ways that are contrary to what they think and don't understand why. By gaining a better understanding of how our spirit interacts and operates in us, we will better understand how living a righteous life is much more spiritual than physical.

The Spirit controls the Physical

Many people try to change behaviors by focusing on changing their actions. They think they can change habits they have acquired over the years by just wanting to change. Habits are hard to change because they are embedded in our mind, emotions and our will. Our behavioral process looks like this:

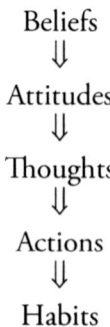

Beliefs
⇓
Attitudes
⇓
Thoughts
⇓
Actions
⇓
Habits

The beliefs we have about various events, ideas, circumstances, people and so on shape our attitude. The attitude we have then shapes our thoughts and our thoughts shape how we act. Finally after doing these behaviors enough times we form habits.

If you want to change a person's behavior you can't start by just telling them to change. This often just hits the physical part of them and never touches their beliefs. This is why cigarette smoking and so many other habits are so hard to change. You can't start at the bottom of the process you must start at the top with their beliefs. Long-term change must deal with and focus on the spiritual part of our being, for this is where we live our life.

So, what is the relationship between our spiritual being and religion? Bible scholar William Barclay said, "It is easy to confuse religion with religious practices …A man might do all the right religious activities and be far off from being a Christian, for Christianity is an attitude of the heart towards God and to man."

Religion is not the same as a relationship with the Living God. Religion is so often ritual and ceremony void of devotion (Isaiah 29:13, Ezekiel 33:31-33). This was the central issue Jesus dealt with in mankind. Actions and words to be genuine must come from the heart. Jesus constantly pointed this out (Matthew 15: 7-9, Mark: 7 1-23, Luke 6:46). The religious leaders hated Him for this.

So often in religion the physical acts don't touch the spiritual part of us. That is why "Christians" can go to church on Sunday and what they hear has no affect on them the rest of their week. For it to affect their actions the inner part must be touched and changed, too. You can't change behaviors in the long term without changing beliefs first. How we think dictates how we act.

The fact that our spirit is real and even more importantly that it controls what goes on in our physical body is essential if we are going to improve and change conduct. We must stop trying to **be** better people and instead **become** better. When we become better, we are transformed into a new creation. God gives us a new understanding and a relationship to Him. Thus we literally **become** new spiritual creations.

When we **become** better, we have realized our wrongful thinking, changed our beliefs and this then filters down to our actions. We think differently and thus act differently, and our actions reflect our change in beliefs. We not only acknowledge our wrongful actions — sins — we confess them (1John 1:9) and then we repent (Matt 4:17, Luke 13:1-5).

We as followers of Christ know God will change us spiritually (Ezek 36:26-27, John 3:3, Eph 2:10) and help us in our time of need (1 Cor. 10:13). This being said, we despise sin and desire to stop. We can't do this on our own. Only God can do it in us by creating us new. We thus **become** new creations.

The other way says I want to **be** better, but the reality is we don't have the power by ourselves to change. The difference is when we fail, or sin, most of the time we say, "Sorry, I will **be** better next time." The problem is nothing has changed inside us so we continue to repeat our wrong behavior and habits. When we try to **be** better, we hope that by trying harder next time we will do better. This aims at external actions not internal thoughts.

To try to do this on our own is like buying a new refrigerator and not plugging it in. The new refrigerator has no power to work of its own. If it has no source of power it is useless. The Holy Spirit in us is the power to change and become like Christ. Without the Holy Spirit, we have no power to change.

God will give us a new life that is open to His power, and a new spirit, through which we will act differently. The saying, "actions speak louder than words" is 100 percent accurate. If you want to know someone, watch what they do, not what they say. How we act tells who we are inside, revealing our hearts. Jesus talked about our fruit and how our actions reveal our inner desires and thoughts (Luke 6:43-45). He said:

> "By their fruit you will recognize them…Likewise every good tree bears good fruit but a bad tree bears bad fruit. A good tree cannot bear bad fruit and a bad tree cannot bear good fruit." (Matt 7:16-18)

We can't cover up who we really are inside for very long because our actions will eventually give us away.

Jesus expanded this teaching in Matthew 15.

> "Don't you see that whatever enters the mouth goes into the stomach and out of the body. But the things that come out of the mouth come out of the heart, and these make a man unclean. For out of the heart come evil thoughts, murder, adultery, sexual immorality, theft, false testimo-

ny, slander. These are what make a man 'unclean'" (Matt 15:17-20)

Here He said the sins of adultery, slander, murder, stealing, and so forth go on inside our inner thoughts. The actions we do are just carrying out our thoughts, which come from our heart — our attitudes and beliefs.

Some people think they can they can shortcut the process by mimicking actions they see in others — trying to get the results without the difficult work of examining their beliefs and modifying their attitudes. Even if you pick a good role model, this technique does not succeed.

Think of certain young people who idolize an outstanding baseball player. They want nothing more than to run or hit as well as their idol. So what do they do? When they play the game, they imitate and behave exactly as their favorite star does, buying the shoes, using the same glove and so on. They even hold the bat as he does or slide into base as he does. Will they succeed in performing as the star? No, because no matter how gifted they are, it is not the habits of the game that makes the star great; it is the preparation of the mind and emotions that flow into the body day in and day out in practice that provide the key. As Plato saw long ago,

> "There is an art of living, and the living is excellent only when the self is prepared in all the depths and dimensions of its beings (body and spirit)."[11]

To play well like the stars, we must train our minds and emotions in practice to be like the top athletes. Then our thoughts will flow into our body to help us perform at a higher level. The key to proper training is to train wiser, not try harder.

This is seen in the Bible when Israel was looking to pick a king to rule them. They looked mainly at physical appearance of potential candidates, they didn't worry about the spiritual side of the men. God eventually choose David, His appearance was not very good as far as strength and height were concerned, but he was a great man inside. God said this,

> "The Lord does not look at the things man looks at. Man looks at outward appearance, but the Lord looks at the heart." (1 Sam 16:7)

It is not enough, or even necessary, to "look the part." For great leaders, and mankind overall, the key is what goes on inside, not outward appearance.

Invisible concepts, Visible results

We can better understand the idea of spiritual beings when we consider concepts such as thought, logic, ideas, feelings, conscience, memory and emotions such as love or hate. These concepts can't be held in our hands or seen by our eyes yet they exist; we do them every day as we live our life. They affect all we do for the better or for the worse. The problem is because we can't see them they are more difficult to understand.

There are specific emotions and thoughts that we must develop in order to be more successful in what we undertake. These qualities are called virtues. Specific virtues such as courage, determination, encouragement and patience are vital to peak performance. These virtues need to be formed in us to make us better able to handle difficult situations. With them we can do great things, without them it will be tough to reach our full potential.

We will talk more about virtues in later chapters, but for now I want to briefly look at cultivating virtue in us, such as the virtue of courage. To develop more courage, we must understand what courage is, how it works, and the thought patterns that inspire it. Finally, to develop courage, we must do things that require courage.

We can build courage just like we build physical fitness. If we want to become more aerobically fit we must do things that work our heart and lungs more. To be more courageous we must pursue activities that require courage. We can grow more courageous just like we can become more physically fit.

There are also emotions, or vices, that will sabotage us in crucial times. Some of these are fear, anger, frustration, doubt and discouragement. When these vices are present, we will not perform anywhere near the potential God has called us to because these emotions sabotage our performance and ability to perform. When these vices are present, they get you to react improperly to situations. Each vice is a cancer. Cancer is destructive and spreads. A little cancer will eventually spread to the whole body unless it is stopped.

When you watch someone who is angry, you see them act in irrational ways. They often make rash decisions and choices, saying and doing things inconsistent with their beliefs and values. They are very irritable and often out of control, and seldom present the best side of themselves. The anger inside them causes them to self-destruct.

Vices tend to cascade. Anger breeds depression; depression feeds anxiety; anxiety fosters rashness; rashness produces errors in judgment; errors cause failure, and failure makes us angry! So 'round and 'round we go, out of control, spiraling down the drain. Soon we are so wrapped up in our own angst that we start ignoring the very virtues that might save us. Vices run counter to virtues and devastate your ability to be at your best.

Vices often paralyze your thinking, limit your physical capabilities and waste your energy. Fear will literally tighten your muscles and not allow them to perform normally. Your muscles actually constrict when you are fearful. Tighter muscles restrict your physical performance and limit your ability.

When vices like fear, anger, frustration, doubt and discouragement are present, you can't think clearly, soberly, or calmly because negative emotions and thoughts limit your physical abilities.

Let me give an example of how this works. My 5 year old was learning to tie her shoes recently. My wife had a book to demonstrate how to do it, but after a few minutes my daughter couldn't do it. She was getting so frustrated she started to cry-- all this emotion because she couldn't tie her shoelaces. She got so worked up and became hysterical. She became irrational and said things that were very illogical, even for a 5 year old.

How we think and the emotions we let in, or not in, have a direct impact on how we perform. We know this instinctively and this is seen by how we cheer for athletes or favorite teams. When we want an athlete to perform better, we shower encouragement on them; we only tell them positive things. This is our "in the stands" mentality. We all know that by giving them heavy doses of encouragement, no matter how bad the situation, the encouragement will help build them up. We know it will stimulate them to perform better.

Conversely when **we** are "in the arena" competing, we have a different mentality. We aren't so optimistic about our own mistakes. When we miss an easy play, we most likely dump heavy doses of discouragement or frustration on ourselves. "I stink," we say to ourselves, or "I can't believe how bad I am today" and our own negative thoughts make us want to give up instead of go on. How we think when cheering for a team is totally different than when we ourselves are playing. *We must become the fans in the stands at the same time we are performing in the arena.*

If I go back to my daughter again and tell you that my wife encouraged her with remarks such as, "you almost got it," or "you are so close" and "good job," you wouldn't be surprised. These encouragements kept her trying a little longer, and will inspire her to try again. What would have happened if instead my wife had made comments that would discourage her? Comments such as, "boy that is pitiful, you are an embarrassment to our family," or "the neighbor girl down the street is half your age and she tied her shoes first try, you are so uncoordinated!" That would have shut my little girl down instantly. She would not have wanted to try again. Of course, my wife would never say such mean, discouraging things to our daughter; why would you say them to yourself? Don't beat yourself up for being so bad; build yourself up to be even better.

Spiritual Maintenance

One of the keys to our sprit is our emotions, specifically how we control our emotions. Sports psychologist Jim Loehr noted this about our emotions,

> "The capacity to manage emotions skillfully in the service of high positive energy…gives us our emotional intelligence."[12]

We must monitor our emotions and thoughts like you monitor the gauges on your car as you drive. To ignore a low fuel light or low oil light is hazardous to the performance of the car. So too we must read our "spiritual gauges" to know when we are in trouble. We must know when we are angry, distracted, impatient, or fearful because these will have an adverse affect on our performance.

The first part of correcting the problem is spotting the problem. Be aware of warning signs of internal trouble. Some signs for anger are: incessant negativity, emotional outbursts, verbal cues such as yelling or harsh words, and physical reactions such as slamming your fist down. We must constantly supervise what is going on inside us.

Second we must then fix the problem. To continue to drive down the highway and pass all the gas stations when your tank is empty is foolish. Stopping for gas will fix the problem. This is exactly what we must do when our gauges show warning signs of anger, or fear, or doubt. We must stop what we are doing and refuel ourselves spiritually. In sports it is called getting a timeout. In life we must stop and rethink why we are angry, fearful or doubting. Many times we are just reacting to situations and our emotions are leading us around. When we stop and regain control of our emotions, we can defuse the vice that is threatening to explode and destroy us.

Third, we must also seek to avoid the problem before it occurs. This is called maintenance. We do regular maintenance on our car so that it will function at its best and not break down. Spiritual maintenance operates on the same principle, requiring us to review what we believe and gear our life around these beliefs. All our thoughts and emotions must support our core beliefs and values, and we must reinforce these beliefs on a daily basis. If our thoughts are consistently in line with our deepest beliefs we will have much greater success at controlling our actions. We must get rid of thoughts, behaviors and emotions that run contrary to these core values and beliefs.

We refer again to Jim Loehr who stated, "The connection to a deeply held set of values and to a purpose beyond our self becomes an issue of our spiritual being. This then motivates us. The quantity of energy we have to spend at any given moment is a reflection of our physical capacity. Our motivation to spend it is largely a spiritual issue."[13]

The more we can tie into what we believe and why we believe it, the more we can perform at higher and higher levels because our entire being is integrated in a common cause. Our body and spirit are united. This will become a stimulus for us and will then have a direct positive impact on our external actions and our ultimate success.

To grow our ability to think more efficiently and effectively, we must learn how and why we think as we do. If we can improve our ability to think better, more clearly, logically and with better reasoning, then we will have fewer mistakes in judgment and execution. This, combined with more creativity and a better ability to take favorable risks, will improve our performance.[14]

The goal must be to change our physical abilities through our spiritual capabilities. Our physical body is important because it is where we live out our life. For me to go get groceries, it is not enough to just think about the grocery store. I have to move my body and go to the store.[15]

The mind and the body must interact. This is also true with emotions. I can think of loving my wife on Valentine's Day but that won't make her as happy as going to buy her flowers and then taking her out to dinner. The key is to get the spiritual to interact with the physical, leading to right behavior. When this occurs we are united, more powerful, and most effective.

Amusing Ourselves to Death

The body and its desire to be satisfied is the main form of pleasure today. If you are what you eat physically, and all you eat are chocolate donuts, then your body will not function nearly as well as it could. (Ever see a chocolate donut on the MVP list?) This holds true for our minds, too. If we feed it worthless information, our mind doesn't function very well either.

Today we feed ourselves many worthless forms of pleasure just because it feels good, and this also has an adverse affect on our thinking. What is most dangerous about this is the lack of nourishment given to the mind as the body alone continues to be pleased. This stunts spiritual growth. The body is fed while the spirit is starved.

Critic Neil Postman writes about this in his book "*Amusing ourselves to Death."* In it he compares George Orwell's book "*1984"* to Aldous Huxley's book "*Brave new World"* He says:

> "Orwell feared the future of those who would deprive us of information, books would be banned and that truth would be concealed from us. Huxley feared that we would have so many "things" that we would be reduced to passivity; he feared the truth would be drowned in a sea of irrelevance and therefore no one would want to read a book. In "*1984"* people are controlled by inflicting pain. In "*Brave new World"* people are controlled by inflicting pleasure. In short the book *Amusing ourselves to Death* is based on the premise that Huxley not Orwell is correct."[16]

His point is that we as a culture have been so enamored by TV and other technologies that life chiefly consists of amusement and entertainment. Las Vegas is the "poster-child" city for society at large. We have ceased feeding our minds information to make us think more deeply. Instead we have replaced critical thinking with amusement and entertainment. This is the main focus of TV, to entertain. TV programs are designed to make people watch them and so the focus becomes: laughter, sex appeal, violence and drama. Deep thinking skills, logic and reasoning are not involved. Sit back and enjoy is all that is required. If you don't like the program you just switch channels because most cable providers give at least 50+ channels to choose from.

Many in our culture have become immersed in pop trivia. People know who was picked on "American Idol" but can't name the vice president of the United States. The information that is passed along in many TV shows is generally worthless. Most shows that give **useful** information, such as history or Biblical discussions, have low ratings when compared to most TV movies, sitcoms or dramas. We are a culture that spends on average 3 hours a day watching TV and feeding our minds **useless** information. The effect this has on us is seductive and alarming.

Malcolm Muggeridge deals with this in his book "*Christ and the Media.*" In it he states:

> "It is a truism to say the media in general, and TV in particular…are incomparably the greatest single influence in our society today, exerted at all social, economic and cultural levels. This influence, I should add, is in my opinion, largely exerted irresponsibly, arbitrarily, and without reference to any moral or intellectual, still less spiritual, guidelines whatsoever."[17]

Jesus Christ deals in truth and reality, TV deals in fantasy. This then makes it more and more difficult for people to separate the two. Good is made to look unappealing while evil is made to look inviting. God is a god of truth and only in knowing truth and reality can we worship Him. Muggeridge further deals with this concept:

> "The prevailing impression I have come to have of the contemporary scene is on an ever-widening chasm between fantasy, in terms of which the media induce us to live, and the reality of our existence as made in the image of God, as sojourners in time whose true habitat is eternity. The fantasy is all-encompassing; awareness of reality requires the seeing eye which comes to those born again in Christ."[18]

Compare this to times gone by, when reading was the norm and literacy was high; when free time was spent reading and thinking. The literacy rate between 1640–1700 is estimated to have been between 89-95% for men in Massachusetts and this was probably the highest concentration of literate males found anywhere in the world.[19] Their ability to read gave them a much deeper ability to think and reason. Reading gives the audience time to stop, contemplate, and draw out assumptions or point out errors. (This is very difficult with TV due to the continuous flow of the program. Fortunately, TV had not been invented yet, in those bygone days of literacy.) Therefore the ability to find truth and rhetoric became key ingredients to the culture. People actually wanted to know and learn, rather than merely be entertained. The discourse was coherent, serious, and rational. These people were deep thinkers with long attention spans. Today is just the opposite. Today human discourse has become shriveled and often absurd, focusing on the shows that were on TV last night.

What Huxley teaches is that in the age of advanced technologies, spiritual devastation is more likely to come from an enemy with a smiling, reassuring face.[20] Postman says this:

> "When a population becomes distracted by trivia, when cultural life is a perpetual round of entertainments, when serious public conversation becomes a form of baby-talk ...then a nation finds itself at risk."[21]

Our spirits have become shriveled and many Americans don't even know it is happening. It is like the frog put in a pot of water that is slowly heated. Since it doesn't sense the gradual increase of heat it will not jump out of the pot and will boil to death. We are in a culture of advanced technology, fast paced living that makes life easier and more enjoyable. At the same time little spiritual growth is going on. Our spirits are shriveling at the expense of physical pleasure and amusement and we don't even know it is happening.

Says Postman,

> "What afflicted people in *"Brave New World"* was not that they were laughing instead of thinking, but that they did not know what they were laughing about and why they had stopped thinking."[22]

We live in a world where developing our spirit is a difficult and serious challenge. We are too busy and have too little time. We have no desire to do something that isn't "fun" or "entertaining." We are bogged down by trivial information such as sports statistics. We are masters of useless knowledge such as appears on games like *Trivial Pursuit, Jeopardy* or *Who wants to be a Millionaire?* We laugh through life and take very little seriously. The bottom line is we have little depth to us. We have empty souls and full bodies. We continue to feed our body and starve our spirit.

<u>Empty Spirits</u>

Alan Bloom, in His book *The Closing of the American Mind* said, "Today's select students know so much less, are so much more cut off from tradition, are so much slacker intellectually, that they make their predecessors look like prodigies of culture."[23] They have emptiness in them that stems from their inability to understand who they are, or how to live a moral life. They certainly can't understand the concept of a spirit-filled life. The concept of giving of themselves without getting back is foreign to them. They live to get all they can, physically, from their one shot at life.

Psychologists call this the empty self. It is constituted by a set of values, motives, habits of thoughts, feelings, and behavior that perverts and eliminates the life of the mind and makes maturation in Christ extremely difficult.[24] J.P. Moreland talks about seven traits of the empty self that undermine spiritual and intellectual growth. They are:

1. **The empty self is inordinately individualistic.**
2. **The empty self is infantile.**
3. **The empty self is narcissistic.**
4. **The empty self is passive.**
5. **The empty self is a slave to the senses.**
6. **The empty self has lost the art of developing an interior life.**
7. **The empty self is hurried and busy.**

So, what does he mean?

The empty self is inordinately individualistic because it is concerned only with itself. People today tend to ask, "What's in it for me?" with little regard for society at large or the wider community.

The empty self is infantile because, like babies, such people are only concerned with what feels good to them. Unlike babies, whose chief concerns deal with eating, sleeping, and feeling warm and protected, the empty-selfers seek material goods, sex, image, fine clothes and indulgent pleasures. These "babies" carry their infantile desires well into their adult life. Some never lose them.

The empty self is narcissistic because people are simply in love with themselves. They are so preoccupied with self-interest and personal fulfillment that they have no time for God and His purposes.

The empty self is passive because it lacks any real values and guiding principles in life. Those take too much effort. Empty-selfers would rather "go with the flow" and let life carry them along with the current … just as long it feels good and keeps them entertained.

The empty self is a slave to the senses because all it knows is the physical world. If you can't see it, hear it, feel it, taste it or smell it, it can't be true … that's the slavish faith empty-selfers put in their 5 senses. Critical thinking and abstract reasoning are foreign concepts, and the notion of anything transcendental is beyond their grasp.

The empty self has lost the art of developing an interior life because it no longer values virtue, morality, deep character, honor and reputation. These hallmarks of intellectual reflection and spiritual formation — once held in such high regard as to outweigh money, position and celebrity — are today considered quaint and irrelevant.

The empty self is hurried and busy because it dare not stop and reflect on its own folly. To do so accentuates its very emptiness and opens the door to pain and loneliness. Stay busy enough and you won't have time to think.

Empty-selfers are people who are filled with this world and all it has to offer. They seek its material goods and technological pleasures. No depth of character is formed in their life. They have very little spiritual life because they are preoccupied with the pleasures and entertainment supplied by the physical world around them. Other people form their opinions for them. They have many acquaintances but no real, deep friends. They spend most, if not all, of their time in shallow conversation about sports teams or trivialities in life. They avoid conversations that push them or challenge them mentally. Their opinions are informed by their feelings, not by facts. They live life on the seat of their pants with no inner or spiritual existence.

Finding our Way Back

Since the spiritual life is the key to righteous living, we must find our way back. This book is written to develop spiritually full individuals through the power of virtue. The goal is to bring the spiritually dead to life through spiritual rebirth in Jesus Christ. From His death on the cross we can become new creations with the Spirit of the Living God dwelling within us. Only by spiritual growth is it possible to live righteous and holy lives. Only by filling empty spirits can we come to understand the shallowness of living merely to meet the physical desires of our body. *The material pleasures of this world will never satisfy the void that can only come from the Living God.*

Knowing the problem is half of the battle, the other half is developing a spiritual life and knowing what it is and how it shapes us. Setting our sights on spiritual targets are where we need to start. The targets of virtue and Truth must be our sole aims. We can change, and it is worth the price. It won't be easy and will take lots of work. However the dividends it will pay out will be well worth the investment. It will give you a relationship with Jesus Christ and bring a purpose and conviction to your existence.

This process is not a passive one; it is active and must start today. You must act in predetermined ways. You must seek virtue and Truth as a drowning man seeks air. When a person becomes alive to Christ they come to know the greatest source of power to overcome any obstacle life throws at them. In Christ we possess an infinitely superior power source when compared to our physical body. We can't change on our own, we don't have the power or the ability. There is One who is able to change us and knocks at the door of our spirits (Rev 3:20). When we invite Him in He gives us access to His power to change and become new, born of the Spirit (John 1:13 and John 3:8).

Our power then is in God. The apostle Paul said,

"I can do all things through Christ who strengthens me."
(NKJV Philippians 4:13)

"Finally be strong in the Lord and in His mighty power."
(Eph 6:10)

And again through the prophet Isaiah God said,

> "So do not fear for I am with you, do not be dismayed for I am your God. I will strengthen you and help you, I will uphold you with my righteous right hand." (Isaiah 41:10)

> "They will say of me, in the LORD alone are righteousness and strength."   (Isaiah 45:24)

Throughout the Bible God is proclaimed time and again to be our strength. Psalm 121 is a great Psalm that teaches just this. He is our source of virtue and empowerment. God gives His strength and power to his servants to do His Kingdom's work. *He never calls us to do anything He won't enable us to do through Him.* No matter how bad our circumstances, no matter how strong our foes and no matter how weak we feel, God is our strength and shield.

When we live through our spirit, there comes an understanding about the difference between eternal treasures that are spiritual, and temporal treasures that are physical. We must separate the here and now (and its physical temptations) from the distant future (and its promise of eternity with Jesus), for the former is **seductive and destructive** while the latter is **productive and constructive.** This desire to store up treasures in heaven must become a hunger in us; one that we long to accomplish.

Jesus talked about spiritual treasures versus physical treasures. In Matthew 6:19-21, He said,

> "Don't store up for yourselves treasures on earth *(physical)*, where moths and rust will destroy and thieves can break in and steal them. But rather store up for yourselves treasures in heaven *(spiritual)* where moths and rust can't destroy and thieves can't break in and steal. For where your treasure is, there your heart will be also." (Italics mine)

Material goods and possessions will not go with us when we die. "You can't take it with you," as the expression goes. Spiritual treasures and values are eternal and will go with you forever. The memories you leave for others, such as love, will be carried on with them even when you die.

Another concept is this: "God is Spirit and his worshippers must worship in spirit and truth." (John 4:24) God is Sprit and He reveals Himself to us in our spirit. This is where we meet Him. He gives us His Holy Spirit to dwell within His believers. His Spirit then can communicate to our spirit and we get to know who He is. We desire what He desires, because He controls us.

When our physical bodies die, as they all will, only our soul or spirit can go on to eternal life. Jesus came to show us how to live life in His Kingdom with spiritual discernment and boldness. His Spirit must dwell within us and control our spirit. He died so that we might live. The life we get comes from His Spirit in us empowers us and enables us.

When you come to understand how wrapped up we are in ourselves physically, and how out of control we are spiritually, you will come to realize how our vices are a vortex pulling us down. Only by being reformed spiritually can we transform our body and its actions through virtue. Until we understand this we will continue to fail in godliness and righteous living because our Human System is formed to fail. (Jer 17:9, Ps 51:5, Gen 8:21, Gen 6:5, Ps 53:3).

The Human System:

The Dynamics of Our Body

"Remember then: there is only one time that is important—Now! It is the most important time because it is the only time we have any power."

Leo Tolstoy

A well-lived life, one that has maximum impact, must be our aspiration. God is concerned with process as much as end results. This process, or training, is the key to growth. We must train to maximize our abilities every day of our life. This means training every part of our body. We must seek to train more than just our body. We must train our mind, our emotions, and our will.

Professional athletes typically spend ninety percent of their time training, in order to be able to perform ten percent of the time.[25] How do they maximize the impact of their training so as to get maximum results from it? The key is understanding that there are two key ingredients in their preparation, time and energy.

The training equation then looks like this:

$$\text{Time} + \text{Energy} = \text{Impact}$$

Here *time* is the allotted hours we have in a day and *energy* is the power we have in that time. Together they combine to make our *impact* on any person or in any situation. To have maximum impact, we need to have quantity time combined with quality energy.

Let's look at *time* first. God gives us a limited number of hours in a day and a limited number of days in a lifetime. Time is short and we must use it with a sense of urgency. The more time you give to something, the more you reveal its importance to you. When you give a person your time, you are giving them a portion of your life that you will never get back. That is why the greatest gift we can give is our investment of time.[26] Time is like money; you can only spend it once.

How many hours of our day are spent wasting time? Time that is lost is gone forever. Jay Carty noted this analogy, "Imagine you have a bank account called t-i-m-e. Every day it credited you with 86,400 seconds. At midnight, whatever you failed to use is lost. A balance is not carried over to the next day and you are not allowed overdrafts. Each day the t-i-m-e account opens a new balance for you. What would you do? You would spend every cent (second) of it in the best way possible."[27] If we looked at our time as limited, we would use it a little more wisely. This is the very point of the rich fool in Luke 12:13-21. The key to time is using it more wisely and more efficiently.

The other ingredient is *energy*. Energy is the amount of power we bring to a situation. Just because you are physically present doesn't mean you are using your full energy. For example; if you are going to a "Key Concepts in Knitting" seminar your wife dragged you to, and you are in hour 4 of an 8-hour lecture, you may find yourself not totally there mentally or emotionally. You are in the room but you are not getting a whole lot out of it because your mind is wandering or you are uninterested about learning this new skill. Just because you are there physically doesn't mean you are there mentally and emotionally.

Jim Loehr discusses this concept of energy in training top athletes and top business executives. He says, "Everything we do requires energy. We often fail to take into account the importance of energy at work and in our personal lives. Without the right quantity, quality, focus, and force of energy, we are compromised in any activity we undertake…to be fully engaged we must be physically energized, emotionally connected, mentally focused, and spiritually aligned with a purpose beyond your immediate self interest."[28] The concept of full engagement, as he uses it, is a great way to think about our energy level. It is a sum total of the 4 key elements of your being – body, mind, emotion, and will. The higher our energy level, the greater our potential impact on others and situations. Being physically present isn't all there is, we must be mentally and emotionally present to increase our total energy output.

The impact we have, or do not have, on any situation or person is a product of these two components, time and energy. They form our habits and our habits form our character. As the saying goes:

> *Sow a thought and reap an action*
> *Sow an action and reap a habit*
> *Sow a habit and reap a character*
> *Sow a character reap a destiny*

The choices we make with our time and energy are the key factors in determining our impact in life, be it for good or bad.

Maximum impact is achieved when you have a high quantity of time combined with a high quality of energy. If you increase one without the other you have minimum impact. Many people have minimum impact in life, be it in sport or on people, because of an improper use of their time and energy concerning the area they wish to influence.

The 5 Key Components of the Human System

The key components to the makeup of our being are a sum total of these 5 areas: physical, mental, emotional, will and Truth. I will define each one as follows:

> *Truth* – Outside of me, reality in the world, absolutes in life
> *Will* – affections, desires, self-consciousness, and the center for moral life
> *Mental* – the center of understanding, thoughts, reasoning and logic
> *Emotional* – the center for emotions, feelings, and our conscience
> *Physical* – the center of bodily life, our bodily actions

These areas work from the top down as they relate to importance in to our human system. Change also occurs from the top down. Here is a diagram of what the humans system looks like in a person redeemed by Christ's blood.

The Human System

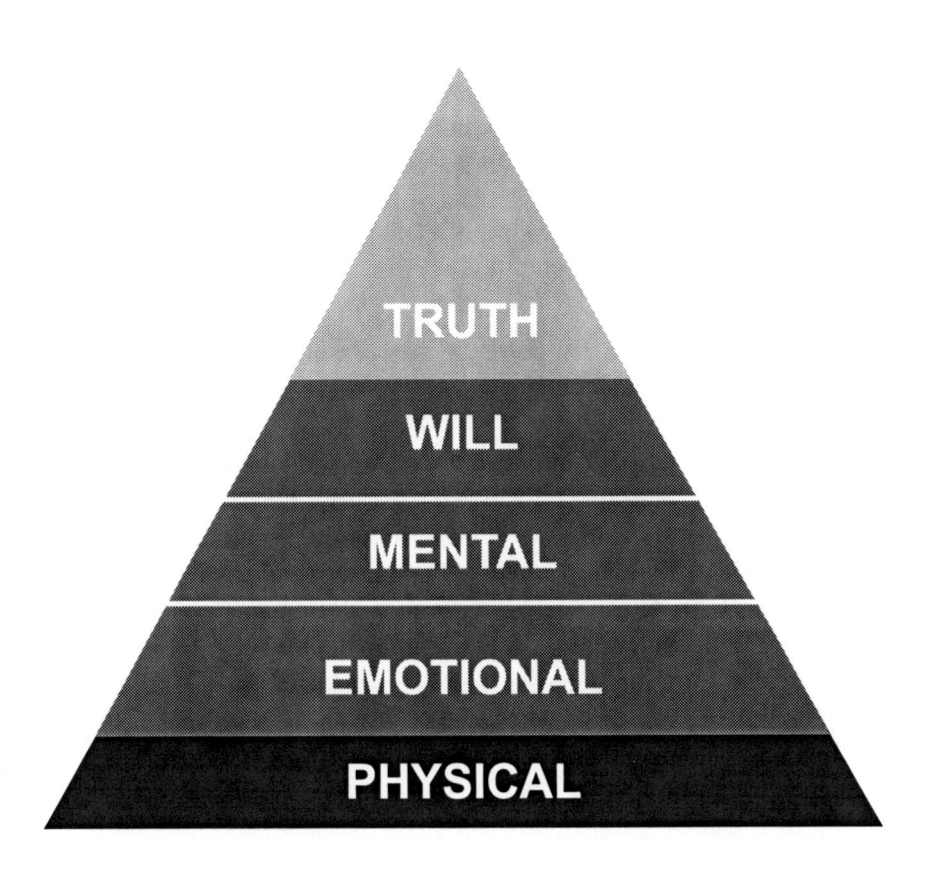

```
        TRUTH
        WILL
       MENTAL
      EMOTIONAL
       PHYSICAL
```

The bottom section is the physical part of us, it is the empirical world around us. It is the area we can measure or test. A piece of wood is so many inches long, a compound is made up of certain elements and so on. It is in this physical base where the main focus of athletics, science and medicine has been in the last one hundred years.

The middle three sections (emotional, mental and will) makeup the spiritual area that we can't see with our eyes. It is made up of the emotions, mind and our will. What goes on in our spirit and how we live it out, is the term we call our "life." In the New Testament there are two terms for "life" in the original Greek language. It is either *bios* or *zoe*. *Bios* refers to the manner of existence or the present state of existence. It is used in Luke 8:14 (KJV) to refer to "riches and pleasures of this life" or it is used in Luke 8:43 (KJV) to refer to "spent all of her living upon physicians."

Zoe is usually referred to as spiritual life. The term refers not just to our existence, but so much more. It is the vitality and abundance of that existence. It is used most frequently in the New Testament in the writings of John. For instance in John 1:4 it says "In him was life and that life was the light of men."(KJV) In John 5:40 it says, "And ye will not come to me, that ye might have life." (KJV)

To have *Zoe* is to have the fullness of life God desires for every person. Jesus said,

> "...I have come that they may have life and have it to the full." (John 10:10)

Many people have life in *bios,* but that is not the highest level of existence. This is life without God and is the part of the pyramid without the capstone of Truth at the top. If we add Truth to the pyramid, then we have *Zoe*. The life of a believer in Christ is the full pyramid whereby they have *Zoe* in them. This is the life we receive from Jesus atonement on the cross as we accept His death for our sin. It is the atonement we have for our sins in Christ's death for us on the cross. This is the spiritual life of Christ in us.

Jesus gives both *bios* life when we are born and *Zoe,* eternal life, when He becomes our Savior and Lord. Only those with *Zoe* have eternal life in the Kingdom of God. They have life *bios* simply because they are breathing. To have *Zoe* they must be alive to God, for only He can give that life to us.

To be born into this *Zoe* life is referred to in the Bible as to be born again (see John 3:1-21).[29] Before this we are spiritually dead to God because of sin. Once God quickens our spirit, we are at peace with God and become His children. Without His Spirit in us giving us life, we are enemies of Him (Luke 11:23, Rev 3:15-16). There is no middle ground, we are either His friend or His enemy (Luke 19: 11-27).

C.S. Lewis said this about life and comparing *bios* to *Zoe*:

> "When we come to man, the highest of the animals, we get the completest resemblance to God which we know of. Man not only lives, but loves and reasons: biological

life reaches its highest known level in him ...But what man in his natural condition has not got, is Spiritual life — the higher and different sort of life that exists in God ...In reality, the difference between Biological life and Spiritual life is so important that I am going to give them two distinct names. The Biological life which comes to us through nature, and which ...is always tending to run down and decay so that it can only be kept up by incessant subsidies from nature in the form of air, water, and food is *bios*. The spiritual life which is in God from all eternity, and which made the whole natural universe, is *zoe.* "[30]

He goes on to add:

"*Bios* has, to be sure, a certain shadowy or symbolic resemblance to *zoe*: but only the sort of resemblance there is between a photo and a place, or a statue and a man. A man who changed from *bios* to having *Zoe* would have gone through as big a change as a statue which changed from being a carved stone to being a real man."[31]

The top section of the pyramid is Truth. Truth is God. God is so many things and Truth is just one of them (John 14:6). When we have Truth in our lives it gives direction and instruction in how to live. Truth then unites us in every area of our being.

It is not what we believe, but rather do our beliefs match up with reality and the facts of this world. Just because we believe something doesn't make it true. For instance I can choose to not believe in the law of gravity, but if I jump off a building I will still fall. Truth is still truth no matter whether I believe it or not.

To live life based on lies and wrong information will be very costly. We may not know the information is wrong but that won't change the outcome. Wrong information often has disastrous effects. In fact doctors, astronauts, and construction workers, for example, rely specifically on accurate facts. They must have only correct information, truth, to do their job. Imagine a doctor operating with wrong information about the human body or a home builder having inaccurate measurements when building a house. Having the correct information in both of these situations is critical for their performance.

Truth is vital to guiding and dictating our right decisions. It gives us the information we will use to decide how to act. We must seek it and strive to rid our life of all lies and falsehood. Once we know Truth, our spirit has direction — a guide to lead us.

This pyramid reveals the makeup of a believer in Jesus because only He can give us life wherein Truth is revealed to us. This truth then gives us His life and power to overcome our sinful nature. It also enables us to tap into virtues and the unlimited power sources that come only from God.

Training our Interactive Self

The physical, emotional, mental and willful aspects of our being interact with each other and are not isolated from each other. These elements constantly communicate with each other and affect each other. For example, the mind thinks a thought and an emotional response usually follows. Consider a man in a store who sees some guy he doesn't know talking to his wife. He may think, "That guy is trying to 'hit on' my wife." Anger then is the emotional response. In the body the heart will respond by beating faster as a result of anger. Here the situation caused a mental idea to be formed and the emotions responded to the thought. This response then had a physical effect as well. Note that it makes no difference whether the idea (the stranger "hitting on" the wife) is true or not; the emotional and physical reactions are the same.

Take another example. You are home alone and hear a noise that startles you (anxiety), your mind then responds with the thought that there is a burglar in the house. Your heart then beats faster. These interactions occur instantaneously without thinking. The point is these four areas are in constant contact with each other.

We can and must cultivate virtue in our will, our minds and our emotions. For instance, we can increase patience, control our anger and be more optimistic in our thinking. We can train each of these areas in virtue by responding in carefully considered ways, which empower us, as compared to habitual ways, which are destructive. We don't have to continue to respond in wrong ways just because they have become habits.

We must seek to train to increase our physical abilities by better understanding our spiritual capabilities. We must seek to unite all areas of the human system in Truth through virtue. Jim Loehr and Tony Schwartz describe energy this way. "We must seek to increase quantity, quality, focus and force of our energy. Physical energy is quantity, emotional energy is quality, mental energy is focus, and spiritual energy (the will) is force. To be fully engaged, to have maximum energy for the maximum duration, we need to be physically energized, emotionally connected, mentally focused and spiritually aligned."[32]

When we respond with virtue, we are providing the body righteous power to act in the appropriate manner. As we continue to develop in this way, we build the quality, quantity, force and focus of our power to act. We then will have a greater impact in what we do because all of our physical body is acting in harmony with all of our spirit.

A Closer look at Vice

We grow the spiritual capacities of quantity, quality, focus and force by undertaking situations where we need specific emotions or thoughts to strengthen us. We must commit to responding with virtue ahead of time, no matter what the situation is. Our tendency to respond with vice is inborn and must be overruled. These wrong actions — vices — can become so automatic we don't even realize that we have other choices of response.

One of the goals of this book is to help you make better choices. By making better choices in life, we will perform at our very best, do it more often and in greater duration.

Vices destroy us and those around us as well. If we "zero in" on the vice of anger we can see how this happens. We get mad and we want to let it out, the release of it helps us feel better. The problem is when we release our anger we most often do harm to others. One of the most typical releases for anger is verbal assaults on others. Yelling at people seldom helps a situation.

Consider if someone has yelled at you, fairly intensely, for thirty seconds. This is hard to just let go. Being yelled at lingers on in our minds and often shuts us down emotionally. Marriage counselor Gary Smalley talks about this and how when we shut off another's spirit, they shut us out. *Acting on our anger is a short-term fix but a long term menace.*

They often stop listening to us and often the hurt we have created lingers for a long time.

The Bible warns us about anger and reminds us that it must be controlled or it will have dire consequences. Here are several verses speaking directly to anger:

> "A fool gives vent to his anger, but a wise man keeps himself under control." (Pro. 29:11)

> "In your anger do not sin. Do not let the sun go down while you are still angry, and do not give the devil a foothold." (Eph. 4:26-27)

> "…Everyone should be quick to listen, slow to speak, and slow to become angry, for man's anger does not bring about the righteous life God desires." (James 1:19-20)

God commands us not to act on our anger. To act on anger is to go against God's command. This is sin. Sin is defined as: "coming short of our true end, missing the mark, a falling away from or missing the right path." The idea is of a law and a lawgiver. To sin is to disobey both the law and the Lawgiver, God. By recognizing that vices such as anger are sin, we then agree with God that it is wrong and must seek to do all we can to steer clear of it.

Our emotional choice must be not to act on anger, but rather to overcome it with virtue. Here the virtue of patience or gentleness will give us the power not to act in anger. We must not give into "feeling angry." Instead, we must pre-determine to act with patience and kindness when we feel anger.

Let's dissect another vice and find out how harmful it is. Worry is another such vice. Worry or anxiety are formed from negative thinking. We must understand how negative thinking affects us and rid ourselves of it. Negative thinking blocks, distorts, wastes, diminishes, depletes and contaminates our stored energy.[33] Negativity (such as worry) distorts and scatters our thoughts, making us less powerful when we get in crucial situations. Negative thoughts have certain qualities about them that deplete energy. For instance here are some characteristics of worry:

- Worry itself is usually more damaging to our lives than the effects of the things we worry about.
- Worry is a thin stream of fear that trickles through the mind, which, if encouraged, will spread out so widely that all our other thoughts will be drained and only fear will be left inside us.
- Worry divides your thoughts and prevents you from being focused and single minded. It is a major distraction.
- Once your mind is divided, it is utterly incapable of giving all needed resources to the effort at hand. It weakens you and makes your body weaker.
- Focusing on the future can lead to worry and focusing on the past can lead to anger, but focusing on the present builds confidence.
- Worry takes the joy out of life.
- Worry often focuses on things we can't control or things that are unknown. Since we can't control them or can't know them, it is silly to focus on them or worry about them.
  o Focus on what you *do* know.
  o Focus on what you *can* control.
- Worry offers no benefit but leads to many problems. "Who of you by worrying can add a single hour to his life?" (Luke 12:25)
- Our biggest worries usually never come true, and hardly ever to the disastrous degree that we imagine.
- Worry is blind and refuses to learn from the past.

Christ himself tell us not to worry; in fact, it is a command. (Matt 6:25-34) When we realize the damage negativity does to our ability to perform, we must choose to not give into it. We must understand that it depletes our power. We must train ourselves with positive thoughts and emotions such as trust and hope. These grow confidence, which is the opposite of worry.

> Our goal is to form good habits — habits of virtue — that make us better and rid our life of bad habits — habits of vice — that make us worse. Habits are powerful, and they can wield their power in good or harmful ways. When we

have good habits — habits of virtue — we have the power to act in right ways. The reverse holds true for habits of vice and their power to influence our action in wrong ways.

Power gives us the ability to act, either rightly or wrongly. The more virtuous power we have, the greater the likelihood we will choose to act rightly. Habits of virtue are great powers for making the best choices.

<u>Unity in the Spirit Creates Unity in the Body</u>

Truth unites us physically and spiritually and when Truth guides and dictates our actions, our physical and spiritual beings act in harmony. This gives us even more power to act in proper ways. Unity of body and spirit is a source of great power, and virtuous habits add to that power. Habits, after all, are simply tendencies to act in regular, predetermined ways. When right actions are done enough times they become habits. Habits and Truth are two sources of power that enable us to act in ways that are for our greatest good.

Self-control is an essential part of that power. We are called to be in control of our bodies. We are told to make our body the slave of our spirit. The apostle Paul said,

> "I beat my body and make it my slave, so that after I have preached to others, I will not be disqualified for the prize." (1 Cor 9:27).

How many people can say they make their body a slave to their spirit? The body and the spirit must act in one accord for the ultimate good of the whole human system. When we make our body our slave, we seek to do only what is right and virtuous, leading to a holy and upright life. We must decide what is best for us and then direct our body to act accordingly.

We make our body a slave to righteous, honorable and virtuous living. The apostle Paul again said,

> "Flee evil desires of your youth, and pursue righteous living, faith, love and peace ..." (2 Tim 2:22)

For this very reason we are called to guard our heart (Pro 4:23). Proverbs tells us,

> "In the paths of the wicked lie thorns and snares, but he who guards his soul stays far from them." (Pro 22:5)

We must diligently guard what goes on inside of us. We do this by growing virtue and getting rid of vice. We can know what to do but if we don't have the power to carry it out we will fail. When our body is united with our spirit, we build power to act in ways that will be for our ultimate good.

We must train to become "the very best version of me," as motivational speaker Matthew Kelly says. To do this we must know what the very best version of me looks like. The life of virtue, where virtue is power to live as Jesus commanded, is just that life. It is the *Zoe*, and it is the abundant life Jesus lived and calls us to live as well.

We can plan for the future, but we must live like today is our last day. We must train as an athlete trains for peak performance by striving to get the most out of themselves. We must invest in our life as a financial planner invests money for the future. The outcome of our life depends on how we invest or don't invest, how we train or don't train.

What we do now will have consequences for us down the road, for better or for worse. Most importantly, it will impact people and relationships we currently have for time and eternity.

Formed to Fail

When you come to understand how wrapped up in ourselves we are, and how out of control we are spiritually, you will come to realize how our vices are a vortex pulling us down. *We were formed to fail.* Only by being reformed spiritually can we reform our body and its actions. We must be rewired to be controlled by our spirit and ultimately by Jesus Christ and His Holy Spirit. Until we understand this, we will continue to fail, because our internal structure is formed to fail due to sin. "The heart is deceitful above all things and beyond cure, who can understand it." (Jer 17:9) This same thought is echoed in other Scripture verses such as: Ps 51:5, Gen 8:21, Gen 6:5, Ps 53:3. Let's now take a deeper look into our inner spirit to see why this is true.

The Problem:

The Battle for our Spirit

> *"The modern skeptical world has been taught for some 200 years a conception of human nature in which the reality of evil, so well known to the ages of faith, has been discounted ...We shall have to recover this forgotten but essential truth — along with so many others that we lost when thinking we were enlightened and advanced, we were merely shallow and blind."*
>
> **Walter Lippmann**

To live life abundantly, over and above a normal life, we must understand there are obstacles we must overcome. These obstacles inhibit our ability to understand our spirit, and our ability to reform it as well. They fight against us in many different ways. They make it very difficult for us to see life as a battle, a battle for our very existence.

In all battles there is an enemy that we are fighting against. This battle is no exception. Our enemy is multidimensional and invisible. It aims to remove truth and replace it with lies. It will tell us to conform to the way everyone else thinks and will tempt us to take the easy route in life. This foe will seek to encourage us to act on our feelings and to feed our physical desires only. This enemy will destroy us unless we actively engage it in combat and fight against it on every front of our life.

The decisions we make determine the side that we are fighting for — good or evil. On the side of good is God, truth, and righteousness. On the side of evil is: Satan, worldliness, and human nature. These two powers battle for control of how we will live and what we will live for. It may seem as if I am overstating the reality of what is going on, but far from it. It is a battle you fight daily in the choices you make. Do you consistently choose good over evil?

Virtuous Choices

We are constantly making choices every day. There are three types of choices we make: Best, bad and terrible.

- The *best choices* are based on accurate information and good reasoning.
- The *bad choices* are based on erroneous information and faulty reasoning.
- The *terrible choices* are based on ignorance and no real reasoning at all.

Only by repeatedly making the best choices can we improve our character.

Terrible choices are obvious, and we all seek to avoid them. No one intentionally makes a terrible choice, but they occur all the time. These choices will surely lead to disaster. This is how drug addicts, alcoholics, gambling addicts, pornography addicts and so on end up where they are. They make one bad choice, which leads to another, and soon they are addicted. They never intended to become addicted but their terrible choices became the road to their ruin.

The most common decision-making errors concern bad choices. Often people have just a little wrong information or apply poor reasoning and this leads to a bad choice. They make the same destructive choices, but in a more subtle way. Any wrong information, or faulty reasoning, whether in large or small quantities, leads to problems. If I asked you, "How much poison would you like in your food?" Knowing that poison is harmful to your health and often can kill you, you would probably reply, "None." The same is true with wrong information and faulty reasoning. A little of it in your choice is just as harmful as poison. It may work more slowly, but destroys you just the same.

Only with all-correct information and good reasoning can we make best choices. Thus Truth is critical. Truly virtuous choices have truth and sound reasoning as their foundation. Saint Augustine said, "No one can doubt that virtue makes the soul good." Thomas Aquinas noted this as well about virtue, "For virtue is a perfect habit, by which it never happens that anything but good is done ..."[34] To act in virtue is to act for the ultimate good of your being as defined by Jesus Christ. Best choices are grounded in ultimate good and ultimate good is grounded in virtue.

Best choices are not always easy to make. Often, telling the truth — especially when you have done something wrong — is difficult to do. Telling the truth is still the best choice, no matter what it may cost you. Another hard choice is to be courageous. In war, for example, it is hard to be courageous because it may cost you your life, but it is still the best choice. *Best choices are not what is easiest but rather, what is right.*

The Battle for You

The spiritual battle over you *is* being fought whether you realize it or not. The stakes are high and the battle is fierce. Every choice you make is for good or evil, there is no middle ground. You choose for God or against Him in every choice you make (Matt 6:24).

Most people don't realize the urgency and importance of their choices. I draw an analogy to an iceberg. Most of the mass of an iceberg is below the surface; about 90 percent of it, in fact. The part you see is only a small part and the most dangerous part is what you can't see. It is easier for ships to avoid ice that they can see, they just steer around it. The part below the water is much more dangerous for them because they can't see it.

Forces we can't see control much of our life. It is this hidden part that we can't see that holds the greatest risk for us. The hidden part guides the choices we make and forms the opposition to our best choices. It is an enemy we can't see so it is difficult to engage in battle. Yet the battle is real.

The three main fronts with which we must do battle in that war against our spirit are: our flesh (our inborn tendencies), the world system, (the beliefs of our time), and the Devil (lies). These three adversaries make living a life of virtue difficult, if not impossible. They wage a hidden assault on our life by getting us to make selections that give us less and less control over our body. Jesus Christ defeated all three of them on the cross and the battle is won in Him alone. We can't do it on our own but the battle is won in Jesus (1 John 4:4, John 10:28-30).

I will go into detail and describe the battle each of these three invisible forces wages against our human system. The first is our flesh.

The Flesh (our inborn tendencies)
The Flesh—Good or Bad?

One of the questions we hear today is: are we naturally inclined towards good or are we naturally inclined toward bad? I use the word "bad," but the Bible often describes morally bad as evil (Gen 6:5, Gen 8:21, Eph 2:1-3). How you answer this question determines your perspective on the human spirit. It determines how you in your natural state will deal with life's choices. If you believe that you are a "good person" with an occasional bad decision here or there, you will seek to stay as you are. Why change since a bad selection is no big deal and you are naturally a "good person?"

Temptations
Circumstances
Trials
People

If, on the other hand, you believe that we are born with a bent toward bad and terrible choices, called sin, your view drastically changes. This view states that I am a sinful person who will naturally act sinfully (with vice). I am self-centered, unreasonable, have an improper view of the world and vices are my natural reaction to life. The worse the situation, the greater my chances to sin. Only a reformed spirit in me can overcome this bent. This view completely changes how you view "you." **Until you understand you are formed to fail internally, you won't seek to change.**

The following diagram illustrates this total depravity inherent in us.

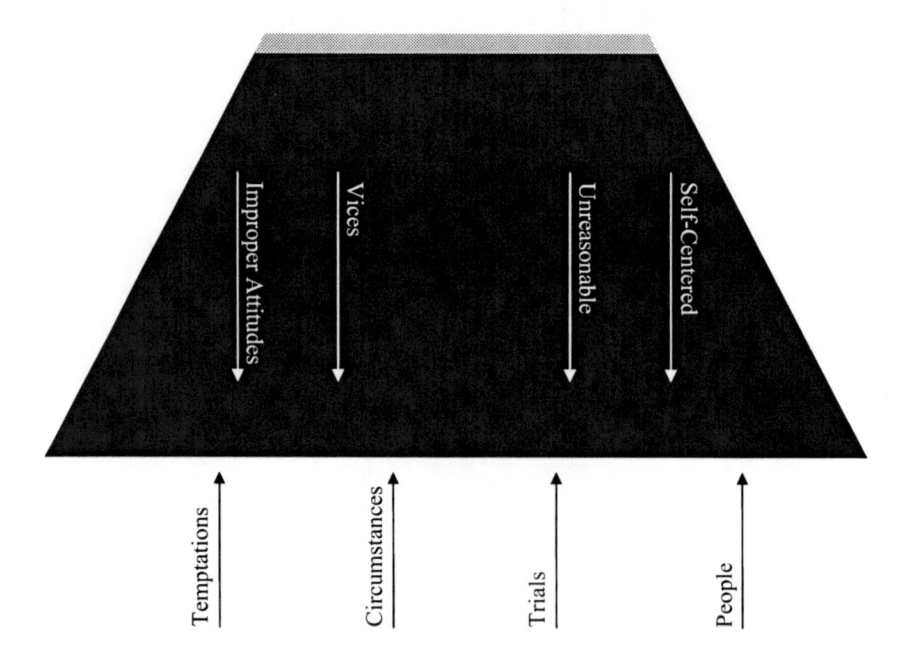

[Diagram: A trapezoid labeled with downward arrows inside — "Improper Attitudes", "Vices", "Unreasonable", "Self-Centered" — and upward arrows below — "Temptations", "Circumstances", "Trials", "People".]

Here in this diagram the gray line reveals that this is a closed system and it is unable to change itself. It shows how the "bad" is stirred up in me when the tests in life grow stronger. This makes sinful responses natural in me. Finally it shows that temptations, circumstances, trials and other people bring this out in me more and more. As we said the worse the situation, the worse my response to them will be.

In support of this view of man I would cite as evidence that technology and advancements in science have multiplied greatly in the last two hundred years, yet the 20th century is beyond a doubt the bloodiest century in history. More people have been killed in the 20th century than in all previous centuries combined. This post-modern area with, all of its technological advances, has not improved man's moral situation. In fact, it has made it worse. All of our great thinkers and experts have not helped either. Our education has not changed man's heart, which — as we will discuss — is bent toward evil. Sin continues at epidemic proportions. We find new levels of depravity. When you read Romans Chapter 1, you would think Paul was writing to our modern society.

Let me cite examples from my own life and see if it resonates this point more clearly. I am a father of four kids; their ages range from 9 years to

18 months. When my kids were infants, like all infants they were selfish, impatient, and self-centered. If I didn't get them what they wanted, or said "no" to their desire, they screamed until they got it. If it took me too long to get it, they cried as well. They didn't like my authority either. If they didn't like what you are doing with them, say changing their diaper, they cried.

As they got older this process changed just slightly. I now watch my 5, 7 and 9-year-old play together; they do the same stuff, just not as often or as bad. If one of them has a bigger piece of cake they get upset. If I give one child a piece of candy and not the others, they get upset. When it is time to stop playing outside and come in for a bath, they get upset. When they have to clean their room (even though they made the mess!) they get upset. Did we teach this behavior to them? Absolutely not, they were born with it and have done it since Day 1. They get upset if they don't get their way. They get better at *controlling* their self-centered emotions as they get older, but they have a definite bent towards vice and their behavior shows it.

I watch other kids and I see the same things: selfishness, impatience and self-centeredness. Someone once commented, "It sure is a good thing babies can't operate guns or there would be a lot more crime in the world." If a baby wants something, you have about 30 seconds to figure out what it is or the volume of their screaming goes up steadily until you do. Babies are born with a sinful nature from the start, and from this they react to the world in vice naturally, just watch them! This is from original sin and was handed down to them from their original parents Adam and Eve.[35] (Gen 3)

Another example I cite as evidence is by observing people in difficult situations. Do they respond naturally in vice or virtue? For example if you are working on a project — say, putting a child's toy together — and it isn't going well after 30 minutes, how do you respond, with frustration or patience?

If you get cut off in traffic on your drive home from work, do you respond with anger or mercy? If you get caught speeding by a police officer do you respond honestly and admit your speeding, or dishonestly and lie or make an excuses? These are just a few of the many examples that show our natural response to difficult situations is to react with vice.

Consider this: if vices are unnatural then why are they our first response in difficult situations? Discouragement, frustration, or fear are not only natural, they are second nature for mankind.

Why do we seem to never totally get over these vices and struggle with them all our lives? It isn't like people *want* to be more angry or worried in their life. How many people have you ever heard say, "I wish I were an angrier person," or "I wish I worried more in life"? Vices make life more difficult yet we can't seem to triumph over them. If they were unnatural, like smoking a cigarette for the first time, we'd hack and cough and say I am not doing *that* again.

To put it another way, if virtuous responses were our natural reactions, why don't more people live them out? Why aren't there more people living out patience, honesty, and encouragement when things don't go their way? Why aren't these virtues the typical "knee-jerk" response to storms or tests?

Take this test: find any 3-year-old and try to teach them to build a "house of cards" say three levels high. Use any standard deck of cards. Watch them as the cards fall on every mishap and they have to start all over; see if they respond with patience and determination, or frustration and anger? Do they seem to want to keep trying (determination) or quit? Do they respond with encouraging remarks to themselves or discouraging ones? Do they grow in confidence, or in doubt?

Think of how people react instinctively, and I think you would see the natural tendency would be vice rather than virtue almost every time.

The bottom line: our instinctive reactions to life's difficult moments show that our natural bent is towards vice, not virtue. Our choices will sway towards vice and not virtue. This is why we must transform our spirit.

God's View on Man

The Bible is not silent on this issue. Here are just a few verses that tell of mankind's iniquity and wickedness from the start:

> "The heart is deceitful above all things and desperately wicked, who can understand it." (Jer 17:9)

> "…every inclination of his heart is evil from childhood." (Gen 8:21)

> "Not a word from their mouth can be trusted; their hearts are filled with destruction. Their throat is an open grave; with their tongue they speak deceit." (PS 5:9)

"...there is no one righteous, not even one, there is no one who understands, no one who seeks God. All have turned away, they have together become worthless. There is no one who does good, not even one." (Rom 3:10-12)

"...but each one is tempted when, by his own evil desire, he is dragged away and enticed." (James 1:14)

This is just a sample of verses that show God revealing man's inner heart to be prejudiced towards vice from the start. A.W. Tozer notes,

"The human heart is heretical by nature and runs to error as naturally as a garden to weeds."[36]

The cause is from original sin and man's fall in the Garden of Eden (Gen 3). It says in Jeremiah 13:23, "Can the Ethiopian change his skin or the leopard his spots? Neither can you do good who are accustomed to doing evil." The concept is simple; people who are born in sin and wired to do evil can't change their spiritual nature by themselves. They need an outside force to make this change for them. Only then can they exchange virtue for vice on a consistent basis.

God pronounces mankind fallen, sinful and worthy of death. The whole point of the New Testament is that man is fallen and on his own will die eternally in his sin. He is separated from God and because of this he is in rebellion to God. Man is cursed from birth because of his disobedience to the Law of God, his sin (Gal 3:10-14). The New Testament is the Good News that God has redeemed man from the curse and bridged the gap between sinful man and God in Jesus Christ. If man was not sinful at birth and in need of a Savior, Jesus never needed to come to die on a cross.

Once we understand that God calls us sinners in disobedience to His Law and commands, we can then go on to seek a cure. The cure is found in becoming a new person with a new spirit. We can't become good on our own, we need help. God can give a man a new spirit, make him reborn (John 3:3) and give him new desires in his heart, desires for virtue and right behavior. It says in 2 Corinthians 5:17 "Therefore if anyone is in Christ he is a new creation, the old things have passed away, the new has come." Again in Galatians 6:15 "Neither circumcision or uncircumcision count for anything, what counts is a new creation."

When we come to God in Jesus Christ we receive a new inner spirit to do battle with our flesh, our inborn sinful nature. This is the hope of the cross of Christ, to change us from the inside out. We will never get rid of our desire to sin in the flesh but with a new spirit we can fight it. Our renewed spirit can battle daily this desire of our flesh towards vice. We can stop making bad choices and overcome them with righteous choices. We have to battle these vices each and every day, but we can overcome them through the strength we have in Christ who reforms us and abides in redeemed man.

Man will naturally have a bent towards sin and vice. Mark Bubeck in his book called "The Adversary" says this:

> "The flesh is a built-in law of failure, making it impossible for natural man to please God. It is a compulsive inner force inherited from man's fall, which expresses itself in rebellion against God and righteousness. The flesh can never be reformed or improved."[37]

The flesh leads us down a never-ending slope of wrong behavior and wrong thoughts and emotions. The worse the situation, the more the natural reaction will be one of vice.

We must view ourselves as God does and understand we are formed to fail. Until this is admitted we will continue to sabotage our own cause. Until you win the battle against yourself, you will never be able to win the battle against other invisible forces. You are the greatest opponent you have to face. As Walt Kelly, the creator of Pogo, so correctly observed, "We have met the enemy and it is us."

The second front we must engage in battle is the world system and the beliefs of our time. It is another powerful force we face that seduces us to conform to the beliefs of our times.

The World System (The Beliefs of our Time)

The War of the World

To quote Mark Bubeck again,

> "As our enemy, the world is the whole organized system, made up of varying and changing social, economic, materialistic, and religious philosophies which have their expression through the organizations and personalities of human beings…The world system begins to surround man with that which intensifies the inner problem he already has as a fallen creature."[38]

In other words the world hits us where we are most vulnerable, the desires of our flesh.

The world system strengthens our desires for more power, possessions, fame and illicit sex. The ways are very seductive and they target our sinful nature in these areas. We seek them out naturally. The world then sells and markets to these appetites. Our inner desire for more money, greed for notoriety, sexual gratification and vanity, make easy targets for advertisers to prey on.

Take for example how the world directs our thinking concerning the selling of sex to society. We are told sex is OK outside of marriage. We are told sex is natural so let's make it great. We have enhancing drugs so we can do it more often, like Viagra. Then mostly we put skimpily-clothed women and men on the covers of magazines, on TV and in movies to stimulate our drive for more sex. This is also encouraged on TV sitcoms and dramas by portraying the "heroes" having illicit sex. Add on top of all of this no responsibility for the consequences and our sinful nature easily falls under the spell of our illicit sexual desires. All humanity is seen as a breeding ground (pardon the pun) for sexual fulfillment.

There are many other things society wants us to believe that are contrary to the Bible. "Groupthink" in our world system influences our opinions and our actions. We already have a bent towards materialism, fornication, and envy. These natural inclinations are just that much harder to resist when they are actively marketed by the society in which we live. Even worse, we begin to think of them, not as the vices they are, but as good, desirable things.

Another problem this world creates is peer pressure or expectations from others. We want others to like us, we want to fit in. We naturally want their approval of our actions and we want them to know we are making it in the world. We often feel the need to make excuses for a poor performance. Patrick Morley, author of the bestselling book *The Man in the Mirror*, said something to this effect, "We spend much of our lives trying to please people we not only don't like but people we really don't care what they think of us in the first place." Yet it is these very people whose approval we so often seek. We get molded into the world as it tells us we should be, instead of being who we are called to be.

Other beliefs the world sells us are seen in slogans of today. Here are some of these slogans and the implications behind them:

> "He who has the most toys at the end wins."— *so we buy more stuff.*
>
> "You only go around once in life, so go for the gusto."— *so we live life for today and don't worry about tomorrow.*
>
> "Don't rock the boat."— *so we don't do things that might offend others even if we believe what they are doing is wrong.*
>
> "We have to keep up with the Joneses"— *so we buy or try to outdo whatever it is our neighbors have or do.*
>
> "I work hard for my money, I deserve this."— *so we splurge because we want a few of life's extras.*
>
> "Everyone else is doing it."— *so we go against our moral conscience and act on our passions.*

We often don't even realize where we get our beliefs, but yet they still occupy our minds and drive our behavior, whether we consciously know it or not. We shop for image in our cars and in our clothes to impress those around us. Driving around a 10-year-old car seems to say that you can't afford a new one. Driving around a new Mercedes says you are making it in life, even though you may be in debt up to your ears. The image we have of ourselves and the image we want others to have of us drive many of our decisions.

This "presenting an image" is clearly seen in the world of advertising. Neil Postmen said this about advertising,

> "Advertising used to be solely for information to be passed along for the benefit of both the seller and the consumer. Advertising made propositional claims of truth and assumed the consumer was rational, literate and analytical. Today this has drastically changed. Advertising tries to sell by the image of a product. It tries to convince you that it will make your life easier. Advertising is seen today as a means of entertainment, it uses psychology to sell, and has no need for reasoning."[39]

Products are sold most often by what image they portray to the consumer. A dress will make you look thin, even if you aren't. A boutique beer is promoted as an upper class beverage and if you drink it you are upper class. If you wear a specific cologne those of the opposite sex will be attracted to you not because of who you are but because of how you smell. So goes the world of advertising.

This happens in other areas as well. We buy into what the world system tells us to think politically. Hence the term "politically correct." This affects more than just politics, though. It affects morals, religion, the economy, world stability, and so on. The world tells us we should believe what they tell us to believe or we aren't up to date. We are out of the loop and need to get with it. We don't want to be seen as old fashioned, so we should think twice about what we believe.

I bring all of this up because the world is constantly selling you its own thoughts and ideas; whether this is from an advertiser to buy their product or "peer pressure" to "fit in." Many of the concepts the world is promoting are false, such as the car you drive revealing who you really are. We must understand that the frenzy to sell more products is why companies advertise as they do. Politically-correct ideas are always political, but they aren't always correct. You must not be swayed by pandering emotionalism or peer pressure to adopt someone else's agenda.

The world has tremendous impact on how we think and what we do. We often "go with the flow" without realizing what ideas we are promoting. We send our kids to the local public school because that is what you are "supposed" to do. We give our child a car, or let them buy one, at age 16 because that is what everyone else does. We wear the latest fashions because everyone else "approves" of that style. We must understand that we can't let the world conform us to *its* values and beliefs but rather, we must transform our values and beliefs to those instructed by God.

Transforming not Conforming

Compare what the world is calling us to be to what we are called to be as children of the Living God. We must take our thoughts obedient to Christ (2 Cor 10:5), be in command of our emotions (Phil 4:8, 1 Tim 6:11) and desire righteousness in our body (Titus 2:11-14). This is the life we as children of light are called to.

This is clearly seen in Rom 12:1-2:

> "Therefore I urge you brothers, in view of God's mercy, to offer your bodies as living sacrifices, holy and pleasing to God — this is your spiritual act (service) of worship. Do not conform any longer to the pattern of this world, but be transformed by the renewing of your mind. Then you will be able to test what God's will is, His good and pleasing and perfect will."

We are called here to not conform to "groupthink" or as the world wants us to think. Rather we are called to change and renew our mind the way God wants us to think. Ways that are good, right, and holy to Him.

There are three key concepts in this verse that we need to take a second look at. The first concept is to "conform." This means to fashion like or to be made in the image of. *We were designed to be a reflection of God, not a reflection of this world.* This world is not something we want to be like (1 John 2:15-17 and Col 3:2). In fact we are told to not seek to be like this world but conversely to overcome the world and its views (1 John 5:4). To do this we must understand how we are called to live and not be of this world. Simply put we must stop trying to "fit in" with others around us.

The second concept is to "renew your mind." The concept is to renovate or restore. This is a complete change for the better. When we renovate a house we change it for the better. Similarly when we renovate our spirit we make it more like Jesus. The assumption is our mind is not currently at its best but by changing it or renewing it we can make it better. This renewal is to seek the mind — the Truth — of God. See the world as He sees it, think of it as He thinks of it. To do this unleashes the power of our mind to change who we are in our physical body. In order to renew our mind as God calls us, we must study His Word in the Bible. When we read the Word of God it renews us because it is alive (see Heb 4:12 and 2 Tim 3:16) and lives in us to shape us in righteousness. When we renew our mind we make it better. The more we enable our mind the more our mind can enable us.

The last concept is "spiritual service." The word spiritual comes from the Greek word *logikos*, which is a derivative of the Greek word logos. It says in John 1:1 "In the beginning was the word (*logos*) and the word (*logos*) was with God and the word (*logos*) was God." The thought here is that if we take the word of God, which is God, into our mind we will be able to serve Him. This is called our spiritual service because we are changing our mind which will conform our actions to His Word. So our spiritual service to God then becomes doing His will in our body. We are His hands and feet in this world.

We need to renew our mind to transform our body. Then our body gives God spiritual service through obedience to His commands. All parents demand obedience from their children and God our Father is no different. We must seek the will of God for our life and live it out daily in our body. We must make our body a "living sacrifice" exhibiting goodness, kindness, gentleness, patience, peace and love to a world so in need of these elements.

Recapture the Wonder

Lastly, the world system tells us man is the measure of all things, and God is on a lower level. We then lose wonder and awe for God and His creations.

So, if a famous artist paints a beautiful picture of a sunset, we may pay handsomely for it and hang it in a prominent place on our wall, but we overlook the free, ever-changing beauty of natural sunsets. Instead of marveling at the limitless beauty and awe of the night sky, we visit a planetarium. We have lost the wonder God has put in each one of our hearts.

Ravi Zacharias in his book *Recapture the Wonder* talks about how as adults we have lost the gift of wonder we had as kids. As we get more and more knowledge we seem to lose this ability to marvel at things in life. He says,

"The tragedy with growing up is not that we lose childishness in its simplicity, but that we lose childlikeness in its sublimity."[40]

Kids have a marvelous imagination which fills them with wonder and awe at life. You throw them up in the air and they say do it again, and repeat this 20+ times. This same action does not bore them but thrills them. They get a present from Santa and just seeing the presents under the tree makes them squirm. They love the simple things in life.

As they get older they lose this because they believe they have figured it all out. Your parents are Santa, there is no tooth fairy, and it takes a roller coaster ride to thrill them. Believing they can find all the answers to life destroys the wonder as they become adults. There is something good about childhood innocence that leads to wonder, which most adults have lost.

I went to the theater with the author of a successful play.
He insisted on explaining everything …
Told me what to watch,
The details of direction,
The errors of the property man,
The foibles of the star.
He anticipated all my surprises
And ruined the evening.
Never again—and mark you,
The greatest Author of all
Made no such mistake![41]

God only gives us so much information. He holds all knowledge and truth. These then are revealed to us by Him, not discovered by man of himself. God alone gives us knowledge and thus we must be humble before Him. We must be meek about His revelations, not proud about discovering it. When we feel we can explain everything, we substitute man for God. Man then becomes the measure of all things. The question is which man, Abe Lincoln or Hugh Hefner, Mother Teresa or Hitler?

When finite man surpasses an Infinite God, man becomes only as enchanted as his last movie or newest technology. When God transforms us in His image, He has infinite power and knowledge to bring you to your knees in worship. His creation reveals His splendor (Psalm 19:1). The result is awe when we look at new-fallen snow on a winter morning or see a breaching whale in the ocean. These are just a few signs of the glory of God, and it far surpasses anything man can conceive or invent.

Ravi Zacharias opens his book on wonder by discussing a homeless man he once saw. He talks about the homeless man going through garbage cans for food and the impoverishment of the situation. How destitute this man was physically. He then makes this comment about mankind today spiritually,

> "We pity the man at the garbage dump because his impoverishment is stark and his disfigurement is visible. But then we sit in front of our television screens or in movie theaters, or thumb through our fashion magazines eyeing symbols of beauty and success—the icons of our time and we do not see the scavenging that goes on within them, the searching through every success to find something of transcending worth, the plastic smiles, the contoured shapes, the schizoid hungers for privacy and recognition at the same time ...I believe it is possible that those who have attained every dream may be at least as impoverished as the man at the dump, perhaps even more, as they bask in the accolades, knowing that the charade is shattered by the aloneness within them."[42]

The spiritually impoverished can hide it much better than the physically impoverished, but they are both just as destitute. The fact that we can hide our loneliness doesn't make it go away. Thoreau said, "Most men lead lives of quiet desperation." This is the situation of the spiritually impoverished man who has lost his sense of wonder in the world. He has been conformed to the world and not transformed by God.

The Devil (Lies)
Is the Devil Real?

We said in Chapter 2 that Truth is the solution to uniting our human system. The dilemma we face is how to separate truth from lies. Lies are the enemy of truth. Lies are half-truths or completely erroneous information. They destroy all in their path and must be avoided at all costs. Winston

Churchill said, "The truth is so vital that it is usually surrounded by a body guard of lies."

Lies are based on deceit. Some deceit is intentional, some is unintentional. In either case it makes little difference, by having wrong or false information you will make terrible choices. Our goal is to understand that the ability to make only best choices is facilitated by true or false information. We must be insistent on gathering only truth as we go through life.

We must understand that lies disperse our power. They take away virtue and replace it with vice. Many people think all information is good information but this is wrong. Information is either right or wrong and we must decipher it. Physicist Andre Sakharov who gave Russia the hydrogen bomb said,

> "I used to think the most powerful weapon on earth was the Atomic Bomb, I now have changed my mind. I have come to the conclusion that the most powerful weapon in the world is the truth."[43]

We need to understand there is a being who is committed to lies. A being who is deceitful and crafty in using his lies to disarm you. That being is the devil. We live in a world where the reality of the devil is questioned. A being whose very intent is to destroy you and all you do. A being you can't see yet who, like God, exists. A being who is evil, whose other name is Satan, which means, literally, adversary, coming from the verb to lie in wait. He is opposed to man and God and all they do. He has forces under his command called demons.

The Bible talks about this being "the devil" around 100 times. It talks about his demons another 100 times. His existence is made very real in encounters he has with Jesus (Matt 4:1-11) and God (Job 1:1-12). Jesus casts out evil spirits (Mark 5:8) and these evil spirits even have names. They cause people to act in evil ways and do things to their bodies (Luke 4:33-35).

I bring this up to underscore the reality of this opposing force we are up against. He is a being we can't see, but that doesn't make him any less real. Like thoughts, electricity, and the wind, there is much we can't see in this world, but which are no less real. Satan exists and we need to understand who he is and how he works. He spreads lies and that is all he does, there is no truth in him.

Satan is "the father of lies," "the one who deceives," "the great dragon," "the murderer." These are other names for him in the Bible. The other descriptive names again reinforce whom he is and what he is out to do. Satan is first and foremost a liar. That is his native tongue. This is seen clearly in the gospel of John.

> "You belong to your father the devil …he was a murderer from the beginning, not holding to the truth, for there is no truth in him. When he lies, he speaks his native language, for he is a liar and the father of all lies." (John 8:44)

This passage is very insightful because it tells how Satan works, he lies. He lied to Adam and Eve (Gen 3:4-5), he lied to Jesus (Matt4:6), and he continues to lie to man today. All lies are from Satan and there is no truth in him. Compare this to God, who is Truth. Just a few passages that deal with God's character and truth:

> "I am the way, the truth, and the life." (John 14:6)

> "When the Counselor comes, whom I will send from the Father, the Spirit of truth …he will testify about me." (John 15:26)

> "But when he the Spirit of truth comes he will guide you into all truth." (John 16:13a)

> "Sanctify them by truth, your word is truth." (John 17:17)

> "…I came into the world to testify about to the truth, everyone on the side of truth listens to me." (John 18:37b)

> "Every good and perfect gift is from above, coming down from the Father of lights, who does not change like shifting shadows. He chose to give us birth through the word of truth that we might be a kind of first fruits of all that he created." (James 1:17-18)

Everything here talks of the truth of God. He is the foundation of all truth just as Satan is the foundation of all lies. In these verses notice: the word of God is truth, God is the truth, God is the Spirit of truth, God testifies about truth, we have birth through the word of truth. God is a God of Truth and no lie can be found in Him.

Notice in this last verse it says God "gave us birth through the word (*logos*) of truth." *Logos* is used again for word here. The word of God, His truth, is used to create, sustain and give life. The Word of God and the truth of God are life-giving in our spirit. This is how we can be reborn by having truth active in our heart. We must then base our life on it. By having truth in us we will then get rid of lies.

God is Dead and we Killed Him

Another way lies work in our world is to deny God's existence. To rid the world of God is to rid the world of Truth. The problem with truth is that once you know it you must make a choice whether to obey it or not. This makes us accountable. It is this very truth that will condemn a man. If a man is guilty and says he didn't commit a crime, a jury is formed to determine his guilt or innocence. They seek the only truth. Once the truth is found, he will be declared innocent or guilty based on the truth.

Truth is crucial in law. Jesus said, "There is a judge for the one who does not accept my words, that very word which I have spoken will condemn at the last day." (John 12:48) The thought here is that the words Jesus spoke will be used to judge us. This is determined by our knowledge of truth and obedience to it. The works, actions and deeds of our life will be compared to Jesus' Word of Truth. If they are equal we will be declared righteous through Jesus' blood. It they don't match we will be condemned to eternal hell (Rev 20:12-13). To know truth and to not act on it declares us guilty because it is a choice we are making.

The world tries to rid itself of God, or truth, so this can't happen. "God is dead and we killed him," said atheist Fredrick Nietzsche. Sadly in our country we are doing the same thing. Our country has been slowly taking God out of our country. We have taken Him out of school, government, families, and finally totally out of individuals lives en masse. We have substituted it with relativism, materialism, pluralism and pragmatism. We have substituted lies for truth. Alan Bloom says this brilliantly,

> "The danger they (students) have been taught to fear from absolutism is not error but intolerance. Relativism is necessary to openness; and this is the virtue …openness and relativism to …all various claims to truth and various ways of life …this is the great insight of our times. The true believer is the real danger. The point is not to correct mistakes of the past and really be right; rather it is not to think you are right at all… There is no enemy other than the man who is not open to everything…In order to make this arrangement work, there was a conscious effort to weaken religious belief, by assigning it to the realm of opinion as opposed to knowledge."[44]

The recent education of openness pays no attention to history, origins, or rights of men. It takes truth out and substitutes openness and relativism in its place. Openness and relativism are the building blocks to lies; a lie says everything is true. Truth is exclusive by definition. If I am a man then by definition of a man I am not a woman. If a car is red then by definition it can't be green. *By accepting everything and rejecting nothing, we deny the very definition of truth.* In fact truth and absolutes are the very thing this new education has come to assault.

The idea that any particular thing can be known for sure is the backbone of truth. It is this concept that has become archaic. Truth now means true for me and nothing more. It may or may not be true for you. This idea is absurd when you consider concepts like math. Is 2+2=4 true for me and not you? This is the very foundation mathematics is founded on. It is true for you, and me. In his book "Relativism, Feet Firmly Planted in Midair" Frank Beckwith and Greg Koukl make this statement:

> "By means of repetition and passive acceptance over time, ideas take on a force of common wisdom, a "truth" that everyone knows but no one has stopped to examine, a kind of intellectual urban legend … the death of truth in our society has created a moral decay in which every debate ends with, 'says who?'"[45]

The results of this are catastrophic. We no longer have right or wrong but moral relativism, we no longer have truth but how you "feel" about an issue is all that matters. We can no longer call behavior wrong because this is intolerant or might offend someone. We have exchanged what *is* good for what *feels* good. Then once our desires have been asserted we attempt to rationalize the choices with moral language. Self-interest is the rule of the day.[46]

Once we take out truth and substitute it with lies, or relativism, we start to work backward and find something we enjoy and then argue vehemently to defend it. Truth works just the opposite. We search with a heart bent on finding the right answer and will stop at nothing until we find it; then no matter what that response is, we must base our life on it. By killing God we have killed Truth, and by killing Truth we have encouraged every behavior. Relativism not only allows bad choices, it encourages them. To believe the lie that the law of gravity is not true and jump off the roof of your house is a terrible choice. These are the type of choices we seek to avoid.

Lies are like fire, they spread rapidly and if not stopped they destroy everything in their path. Satan has infiltrated this world with his lies of relativism, materialism and individualism. We must put out the fire with the Word of Truth, God's Word in the Bible. Our world has symbolically associated Satan with fire, this association is very accurate.

The Call for Wisdom

As I have tried to present in this chapter, our ability to reach our full potential through a reformed spirit is a battle. This battle is fought on three fronts; our flesh, the world system and lies. It is a battle that must be fought and must be won at all costs. It is our life that is at stake. One of the best weapons in this battle is wisdom. Wisdom is a virtue. God tells us over and over again to be wise.

Wisdom is the ability to judge correctly and follow the best course of action, based on knowledge and understanding. Charles Stanley states it this way:

> "Nothing man may acquire, earn, or achieve in the natural realm is as valuable as wisdom. One of the reasons God places such a high value on wisdom is no doubt because the stakes are so high related to living wisely. On the other hand if you chose to walk unwisely you can expect a far different set of outcomes." [47]

Wisdom is of God and is opposed to the wisdom of this world. God promises to bless those with wisdom and curse those without it (Deut 28:1-68). In the fourteenth chapter of Deuteronomy God gives 14 verses of blessing to those who follow Him and 54 verses of cursing to those who don't. Wisdom is more valuable than pure gold or silver, and nothing you gain can be compared to her (Pro 3:14-15). Happy is the man who gains wisdom (Pro 3:13). The man that has wisdom has long life and riches and honor (Pro 3:13, 16). The ways of wisdom are pleasant and the paths of wisdom are peace (Pro 3:17). Finally wisdom is a tree of life (Pro 3:18).

Wisdom is the ability to gather truth in your life. It is an ability to discern truth from lies. Most importantly it is the ability to apply truth. To become the very best that God has commanded us to be requires that we make only best choices, this is having wisdom.

The writer of Ecclesiastes was a man, believed to be King Solomon, the richest man in the world at the time, who had seen it all and done it all. This is what he has to say for all this world has to offer:

> "Come now I will test you with pleasure to find out what is good. But that also proved to be meaningless …I tried cheering myself with wine …I undertook projects: I built houses for myself and planted vineyards …I bought male and female slaves …I amassed silver and gold for myself and the treasure of kings and provinces …and many concubines, man's delight …and whatever my eyes desired I did not keep them from me, I kept my heart from no pleasure. Then I considered all that my hands had done and the toil that I had spent on doing it, and behold it was all vanity, a striving after the wind." (Eccel 2:1-11)

After seeing all and doing all he says it is chasing after the wind. He ends the book with words to his son. The design is to teach him lessons the writer has learned after making many mistakes. By the end of his life he came to realize the value of truth. By not having or applying truth he came to realize the consequences of bad and terrible choices. If he had these choices to make again, he probably would have made different ones. Sadly he realized these consequences late in life, as most people do, and the costs of them are very high.

He spoke these words of regret, yet words of warning to those who read them. They are the warnings of an old man to the young men in this world, words to the wise. These are words we need to ponder as we consider wisdom:

> "Be warned my son ...Now all has been heard; here is the conclusion of the matter. *Fear God and keep his commandments*, for this is the whole duty of man. For God will bring everything into judgment, including every hidden thing, whether it is good or evil." (Eccel 12:13-14) *(emphasis added)*

The only way to avoid the snares of: our flesh, the world, and the devil are to gain wisdom. These are forces we battle spiritually and each one is a very formidable foe. We need to understand how they affect us and our ability to perform. We need to understand how to overcome them. Most of all we need to understand these three forces are already affecting us and will sabotage our ability to know and serve Jesus Christ. They drain power from us and work behind the scenes. By actively pursuing wisdom we become more able to fight. Jesus said,

> "...the one who is in you is greater than the one who is in the world."   (1 John 4:4)

Our strength is in Jesus. Seek out His truth and don't stop until you find it. Its benefits are great, but the consequences of its loss are even greater.

We have finished this chapter talking about lies and the power it has to thwart us from reforming our spirit. In the next chapter I want to talk about its counterpart, Truth and the power it has to transform us.

The Truth:

The Power to Unite

Truth: that long, clean, clear, simple, undeniable, unchallengeable, straight, and shining line, on one side of which is black and on the other of which is white.

William Faulkner (1897-1962)

Truth is not merely a moral concept; it is a reflection of the way things actually are. It is the fabric of reality. To veer away from the truth is to swerve into the realm of fantasy. To deliberately and perpetually reject the truth is nothing short of insanity. Apart from truth, a civil society cannot long survive.[48] Truth reflects reality. Saint Augustine said, "Truth is the affirmation of what is."[49]

Truth comes in several flavors: scientific, mathematical, historical, moral and spiritual. All are important, but the first three — science, math and history — are merely information. It is with the last two, moral truths and spiritual truths, where real power lies, and those are what we will deal with here.

There are three things about truth we have to understand.

1. Truths are based on standards.
2. The quest for truth occurs in the mind.
3. Truth gives us the power to choose rightly.

Truth is the Standard – One test for truth is comparison to a standard. Once we know the standard and accept its accuracy, we can gauge how true things are by comparing them to this standard.[50] An obvious example is measuring an object. We can use a yardstick or tape measure to see how long it is. Because we trust the yardstick to be an accurate standard, we can accept the length of the object (as measured by the standard) to be true. The tape measure is an accurate way to size up an object because it is a set standard of measurement.

This is also true of humanity. The standard to which man must compare himself is Jesus Christ. We must understand how we compare to Him and His teachings. We must measure all areas of our life by Him. This is stated in numerous Scripture verses:

> "Do not lie to each other, since you have taken off your old self with its practices, and have put on the new self, which is being renewed in knowledge in the image of its Creator." (Col 3:9-10)

> "You were taught, with regard to your former way of life, to put off your old self, which is being corrupted by its deceitful desires, to be made new in the attitude of your minds; and to put o the new self, created to be like God in true righteousness and holiness." (Eph 4:22-24)

> "His divine power has given us everything we need for life and godliness through our knowledge of him who called us by his own glory and goodness. Through these he has given us his very great and precious promises, so that through them you may participate in the divine nature and escape the corruption in the world caused by evil desires." (2 Pet 1:3-4)

> "And we, who with unveiled faces all reflect the Lord's glory, are being transformed into his likeness with ever-increasing glory, which comes from the Lord, who is the Spirit." (2 Cor 3:18)

Jesus is the standard of measurement for man because Jesus is the truth. Our life must conform to His truth. Our beliefs and attitudes that don't measure up to God's truth must be changed. As we conform our attitudes and beliefs to truth, we unite with it and become more and more like it. This is the goal of virtue and righteous living, Christ-likeness. We will not reach that goal in this life, but it is still the target toward which we aim. One day we will see Jesus as He is because we will be like Him. This is a promise God gives to Christians (1 John 2:3).

Truth then has the power to unite us in all that we are and do, because it alone holds the only reflection of the way things are meant to be. When we look at the power in truth, we see it not only reveals a divine standard of measurement, but it gives us specifics on how to conform. In other words, once we know what the standard is, we can then work backwards to find out what we must do to match it. It becomes our guide. The differences between the standard and us are the changes we must make, adding or subtracting, to conform to its likeness. What we add or subtract must be the difference to help us match it. Much of what we need to add is virtue, much of what we need to subtract is our vice.

The battle for the Mind- The battle for truth occurs in the mind because that is where we process information. The mind also determines where our thoughts are going, be it for good or be it for bad. What we think about and how often we think about it determines what we will do and ultimately what we will become.

To be right we must think right. A.W. Tozer said,

> "What we think about when we are free to think about what we will—that is what we are or will soon become... Our voluntary thoughts not only reveal what we are, they predict what we will become…But we can by Spirit-inspired thinking help to make our minds pure sanctuaries in which God will be pleased to dwell."[51]

Our minds are bombarded with ideas, pictures, lifestyles, ways to think, and so much more. How we process this and then how we use this ability to think determines our beliefs and our attitudes. Only by choosing good and right thoughts, the dwelling place of truth, can we make our minds holy and set apart for Christ.

The Apostle Paul said this about our thoughts,

> "Finally, brothers, whatever is true, whatever is noble, whatever is right, whatever is pure, whatever is lovely,

> whatever is admirable—if anything is excellent or praiseworthy, think about such things." (Phil 4:8)

He is telling us to control how we think and what we think about. Tozer talked about creating a favorable moral climate to grow our faith, love, and reverence for God. We do this by thinking about God and holy things.

When we think about how much harm someone or something has caused us, we create a negative environment — a perfect place for sin to dwell. Hurtful and harmful thoughts lead to hurtful and harmful action. Conversely, when we choose not to dwell on hurtful and harmful thoughts, we create a positive environment for godliness to dwell.

Truth is perceived in the mind, contemplated in the mind and acted on by direction from the mind. When we think right we live right. To grow in Christ-likeness we must think on virtue, holiness and righteousness continually.

<u>Truth is the Power to Choose Rightly</u> — To know truth is to know reality and to know reality is to have power to make the right choices, every time. As we come to rely on truth as our standard for making choices, picking right choices — even best choices — becomes easier and easier. Truth is power, and the more power we build up in ourselves, the greater our ability to make best choices.

When jurors in a trial hear testimony in a case, what is required of every witness as part of their oath? To tell the truth, the whole truth, and nothing but the truth. Our courts recognize that good decisions can only be rendered through a complete knowledge of the truth. What's true in law is true in life.

Truth does not lose its value over time. It is just as valid a guide today as it was in biblical times. In the march of time, moral and spiritual truths still lead the parade. Scientific "truths" have undergone many changes and modifications over the centuries — for example, who today believes that the sun revolves around a flat earth? — but moral and spiritual truths have survived unchanged since Moses brought the tablets down from Mount Sinai.

The Bible is not outdated. The Word of God will endure forever (1 Pet 1:25). We often think we are so advanced that moral or spiritual truth no longer applies to us today, but this is just intellectual vanity. Truth is never outdated. Fads and trends will come and go, but God's truth will never diminish.

The Offensive Nature of Truth

Truth is objective, not subjective. Likewise, truth is exclusive, not inclusive. If my car is red, that excludes using any other color to truthfully describe it. This means it is not brown, or blue, or green, or any other color than red. This seems obvious enough, even trivial, in the case of car colors but when we're dealing with moral truths, people tend to see "colors" like a chameleon: changing and different in every situation! Truth can be very offensive to people because it exposes their true moral colors.

For example, the biblical declaration that homosexuality is a sin (1 Cor 6:9-10), will offend many people. Followers of non-Christian religions are offended when we speak the truth, that Jesus is the only way to eternal life (Acts 4:10-12), even though the distinguished international thinker, Ravi Zacharias, has pointed out, "It is more rational to say Jesus is the only way to eternal life than to say all religions are right." Even when backed by logical thought, the truth will still be offensive to many. It leaves no wiggle room, and lots of people don't like that.

To say truth is exclusive is to tell those who are outside of the truth that they are wrong. Not partially right, or half-right or almost right ... but *wrong*. This is not only offensive to them, it is telling them they must change, and that is something many people are just unwilling to do. Truth "gets in their face" and they raise their defensive shields. Truth is black and white, but many want to see it in shades of gray. Truth allows no middle ground, and that is unacceptable to many. They want to "just get along" — the "you go your way, and I'll go mine" compromise. Truth will never make this compromise.

People are quick to deny the truth, especially when it threatens their way of life. To see this denial in action, watch how an alcoholic reacts when told they have a drinking problem, that they need help, and that it will require a lifetime of recovery. They don't want to hear that. They don't want to admit to it, they don't want to shoulder the blame or accept the shame, and they certainly don't want to leave their comfy little world of alcoholic friends and boozy good times. Do you think their reaction might be, "Oh, thank God, someone really cares about me and wants to help"? Not likely. Most often, the alcoholic will vent their anger at you because you told them the truth. They don't want to change and truth is telling them to change. Emotional outbursts and outright denial are the most likely responses to the terrible offense of truth. The truth hurts, even when it has the power to make you free.

When people or nations turn their back on truth, disaster is soon to follow. We must have the courage to admit the truth and then make the changes truth demands of us. If not, moral bankruptcy soon follows. History is the mirror that reflects the future of people or nations that ignore the truth. They are destroyed from the inside out and fall, just like Rome.

We live in a society where we don't want to hurt any ones feelings so we don't speak truth because it might offend someone. Imagine a doctor not telling his patient he had cancer because he didn't want to hurt the patient's feelings. The patient might not like the truth, but the doctor has to tell it.

To quote James Robison,

> "We never have to apologize for the truth. It is able to withstand every charge. It is able to bear up under every challenge. It is sufficient unto itself. In due course, it will prove its own value and veracity."[52]

Truth is the greatest weapon mankind has to use against the forces of evil. If we recognize and then apply truth in our life we can navigate our lives through any situation. Without truth we are rudderless. With truth we are powerful and effective.

I recently heard a story about two evil and wicked brothers. One day one of the brothers died. The other brother went to a pastor and said, "I will pay you a lot of money if will you do my brother's funeral. I only ask that you call him a 'saint' in the eulogy." After much thought the pastor decided he would do it. When the funeral came, the pastor said these words, "This man was a rotten, good for nothing cheat, he was a scoundrel of the worst kind, he was despicable and vile …but compared to his brother, he was a saint."

No matter how bad we are, we can always find someone worse to point to. If we use a lower standard, we can feel better about ourselves than what the truth reveals. But that is false relief. When truth is the standard, we should see ourselves as we are. This is how God sees us and how we must see ourselves. Oswald Chambers said,

> "The moral law does not consider us as weak human beings at all; it takes no account of our heredity and infirmities; it demands that we be absolutely moral."[53]

The Power of Words

While gestures and expressions play their part, we communicate with each other mainly by using words. For accurate communication, all parties to the conversation need to share a common vocabulary, where the words being used have the same meaning to everyone. When they don't, communication breaks down into confusion and misunderstanding.

Over time, some words take on different meanings — often because of changes in the social landscape. For example, "the Gay Nineties" can have wildly different meanings, depending on whether you're referring to the 1890s or the 1990s!

Take another word, "discriminate." In modern dictionaries, this word has two quite distinct meanings:

1. a.) To make a clear distinction; distinguish: discriminate among the options available. b.) To make sensible decisions; judge wisely.

2. To make distinctions on the basis of class or category without regard to individual merit; show preference or prejudice

Up until relatively recent times, the first definition was in common usage, and it was a compliment. A personnel manager would be praised (and probably promoted) for "showing discrimination in the selection of employees." Today, the meaning of the word has swung almost completely over to the second definition, and any personnel manager who "shows discrimination in the selection of employees" is looking for a lawsuit.

Today, if you refuse to accept homosexuality as a valid and proper lifestyle choice, you are not admired for your strong character and moral resolve; you are reviled as "intolerant," "bigoted" and "prejudiced." Because of our permissive society's insistence on moral relativism, Christians are under attack for our beliefs in the moral codes set down by God. If we say that homosexual behavior offends our sense of right and wrong, that it runs counter to our understanding of God's will, and that we will not tolerate it or excuse it, then it is *US* who are branded "socially unacceptable."

In today's society, moral correctness has been replaced with political correctness. Truth is ignored, because truth offends and it is socially unacceptable these days to offend *anybody* (except, apparently, Christians).

Think words have no power? Think again.

Years ago a former US president was put before a grand jury. One particularly thorny question (one that he really wasn't interested in answering!) contained the word "is." To evade the question, he demurred because the answer depended, as he put it, "on what the definition of 'is' is." This has become an infamous example of what we call *word parsing* — twisting the meaning of words to suit our immediate purpose.

These are just word games of course, but if we as a society can no longer agree on what "is" is, we are in deep, deep trouble. We are no longer engaged in honest communication; we are waging a war of words.

We make up new words to paint a bad picture of people who disagree with us on certain points of view. A person who disagrees with homosexuality is a "homophobe." We even make up terms to obscure and "candy coat" concepts which, if given their true meaning, would be repugnant to most of us. Killing the elderly infirm has been softened to "euthanasia" (what a warm, fuzzy-sounding word to disguise what is really meant: to get rid of sick people because they are too expensive and inconvenient to keep around!). Political correctness demands "death with dignity" instead of the more accurate and dismal term, suicide. The homosexual lifestyle isn't "deviant," it's "alternative." Abortion activists prefer to be called "pro-choice," which sounds so much nicer than what they really want: the so-called "right" to kill infants in the womb for the mother's personal convenience.

When words lose their meaning, or misleading terms are used to hide ulterior motives, truth becomes harder and harder to find. Lies become easier to spread because they masquerade as truth. As Samuel Clemens (Mark Twain) said, "A lie can travel halfway around the world while the truth is putting on its shoes."

Word games are designed to confuse the real issue and take the debate off of truth. The next step down is relativism where truth is kicked out of the arena of ideas altogether. To the relativist, all viewpoints are acceptable and none are superior; everything is a shade of gray and anything goes.

Compare this to Jesus who is the Word (John 1:1). In Him there is no deception. Everything is black and white with no grey. Words have specific meanings because He holds all knowledge and calls things as they really are. He knows our thoughts (Matt 9:4) and our intentions (John 6:64, John 2:24-25) and to Him everything is laid bare, exposed for what it is (Heb 4:13). We can deceive others for a time on earth with our words, but we can't deceive Jesus. It is before His Throne we will one day stand and give an account for our life and our actions (Rev 20:11-15).

Truth is designed to lead and give direction. When a person or society has lost truth, they have lost their direction.

Truth is a Compass

During merit badge training, every Scout learns how to use a compass — to read maps, navigate rough terrain, and find their way home when they get lost. Truth is our compass to read the moral maps that God has provided us, to navigate the rough terrain of our life on earth, and to find our way home to God when we are lost. Truth is a navigational instrument to guide us in our actions and give us confidence that we are on the right course.

Truth is a guide, a moral compass. It tells you where to go. If we lose it we lose our direction. I heard a story recently about two Australian sailors who were traveling in London. They made their way into a tavern and proceeded to drink themselves silly. They left quite intoxicated and tried to find their hotel. As they were walking they ran into a very thick and dense London fog. They became disoriented and lost. They were trying to decide which way to go when all of a sudden they saw a man walking towards them. When he got close enough they staggered up to him and said, "Beggin' yer pardon, guv'ner, but could you tell us where we are?" The man they were talking to was a highly decorated English naval officer who had many medals on his chest, but because of the dim light and the fog, the besotted sailors didn't notice. The naval officer, rather offended, looked down at them and said, "Do you know who I am?" To which the one Aussie turned to the other and said, "Now we are in a heap of trouble, mate. We don't know where we are and he doesn't know who he is!"

Society today has a lot in common with those drunken sailors. We're lost, with no idea where we are, or who we are. The only difference is the two drunken Aussies knew they were lost and needed help. Post-Modern America doesn't even know we are lost and continues to stagger around in a fog. We don't know who we are in history, or the essence of when life begins; we don't know what constitutes a family and we don't know whether we descended from apes or were created by God.

If we don't know history and who our founding fathers were then we don't know our identity as a nation. If we don't know whether we came from apes or the Living God (Gen 1) then life becomes survival of the fittest. If we don't know when life begins or ends, then killing a living human being is "euthanasia" or "abortion." If we don't know what constitutes a family then two men, two women or two squirrels can make up a family. (They would all be protected of course, and have equal rights under the U.S. Constitution.)

Valid opinions are based on truth, and truth is based on facts and reality. When truth is ignored or twisted to suit the occasion, all opinions become equal. Your opinion is just as valid as my opinion. Truth never compromises, but opinions often do. The gap between truth and ill-informed opinion is as wide as the gap between right and wrong.

Truth is Knowable

Saint Augustine said that if man is incapable of knowing truth then morality and theology are impossible. Truth, as we have said, is reality — the affirmation of what actually is — and man *is* capable of knowing reality, and therefore, truth

The mathematical truth that 2+3=5 is easily confirmed using the fingers on one hand. The scientific truth that water freezes at 32°F can be demonstrated with a thermometer. The historical truth that George Washington was our first president is well documented. These kinds of truths are called facts, and they are readily knowable.

Truth is knowable in other areas just as certainly. All we need to do is find it. Our ability to know truth and apply it will determine our ability to be serve God. God desires for us to find Him and know His Truth. God said this about our finding Him,

> "You will seek me and find me when you seek me with all your heart." (Jer 29:13)

> "I will give them a heart to know me, that I am the LORD. They will be my people and I will be their God…" (Jer 24:7)

> "I am the LORD there is no other. I have not spoken in secret, from somewhere in a land of darkness I have not said to Jacob's descendents 'Seek me in vain'…" (Isa 45:18(b)-19)

> "Ask and it shall be given to you, seek and you will find, knock and the door will be opened to you." (Matt 7:7)

God clearly reveals in these verses that He wants us to find Him. He desires a relationship with us, but He can't and won't do all the work. Just like any relationship, both sides must work together. God also tells us we have to *want* to find Him. The more we want something the harder we work for it. The harder we work at finding it, the greater our chances of discovery.

Thousands of California Gold Rush prospectors spent their lives looking for gold, and the few that found it struck it rich. But most of them, search as they might, never found any. They were just looking in the wrong places, and in that way, they were just like people who never find God ... because they're looking in the wrong places. God wants to be found and longs for us to seek Him. And when we look in the right places, we will find Him.

Jesus told three parables in Luke 15 of lost possessions that were sought after because of their great value. He used them to stress the point that when we desire something of great value we will look all over for it until we find it. God will not write His name in the clouds to prove He is there but to those who earnestly seek Him with all their heart, they will find Him. He is knowable and can be found but we must search for Him as diligently as we search for lost possessions.

One more example of how God reveals Himself to those who are really looking is found in the book of Romans. It says this:

> "For since the creation of the world God's invisible qualities — his eternal power and divine nature — have been clearly seen, being understood from what has been made, so that men are without excuse ...Although they claimed to be wise they became fools." (Rom 1:20,22)

God is seen in creation, all of it. The problem is man refuses to acknowledge God and His creation. We have educated ourselves in earthly knowledge to such an extent that the God of the heavens is no longer believable. We have become too smart to believe in a God. So even though the evidence is there, many people refuse to accept the evidence and deny God's existence.

Look outward at the billions upon billions of stars, look inward at the intricacy of the human body or even just the eye itself, or look at all of the information stored in one strand of DNA. These are just a few of the many examples that demonstrate the awesome power and brilliance of our God. Yet many refuse to acknowledge God as He reveals Himself in His creation, they refuse to accept the very evidence before them. *You will never find truth if you claim there is no truth to know or deny its existence.*

Truth *is* knowable, and only when you find it will you exclaim with the Psalmist,

> "For the LORD is the great God, the great King above all gods. In His hands are the depths of the earth, and the mountain peaks belong to him. The sea is his for he made it, and his hands formed the dry land. Come let us bow down in worship, let us kneel before the LORD our Maker for he is our God." (Psalm 95:3-7(a))

Virtue by Mastering Truth

To master truth we must be obedient to it. This obedience develops our ability to make truth part of our very being. As we apply truth, we come to experience it and this experience gives us a better perception and appreciation of the power it can give to our life. This obedience not only shows we apprehend truth, but more importantly shows our love for it. It then becomes woven into our vary nature and becomes one with us.

By living out truth, we show the importance of it in our life. We grow in virtue and reflect Christ more and more each day. This then becomes a life worth living because of the impact it will have for the Kingdom of God.

Ownership of truth can only be proved by constant use and obedience. The more constantly we do something, the better we get at it. Continuous practice simplifies our tasks and clarifies our concepts. We can own any given truth through constant application. Using techniques over and over also makes them clearer and more habitual. We then use them without thinking because they are a habit to us — a *good* habit!

Through obedience to truth you acquire hands-on appreciation of the concept you are trying to study. When you apply truth in your life, you gain a greater understanding of it. This leads you to discover things you weren't aware of before. It's called experience. The more you apply and use truth, the more you gain valuable experience. Knowledge grows through experience.

If you want to see how important something is to a person, watch what they do. If you want to know how well a person understands a concept watch how they apply it. The more proficient we are at any truth, the closer we come to mastering it. This is true with virtue as well. If you want to know the power and unity provided by truth, you need to live it out in obedience and do this on a consistent basis. As you live out truth more and more in your life, you will grow in virtue.

Much of the concept of knowing, understanding, and living out truth happens in the mind. I want to take time now to understand how we think and how the mind affects our ability to live a life of virtue and have a maximum impact for Christ.

The Mind:

Where Choices are Formed

"The God of the Jews was to exist in the Word and through the Word, an unprecedented conception requiring the highest of abstract thinking."

Neil Postman

"Our society has replaced heroes with celebrities, the quest for a well-informed character with the search for a flat stomach, substance and depth with image and personality. In the political process, the makeup man is more important than the speech writer, and we approach the voting booth not on the basis of a well-developed philosophy of what the state should be, but with a heart full of images, emotions, and slogans all packed into 30-second sound bites. The mind-numbing, irrational tripe that fills TV talk shows is digested by millions of bored, lonely Americans hungry for that sort of stuff. What is going on here? What has happened to us?"[54] Christian apologist and author J.P. Moreland makes this statement in his book "*Love God with all your Mind.*"

His statement hits our society right where it hurts, with the truth. We are a bored culture. We are a culture in which we seldom use our minds. We are a culture which would much rather be entertained than forced to think. We are a culture which knows more about sports than we do about history. Sadly, we have lost our ability to think critically and don't even know it.

Os Guinness drew a similar conclusion stating, "...a leading problem in American Evangelicalism is anti-intellectualism."[55] In his book *Fit Bodies Fat Minds* he builds the case that the average American Evangelical worries more about his body than he does about his mind, hence the mind is quite underdeveloped while at the same time the body is overdeveloped. He further observes,

> "Anti-intellectualism is a disposition to discount the importance of truth and the life of the mind. Living in a sensuous culture and an increasingly emotional democracy, American evangelicals in the last generation have simultaneously toned up their bodies and dumbed down their minds. The result? Many suffer from...having fit bodies and fat mind."[56]

Without our inability to think properly and correctly, we are destined to make bad choices. We will achieve far less than our God-given ability can attain. The mind is crucial to performing as God commands us and must be nourished, maintained and developed. Left to itself it will run wild, controlled by emotions grounded in vice and desires to satisfy our physical pleasures.

Today, man cultivates a fit body at the expense of an unfit mind. Friedrich Nietzsche predicted this would happen and said boldly, "Because of the 'death of God' they would rather confuse heaven with happiness and happiness with health."[57] Even more audacious, Bertrand Russell said, "Most Christians would rather die than think—in fact they do."

From this inability to think, Christians have lost the thinking battle with secular man. The average secular thinker can run circles around the average Christian thinker. So much so that many Christians explain what they don't understand as "you just have to have faith." Regrettably, the solid logic, facts and reasoning behind the Christian religion get passed over.

The mind is central to who we are and how we act. How you perceive an activity, for good or bad, instantly determines your motivation to act or not act. The fact that we as human beings think is obvious, the question is how well?

The mind must be trained to interpret and decipher information. If we are unable to translate and discard information it will form an endless string of useless, contradictory and sometimes false dichotomy of "facts." This in turn will lead us to ineffective or defective thinking. The ability to think rightly is developed from logic, reasoning and rational thought processes. These must take place if we are to think as God commands us.

We form first impressions of others without even knowing it is happening. Think for a moment when you meet someone new. You instantly form an opinion of them based on their looks, clothes, use of words, expressions and so on. These may be right or wrong, but we form an opinion and this will form a judgment of this person until we have something that changes it. The opinions we have are often based on faulty information or minimal information, yet we still carry the belief about that person or idea with us. Much of what we use to judge people, ideas or events is done very randomly and haphazardly.

In this chapter I want to delve into the process of faulty thinking, I want to explore how our mind works and finally I want to discuss how to use your mind to get the most out of it.

The Right and Wrong of Thinking

We are all born with the ability to think, but the problem is that we often don't think correctly. There are right and wrong ways to think, and this must be the chief end of all our thoughts. Until we recognize this, we will never get rid of faulty and incorrect ideas.

One view today is relativism. This view states there are no absolute truths and no way of finding them. Therefore there are no right or wrong moral values that transcend culture or an individual. The only things we have are opinions, and since these are merely opinions you are free to do as you choose. The only thing you can't do is force your opinion on someone else. Everything is OK as long as your actions don't hurt me or my key interests. It is all relative. The only absolute is the absolute that "there are no absolutes." Today truth is gone the way of the dinosaur — it is extinct as we noted last chapter.

There are two popular arguments put forth to defend ethical relativism:

> Argument 1 says cultures and individuals differ in certain moral practices, there are no transcultural values. There are several problems with this argument. First, just because people disagree doesn't mean there is not truth. For example just because you and I disagree whether the earth is round doesn't mean the earth has no shape.[58]

Argument 2 says that sometimes apparent moral differences are not moral differences at all, but factual differences. During the Salem witch trials certain individuals were put to death who were believed to be practicing witchcraft. We don't execute witches today, but not because our moral values have changed. We don't execute witches today because we don't believe that the practice of their craft has a fatal effect upon the community. We share the same values as the residents of Salem, we just disagree that they were factually wrong about the effect witches have upon the community.[59]

Another argument is that some basic rules of logic and reasoning must be applied. Francis J. Beckwith, in his book *Politically Correct Death*, shows much of the right and wrong in reasoning correctly and incorrectly. He states that an argument is made up of a premise and a conclusion. When an argument is valid, then the conclusion must be true assuming the premise is true. Putting this another way, the conclusion follows the premise.[60] For example:

1. John is a bachelor.
2. Therefore John is not married.

This is a valid argument. However here is another argument where the argument is not valid:

1. All girls like dolls.
2. Sally is a girl.
3. Therefore sally likes dolls.

The problem is that statement #1 is not true. All girls don't like dolls, and therefore you can't make conclusion #3. Premise #2 is valid, but since one of its premises is false the argument is invalid.

Another invalid argument is:

1. Bill is not at work.
2. Betty is not at work.
3. Therefore Bill and Betty are out together.

Even if we assume premises 1 & 2 are true, the conclusion still doesn't follow. It is quite possible that Bill and Betty are both not at work and yet not out together. The premises are both true, but the conclusion is false. So an invalid argument is one in which the conclusion doesn't follow from the premises, even if the premises are true.[61]

An ideal argument is one in which the premises are true and the conclusion is valid and sound. For instance:

1. Larry Jones is a bachelor.
2. All bachelors are unmarried men.
3. Therefore Larry Jones is unmarried.

This argument is valid, for if both premises are true, the conclusion can't be false. Since both premises are true and the conclusion is sound then this is a valid argument.

Once we come to understand there are right ways and wrong ways of thinking and arguing, we can then take the next step. That is to think as clearly and rationally as we can. We will then see moral relativism and moral absolutes can't both be right. *The ability to think with coherent and consistent thoughts and ideas will then grow our mental facilities.* We will then benefit with a sharper and better mind that will guide and direct our actions that will lead us to best choices.

Jesus often revealed faulty thinking when he was asked a question. Ravi Zacharias exposes how Jesus would often question the questioner to try to break down the assumptions implied in the inquiry. Often the questioner will try putting the person he is questioning on the defense by assuming things in his question. Jesus was a master thinker and was able to expose these wrong assumptions (Matt 22:15-22, Mark 10:17-23).

<u>Emotions often lead the Mind</u>

Today emotions lead the way in the opinions many people have. Emotions are the guide for much of our political campaigning and advertising. Because of the mindlessness of our culture, people don't persuade others of their views (religious or otherwise) on the basis of argument and reason, but rather by expressing emotional rhetoric and politically correct buzzwords. Reason has given way to rhetoric and evidence to emotion.[62] Arguments are currently based on emotions, and response is seldom given to the concepts being advanced. This then becomes the reason many people hold the views they do; they are grounded in emotion not on facts or truth, and the result is many false ideas being promoted and gaining popularity.

One of the main reasons for faulty thinking is that our mind is often led by our feelings. This should be just the opposite. Emotions are very powerful and seductive — so powerful they can override our logic and reasoning skills.

Emotions make us act impulsively, inconsistently and irrationally. We seldom think when our emotions are strong, we just act. This is seen often in sports. Watch a player argue a call with a referee. He often loses control and says and does things totally irrational because of the emotion, often anger, that is fueling him. Does he consider: that *he* may be wrong, that one call doesn't make the whole game or if he wants to disagree that yelling and screaming does no good and makes the official less likely to discuss it?

Fortunately, emotions don't last long. Unfortunately, when the emotions subside, we still have to live with the consequences of our emotional choice. For example, a car salesman tells you how great a new car is, you test drive it and love it. If you act on the emotion and buy it, even though it is way out of your price range, you will most likely regret your choice. In four-to-six months when the car payments come around and the emotion is gone, we realize we can't afford the car. Now we must sell it because we are in over our head financially. The same is true with affairs in marriage. People act on emotion and then they must deal with the consequences later.

Emotions are often wrong. We say, "I *feel* this is the right choice," but feelings should never be the prime motivator for choices, especially big ones. If our feelings are based on pride, greed, insecurity, fears, jealously or impatience we will be misled. If these or other deceptive emotions are the center of our choices, then these decisions will often be bad. We must make sure wrong emotions don't control our lives. This can be easily demonstrated with greed or fears. When greed guides us, we make decisions simply to get more and don't care about who we step on in the process. Greed becomes a hunger we must feed. Jesus said, "Watch out! Be on your guard against all kinds of greed; a man's life doesn't consist of the abundance of his possessions." (Luke 12:15) When we are ruled by greed, we will do anything to get more material possessions or money. Greed leads to many bad choices.

Fear is another bad emotion by which to gauge choices. Here, we do anything to avoid our fears. We will avoid going to the doctor for fear of what he will say, or avoid a task for fear of failing. Fear of failure, fear of rejection, fear of others' opinions of us, along with many other fears often guide us into bad choices.

We also must not confuse a feeling with a commitment. Many people confuse the feeling of love with the commitment of love. Marriage is based on the commitment "until death do us part." In the Old Testament, death was the only way to get out of marriage. Jesus states this in His teachings (Matthew 19: 1-12). Marital love is based on the commitment "until one dies," and this is the key to the marriage covenant, not the *feeling* of love. You don't always "feel" in love.

Feelings will come and go, but true commitment lives on. For example, a mother may not feel like changing her baby's dirty diaper, but she does it out of a committed decision to love her child, clean diaper or dirty.

This same concept is demonstrated with courage. We don't often feel courageous when confronted with evil, but we must choose to act in the right way. Courage isn't lack of fear, it is acting in spite of fear. It is acting on what we know to be Truth and acting rightly in the face of evil.

Emotions as a Supporting Cast

On the other hand, when correct emotions back correct thinking, these emotions play a strong supporting role in making the best choices. *When our mind directs our feelings, these proper emotions will reinforce and encourage our choices.* The mind can be a very powerful leader of feelings if we so choose. Our mind can then gain energy from these supporting emotions helping us to make right choices in tough situations.

You can evoke thoughts by feelings or you can evoke feelings by thoughts. The latter is far superior and empowering. We must use our mind to induce these supporting emotions. These "emotions of virtue" can be a very potent force to support a choice we have made. In other words, if our thoughts lead us to form an emotion grounded in virtue, we will be made stronger in our resolve because of the emotion. This will often ground us in our commitment to see the decision through, no matter how bad the situation gets.

Take for example the energy we have in the memory of another person or situation. When this memory is good, it can invoke very powerful emotions in us. These emotions can fuel us to do great things. If someone died to save our life this can create such powerful emotions in us that can help us accomplish great things, despite obstacles. When we think back on the 9/11 terrorist attacks on New York City, many great deeds came after it as a result of this tragedy. Acts of courage, determination, and passion sprang up all around New York City. When we think back on those selfless acts of heroism, the memories inspire us to display similar courage in the face of daunting circumstances.

When our thoughts lead our emotions, our emotions support action such as courage or perseverance. Such thought-driven emotions develop great power in us for wise and proper action. The more we develop these supporting emotions, the greater our potential for good.

The Mind and its Makeup

The thoughts we have lead us to the perceptions we have of the world around us, and those perceptions become central ingredients in the formation of our life. Often our perceptions of reality are biased. Our perceptions are colored by our interpretations of the experiences we have had in our life. These self-centered perceptions are called prejudices. Most of us aren't even aware of the prejudices we hold. The problem is, these prejudices lead us to preconceived notions based not on rational thought, but on irrational feelings and biases.

We often form a belief based on these biases and then try to find information to support that belief. If our bias leads us to wrong beliefs, then our perception of reality will be skewed. The longer we hold these beliefs, the harder they are to change. The further our beliefs are from the Truth, the worse our decisions will be. The more wrong beliefs we have, the more wrong decisions we will make.

The quality of our choices is directly proportional to how well our interpretation of life experiences compares to actual Truth. How we interpret our life experiences — emotionally or rationally — will have a great impact on our beliefs and ultimately, our decision-making capabilities.

Let's use the example of marriage. If you were the product of a marriage that ended in divorce, you may have a skewed view of marriage because of this. If you were greatly hurt by the breakup of your parents, then you may believe marriage is bad and may not want to enter into it. Maybe you'll form the impression that marriage is not for a lifetime, but only until someone better comes along.

If your parents were married for fifty years and they had a great marriage, you may believe marriage is the greatest way to seal a relationship. Your experience with marriage will skew your attitudes, be it for good or for bad.

Ideas are very general models or assumptions we make about reality. They are patterns of interpretation, ways of thinking about and interpreting things. The danger is: many of these idea systems are false, based as they are on false premises, prejudices and faulty interpretations. Take for example the idea that a "little" lie is OK. You may believe this because you have never gotten into trouble doing it and have even gotten out of many difficult situations with "little" lies. You tell "little" lies because you believe no one gets hurt. This is in direct opposition to Christ's teachings on telling the truth (Matt 5:33-37, John 8:44, Eph 4:25, Col 3:9-10).

Our task is to find out which idea systems are false and which are true. This is a very difficult task because of our biases based on life experiences, conformity to the world system of thinking and misguided motivations. Once we can exchange our false idea systems with Truth, our ability to think clearly and properly, and ultimately make best choices, will improve.

The Strength and Importance of a Belief

The strength of a belief, combined with the importance it has to us, will directly impact our decisions. Here are 4 situations and the likely outcome of each, based on the strength and importance of the beliefs held:

Situation 1: If it isn't that strong of a belief and it isn't that important to us then we probably won't act on it. This is seen in our moral judgments. If we don't believe drunk driving is wrong, and it isn't that important to us, we may well be inclined to drive drunk.

Situation 2: Even if we believe something strongly, but it isn't that important to us, it may not impact our decisions. Since the belief is not that important to us, we probably won't act on it. If we believe exercise is very good for our personal health but being healthy isn't that important to us, then we probably won't exercise.

Situation 3: Turning the last situation on its head, even if something is very important to us, if we don't really believe in it we most likely won't act on it either. For example, if we are planning a picnic, having good weather may be quite important to us. Now, even if the weatherman says there is an 80% chance of rain, we may stick our hand out the window, feel no raindrops, and decide that we don't believe the weatherman. Since we don't really believe it will rain, we have our picnic outdoors anyway.

Situation 4: Finally, if we believe in something very strongly and it is very important to us, we will almost certainly act on it. Imagine yourself trapped on the roof of a burning building. In the street below, the fire brigade moves a safety net into position and the Chief yells, "Jump! We'll catch you." Now, escaping a flaming death is certainly very important to you, but it is your belief in the Chief that will give you the courage to step over the edge.

In these four situations, three of the four will prompt us to act against our own best interests, and only one will persuade us to act wisely. Therefore, for someone to act properly they need to believe in something strongly, and it must be very important to them. Our actions are directly tied into the strength of the beliefs we hold and the importance they play in our lives.

God indwells Words

In the Old Testament the utterances of God are called "The Word of the LORD." In the New Testament it is called "the word of God" or simply the "Word." God reveals Himself to man by words. The gospel of John (verses 1:1-18) starts with what has been called by Bible scholar William Barclay, "one of the greatest adventures of religious thought ever achieved by the mind of man." Through careful study of these verses we can gain much in our study of the mind.

In the beginning was the Word and the Word was with God and the Word was God. He was with God in the beginning. Through Him all things were made; without him nothing was made that has been made. In Him was life and that life was the light of men. The light shines in the darkness, but the darkness has not understood it. (John 1:1-5)

In studying these verses, we need to first understand that the Word here is translated in Greek *Logos*. *Logos* is defined as something said or thought, and is also translated as reasoning (thinking and calculating). This implies that when we think, we typically think in words.

God **reveals** Himself through words. The Word of God is the written word of God in the Bible. This is the expression of who God is and what He is like. It reveals His personality, character and commands. God is what He says. Puritan Reformer John Owen noted the power of God in the truth of His word when it is illuminated by the Holy Spirit dwelling within believers:

> "Oftentimes they go for water to the well, and are not able to draw …they seek the promises for refreshment, and find no more savour in them than in the white of an egg; but when the same promises are brought to remembrance by the Spirit the Comforter, who is with them and in them, how full of life and power are they!"[63]

In this quote we see how the Trinitarian God (Father, Son, and Holy Spirit) works in believers to strengthen them. To quote Sinclair Ferguson on this, "…the knowledge of the truth had become the knowledge of the power of the truth." Thus the Holy Spirit brings the power of God in His word by opening it and explaining it to us. This is something an unbeliever simply cannot do because the Holy Spirit is not in them.

God also **creates** with His words. He spoke and created the universes and all that is in them. He spoke and formed the animals. He spoke and formed man (Gen 1-2). God brings life by His spoken Word.

Finally, God **rules** in His word today as He reveals it by His Holy Spirit. This is seen in Paul's writings to the Corinthians:

> "…but God has revealed it to us by His Spirit. The Spirit searches all things, even the deep things of God. For who among men knows the thoughts of a man except the man's spirit within him? In the same way no one knows the thoughts of God except the Spirit of God. We have not received the spirit of the world but the Spirit

who is from God, that we may understand what God has freely given us. This is what we speak, not in words taught us by human wisdom but in words taught by the Spirit, expressing spiritual truths in spiritual words." (1 Cor 2: 10-13)

Paul clearly is teaching that Christians can know God's will, God's wisdom and God's ways for their life through the Holy Spirit, revealing this to them in words. As God's Spirit abides in us, He will speak, guide, counsel and teach us in our daily life. God rules us through His Spirit, and we must be obedient to His counseling.

Through the Holy Spirit, God implants in us His revealing word, His creative word and His ruling word. This word then becomes the word of life to us and in us (1 John 1:1).

The Inspiration and Teaching of Words

The power of words is seen in another way. Throughout human history words have been far more than just sounds. They are a means of sparking a fire in us and motivating us to act. Words often come most alive when they inspire us to act. These words can be our own or from others.

The power of words is seen in great orators. Winston Churchill's ability to motivate the English people in World War II to defeat the Nazi regime is an example. It is seen in the abilities of Vince Lombardi and Knute Rockne to inspire their athletic teams. Words are powerful tools in the hands of great motivators.

Words inspire in another way when they become a witness to history. They speak of men and women who have lived exemplary lives in the past, becoming a living testimony to us that they made it through those tough times, often inspiring others to do the same. The words of their history give us evidence of all they did. It reveals how many of them died for their faith. Their martyrdom encourages us and tells us to keep fighting no matter how grim the situation (Heb 11:1-12:3).

Reasoning by Words

Another way God uses words is that they help us to reason correctly. This is the other way *Logos* is used in the Bible. The reasoning of God is seen in the Wisdom literature of the Bible such as Proverbs, Psalms, and Ecclesiastes. This is the thinking of God as revealed through His sages. It is practical wisdom for living and managing of life, not philosophical. In the first nine chapters of the book of Proverbs wisdom is personified often and is made to come alive (see also Heb 4:12). It is seen as life giving, and eternal power is given to it.

We have these "words of wisdom" to help us sort through the choices we must make in life. The Word of God *(Logos)* and reasoning of God *(Logos)* form a powerful means to enable man to live life the way it was meant to be lived. From this we receive joy in our living (John 15:11, John 17:13) and blessing from God by living as He has called us to (Ps. 1:1-2, Jer. 17:7)).

When God's Word dwells within us, we can reason properly because we know His commands and desires for us. This then leads us to know His will for us. We then reason in accordance with intent and meaning based on the laws and rules He has set in place. This in turn will help build virtue in us and form in us the mind of Christ (1 Cor 2:15-16). We are called to have the mind of Christ and only by the Word of Christ in us can we have the mind of Christ.

As we develop the mind of Christ we are then in constant fellowship with the Living Almighty God. His desires become our desires and as we ask of God, He will grant our requests only according to His perfect will. Our joy is His will being done in our lives. We live in Him and He in us by His word and thus we bear fruit by doing His will (John 8:31-32, John 15:1-17).

Renewing your Mind

The Apostle Paul tells us in Romans 12:2 not to conform to the thinking of the world. Do not let the thinking of the world be your guide, but rather let God transform our thinking. As a caterpillar changes into a butterfly (metamorphosis), we too are called to undergo metamorphosis, to change our minds to that of Christ. The way we are to do this is to renovate our mind by matching our beliefs with God's.

The Word (Jesus) came so that we might have life, and have it in the full (John 10:10). So then by storing the Word more and more in us we have life. We do this by memorization, meditating and mimicking it.

Memorizing the Word —The more we know God's Word the more it lives in us and we think on it constantly. When we memorize something, we store it, so to speak, in us and thus have it for retrieval at any time. It inhabits our mind. It lives in our spirit and brings the thoughts of God to us minute by minute. We must make a discipline of memorizing the Word of God on a regular basis.

Meditating on the Word — The process here is to gain understanding of what we have stored. To store the Word in us and not understand it does us little good. When we meditate on it, we seek to understand it and apply it to our life. To meditate is to ponder or to contemplate, and this gives greater meaning to the Word in us.

Mimicking the Word — This is to be obedient to what we know and live it out by seeking to duplicate God's word in our behavior on a daily basis. We imitate Christ by living as He lived. Thus, we then begin to take on the characteristics of Christ in virtue, holiness, godliness and love. We then think, react and live as Christ to a watching world.

God commands us to study his word and meditate on it constantly (Josh 1:8, Ps 1:2, Ps 119:15-16, Pro 2:1-5). Through this we will know Him as He reveals Himself to us in Truth. Then as we know God and His Truth, we will be successful in all we do (Josh 1:7, Gen 39:3, Gen 39:23, Ps 1:3). Our mind is where we start this process and get to know and understand God (Jer 29:13, Joel 2:12, Matt 22:37). By knowing Him we transform our life to His. The key is to renew our mind through the Word of God and be transformed by it into a person of God.

Training your Mind

You can't live out what you don't understand, and you can't understand what you don't know. Therefore, our training must focus on gaining knowledge and understanding it. The greater our understanding of any subject the greater our effectiveness in applying the information. We must train to understand, and understand how to train.

The key to growth in any new field is growing your mind and using its ability to think and process more and new information. This training requires dedication and discipline. Ignorance and laziness are the enemies. The Bible calls us to train in numerous areas. For instance:

- "…Train yourself to be godly." (1 Tim 4:7(b)).
- We are called to train up our children in how they are to live   (Pro 22:6).

- We must train ourselves to distinguish good from evil (Heb 5:14).

Besides these areas we must train our mind. We must train it to be ready to give a reason for the hope we have in Christ Jesus (1 Pet 3:15). We must train our mind to think on whatever is true, right, noble, lovely, admirable and pure (Phil 4:8). We must train it to test everything so that we know what is of God, and what isn't (1 Thes 5:21, Acts 17:11, 1 John 4:1). These are just a few examples of how we must train our mind to think.

Our mind can only act on and process what it has available in its information warehouse. We limit its resources (ignorance), by providing it with minimal bits of information. This in return restricts the ability our mind has to form correct ideas and thoughts. We also restrict our mind when we don't apply the key tools of reasoning and logic in applying the correct information we do have.

The greater our thinking ability is, we can make "best choices" more quickly and more consistently. Some decisions require immediate action, within seconds, and to do this we must be able to think correctly, very quickly. Other times we have more time to process the information and this makes it easier to make right choices. In order to think quickly and correctly, we must train our mind on a consistent basis. One good choice followed by one bad choice does us little good. Consistency is the key to training.

To become a better thinker is simply to become better. Remember our goal is not just to think, but to think well and properly.

<u>Guard Your Heart</u>

To develop the mind of Christ we must monitor what we allow to get to our mind. (Pro 4:23). Ideas and images can have a lasting affect. Nothing enters the mind without affecting it for good or evil. This means the TV shows we watch, the music we listen to, the friends we choose to hang out with and so on. All of these factors affect our mind and how we think. Our thinking processes are constantly being formed and the things we allow into our mind helps form these processes. Without a filter on our mind, whereby we protect our mind from harmful images and ideas, it will be difficult to cultivate a good, truthful and virtuous mind.

We must guard what we allow our eyes to see. We must guard what we allow our ears to hear. We must guard what we allow our minds to think about on a regular basis. No one knows our thoughts but us, and therefore no one can monitor our thoughts but us. We know what we think and how we think. We know where we look or what we listen to in private. The question is do we know the tremendous impact these are having on the way we think?

We must watch over our mind like a new mother watches over her newborn baby. Most people don't do this. They say violence on TV doesn't affect me, or sex on TV won't influence me. If what we watch doesn't affect us, then why do sponsors spend millions of dollars to buy ad space for Super Bowl commercials on TV? The fact is it does affect us.

The cultivation of a great mind is seen in the writings of the great Protestant Reformers. Thinkers like Luther, Calvin, Owen, Whitefield, Edwards and Spurgeon. The depth of their thinking and knowledge of God is inspiring. They became great thinkers by training their minds how to think and what to think. We alone hold the key to our minds and the power to choose and direct our thoughts (renew our mind in the Word). We must desire to become a great thinker as well by seeking to form the mind of Christ in us (1 Cor 2:16).

The Emotions:

The Destructiveness of Impulse

"Feelings are part of each one of us. They can either be friend or foe, depending on how you utilize them ...I understand that faith is not a feeling but a choice to take God at His word."

Ney Bailey

Emotions are feelings, sensations or desires. They are inside us and affect all of us. These desires, or lusts, seek to have us satisfy them. The problem is that most of our lusts are from sinful tendencies dwelling within us. As we have already noted, we are born with a bent towards sin. In the King James Translation of the Bible this evil desire, or lustful passion, is called concupiscence. This word is derived from the sense of a yearning or longing inside us. It is to have our heart set upon a thing. Typically, concupiscence is a longing for something that God has forbidden.

We are commanded to overcome these evil desires and live contrary to them (Rom 6:12, Gal 5:16, 24, Eph 4:22, Col 3:5, 2 Tim 2:22). The fulfillment of these sinful desires brings about a satisfaction and therefore creates a recurring desire to gratify them. The more we give into these lusts, the stronger they becomes in us. They will also demand a stronger fix the next time in order to satisfy them, as seen in most all addictions. The craving grows so strong that it totally dominates the person. They can't go on until they get their "fix" and feed the hunger caused by the addiction.

In Romans 1, Paul tells us how this came about. God gave sinful man over to his sinful desires after the fall. As a result, man became ungrateful to God, was vain in his imaginations, refused to glorify God, and claimed to be wise but was a fool. Man exchanged the glory of the immortal God for images resembling mortal man or birds or animals or reptiles. Paul finishes the chapter by telling how these evil desires grew worse, and he describes what they were and are (Rom 1:29-31). To lose our fear of God and be given over to our sinful lusts is a most desperate and hopeless situation. It is from this desperate situation that most of our emotions originate.

When we learn to control these passions and lusts as God commands us and seek righteousness in Him and through Him, we can then learn to tame them. Just because we want something doesn't mean we should have it. To consistently say no to these evil desires can only happen through the power of Christ working in us as believers. These emotions can be resisted, but only Jesus Christ in us can do it.

Emotions are very powerful and when they control what we do, they become an insatiable hunger deep within us. To know the power they hold over us, we need just to look at addictive behaviors. Take such addictions as alcohol, illegal drugs, sex, food and gambling to name a few. Once we start to feed them, they become harder to control. Eventually our inability to say "No" to the desire forms the addiction in us.

Feelings don't consider the consequences, they just want to be fed. We have several alcoholic beverages after a long day and they do make us feel better. Next time we are feeling low or need this "high" the desire in us perks up and seeks to be realized. Many people gratify these feelings by substances or activities. We want a "cheap high" so we drink alcohol and it produces temporary relief. It then becomes a stronger and stronger desire in us that we no longer can control, rather it controls us. We didn't mean to become addicted but we did.

It is easy to assume that all feelings are legitimate, but they aren't. If we have certain feelings, just because we "feel" them doesn't make them valid. Feelings are in the front row of our lives and hunger for attention. In the triangle drawing in chapter 3 it is seen that feelings are the next level up from our physical body. Thus our desires are closely linked to our physical body. Our physical desires for pleasure are closely linked with emotions. It is critical to understand that feelings are never justified just because we "feel" them.

Thoughts, on the other hand, are open to challenge and invite the question, "why" — not so with feelings. Feelings don't lead us to ask any questions; they just create in us a longing to be satisfied.

This reveals the deceptive nature of feelings that flows from our sinful nature. The evil desires in us control our actions and create a stronger appetite for things we often shouldn't be involved in, but the gratification we receive physically or emotionally supports their drawing power.

We must be alert to the fact that emotions and feelings must be tamed. They create in us a spontaneous or impulsive temperament that acts first and thinks later. We must reverse this order and think first, and act later. When we do, we will be able to resist many temptations that feed on our impulsive nature. By thinking through our emotions, we will at least be more alert to the consequences of spontaneous behaviors. Wrong choices stem from our inability to resist temptations; indeed, most wrong choices originate with our desire to yield to temptation.

The Opportunity of Temptation

Temptations are fueled by desires in us. If we have no desire for something, then we are not tempted by it. Different people are tempted by different things, but temptation works the same way in all of us — when we are tempted, our desires are locked in conflict with our beliefs. Temptations are given a negative image but often in the Bible they are neutral. They are a test to see if we will act in a godly and righteousness way. Paul talks about this in his letter to the Church at Corinth;

> "No temptation has seized you except what is common to man, and God is faithful He won't let you be tempted beyond what you can bare, but when you are tempted He will provide a way out so that you can stand up under it" (1 Cor. 10:13)

It is clear that God won't let us be tempted beyond what we can withstand but wants to see where we are in relationship to His holiness. Temptations are tests. If we resist our desires to give into sin, we become stronger.

On the other hand, if we give in to them, we become more predisposed to the same temptations the next time. The temptations that test us become inducements to do evil only when we let them linger and become a lust growing in us (James 1:14-15). It is like the bait in a trap set by a hunter. An animal is often unable to overcome the desire for the bait so it ignores any danger and often gets caught. So too with humans who become so engrossed by a desire they ignore all common sense and "take the bait."

Temptations are predicated on desire. Temptations work because of our lusts. For temptation to work it must first get your attention. Once your attention is grabbed, the crucial issue is whether the temptation can keep your attention long enough to keep your desires aroused. If it does you will most likely give in to it; if it doesn't you will very likely overcome it. *Bottom line: the longer you linger the greater the lust.*

We must remember 1 Corinthians 10:13. We are not tempted beyond what we can bear. We can stand up to temptation because God won't allow us to be tempted beyond what He knows we can withstand. God provides a way out of every test, and we must find it. Maybe it is a Bible verse that reveals the sinfulness of the temptation, or an understanding of the consequences of failing the test. Maybe the way out is simply to pray and ask for strength to say no when we feel tested. There is a way out and we must find it.

When you feel yourself being sucked in by your lusts and desires, the best advise is: RUN! GET OUT OF THERE, NOW! You must flee and get away from it. This is the best and most effective way to overcome temptation.

Bait is used by fishermen to lure fish onto their hooks. They use strong bait that will have a direct affect on the fish. Once the fish bite the bait, they are caught. Like fish, we often only see the bait. We never see the hook until it is too late. All temptations are bait, and we must realize there is a hook hidden within. If we take the bait, we will be caught.

When we replace wrong desires with right ones, we form habits of virtue. It works like this: when you feel tempted to gossip about someone, remember God has provided a way out for you in this situation — silence and prayer for the individual. By replacing the habit of gossip with silent prayer for this person, you have substituted prayer for gossip. This works for other temptations the same way. Remember the desire that drives temptation is inside you and you must replace it with righteousness.

We can overcome sin only through the power of Jesus Christ. We just need to realize we need a power stronger and greater than ourselves. Only Christ is stronger and more fit to help us. Failure in temptations is no one else's fault but our own. Our own inability to control ourselves is the reason for our wrong behavior when we are tested.

Since feelings, emotions and desires conspire to make us act on impulse and to neglect rational thinking, we will often give in. If we can engage our mind and ignore our emotions, we can reestablish control over our actions. When we are able to understand the wrongness of a certain behavior, we increase our chances to overcome it.

Paul says there are no "superhuman" temptations we can't overcome. We aren't alone; others have faced these same emotions and tests and have overcome them. If they can do it, so can we. We must use their example as our encouragement. Remember, tests are opportunities for growth in virtue, but only when we resist the lusts they create in us.

Faith: the Key to Battling Feelings

Emotions are very powerful because they get us to act impulsively without thinking. We must also watch how our mind can be attacked by thoughts linked to temptations. We must make all our thoughts captive to Christ (2 Cor. 10:5), and get rid of the ones that aren't growing us in righteousness. If we don't, they will take us captive and imprison us in wrongful behavior. We will be held as a slave to our lusts and desires.

These lustful thoughts won't go without a fight. They will speak to our body and tell us how good it would be to satisfy them. These desires will seek to get us to think wrong thoughts that arouse our emotional lusts, and then the battle will be even harder to fight. This is how pornography works. The visual images arouse powerful lusts that demand to be satisfied. This is what makes pornography one of today's most powerful addictions. We must monitor our thoughts so they engender correct emotions, not improper ones. Our thoughts must be controlled by righteousness. Therefore, we must monitor what we allow our eyes to see because wrong images stimulate wrong thoughts and wrong desires within us.

To break the hold of these mental and emotional desires, we need faith grounded in the Truth which is found only in God. Jesus said, "If you have faith as small as a mustard seed you can say to this mountain 'move from here to there' and it will. Nothing will be impossible for you." (Matt 17:20)

We must trust that righteousness is our goal. We must trust that we can overcome temptations. Most of all we must trust in Christ in difficult times. In His strength we are made strong. In Paul's letter to the Corinthians he tells of "having a thorn in his flesh." He didn't say what it was but it was a great burden to him. He asked Christ to remove it and was told "No" three times. Jesus said this to him:

> "My grace is sufficient for you, for my power is made perfect in weakness." (2 Cor. 12:9)

Paul then recounts how this was true in his life. He says:

> "That is why for Christ's sake, I delight in weaknesses, in insults, in hardships, in persecutions and in difficulties. For when I am weak, then I am strong." (2 Cor. 12:10)

When we trust in God and in His power, we are in touch with the most powerful being in the universe. We are able to bring down enemy strongholds and grow in the power that is in the Living God who made and sustains all things. We are called to:

> "Be strong in the Lord and in his mighty power." (Eph 6:10)

> "For the LORD your God is the one who goes with you to fight for you against your enemies to give you victory." (Deut 20:4)

> "But those who hope in the LORD will renew their strength, they will mount up with wings like eagles, they will run and not grow weary, they will walk and not grow faint." (Isa. 40:31)

> "I can do all things through Christ who strengthens me." (Phil 4:13)

The issue becomes one of trust. Trust in who we are in Christ and live in His power, not ours. The Apostle Paul said, "For we walk by faith, not by sight" (NKJV 2 Cor 5:7). If we walk by sight and not by faith we will trust in our own strength and abilities and be defeated almost every time. No, God demands we trust Him and His mighty power, not ourselves. This is the key to faith.

Jesus demanded faith in Himself or it would be impossible to be born again in the spirit. He demanded trust in what He said and did. Without this trust, we couldn't be one of His disciples. Jesus demanded us to have hope, this hope for eternal life with Him. It is through this hope of eternal life that the salvation He secured for us is anchored in our souls.

When our belief in Christ is strong, we are certain of who God is and therefore who we are in Him. Faith is being sure of what you hope for and certain of what you can't see (Heb 11:1). This starts the great faith chapter in the Bible. The book of Hebrews, chapter 11, relates the story of people who trusted God more than anything else. They were rewarded for their faith as a result. They trustingly took God at His word, and God blessed them for it. In the same chapter of Hebrews is another great verse of faith:

> "Without faith it is impossible to please God, for who can come to Him wondering whether He exists and whether He rewards those who earnestly seek Him." (Heb 11:6)

In both of these verses, Hebrews 11:1 and Hebrews 11:6, it is clear that faith is taking God at His word as it is revealed in the Bible. From this faith our salvation comes. Without this belief in Jesus we will die in our sins (John 8:24). We trust that God has called us to live by righteousness and holiness, resisting the worldly temptations and lusts of our sinful nature. We rely on the God who is our strength, our strong tower in times of trouble (Pro 18:10). He is our shield and our rock, the stronghold of our life (Psalm 18:2, 27:1). It is our faith in Him that makes us strong in difficult times.

Compare this to people who base their decisions on their feelings. They are inconsistent because feelings change. Feelings can't always be trusted. Giving into lustful feelings and evil desires only brings momentary contentment, not lasting fulfillment. They drink water but are thirsty as soon as they finish. Only Jesus gives living water that never runs dry (John 4:10). People controlled by emotions go from pleasure to pleasure seeking lasting fulfillment but never finding it. Faith in Christ is a life-long trust relationship, knowing the One we trust is worthy and reliable to meet all of our needs. Feelings are moment-by-moment impulses, giving us a short-term fix with no long-term promise.

Faith builds a fence around our lives that keeps good things in and bad things out. Without this faith-based fence, we will give in to harmful desires and lusts. This fence makes decisions easier because it establishes limits to our behavior. Stay inside and good choices come naturally; stray outside and bad choices lurk in the shadows.

We must build fences in our lives to help keep wrong emotions in check and help us to steer clear of temptations as best we can. When the fences that God has put up for us surround our lives, we are safe from the harm that stalks us outside.

Jesus used the analogy of a sheep and how susceptible sheep are to wolves. The good shepherd seeks to keep the sheep safe from the wolves, but the sheep must trust the shepherd and not go wandering off on their own. Jesus said he was the Good Shepherd (John 10:1-21) of his flock. He would lay down His life for the sheep and we must trust Him. If we don't, the wolves will devour us.

<u>Feelings are Good Servants but Bad Masters</u>

Feelings play a good supporting role in our lives, and that is how God designed them. If we direct them by truth and form them in virtue they can give us added energy that takes us to new heights. They can support key values and behaviors in our lives. As servants, they can give us staying power beyond our normal abilities.

However, feelings make terrible masters. They have an insatiable appetite for hedonistic pleasure. They demand attention and won't take no for an answer. They seldom have our best interests at heart and they direct us to selfishness and self-indulgence. As a master, they will encourage us to seek ecstasy and pleasure, ignoring the threat of discomfort and pain to follow. This lowers our standards and brings us down.

No one can master their feelings at the moment of choice by willpower alone. Our willpower isn't strong enough for this. Think of the person on a diet who tries to resist chocolate cake by sheer willpower. Every time the cake comes around the ability to say "no" becomes harder. They might be able to do this part of the time, but eventually they run out of energy to keep up the fight.

A person grounded in truth knows they don't have to accept their feelings, and they don't have to fulfill them. This is crucial in our ability to overcoming how we "feel" about ideas, concepts and people. Truth is the only source of legitimate contentment.

People grounded in faith don't completely resist feelings but live in such a way they don't base their views only on how they feel. The understanding must be that wrong feelings will lead us astray. They will lead us to make wrong choices and lead us to false information and conclusions. The people grounded in truth have feelings that recognize reality, not disguise it behind the false face of desire. Feelings that support truth strengthen us and enable us to overcome in times of temptation and tests.

Truth-based feelings support us, desire-based feelings manipulate us. When we are faced with contradictory information, we must examine it in the light of truth and resist the impulse to react on "feelings."

We must get off our emotional conveyer belt because it often carries us right into the buzz saw of sin. To get off, you must first want to halt your hedonistic feelings; you must develop revulsion towards them. To develop this righteous revulsion, we must understand what it means to be mastered by feelings compared to being served by them.

Self Control or Out of Control

When feelings, emotions or moods control us, we will act irrationally and be dominated by an inability to control ourselves. Self-control, on the other hand, is the reining-in of one's emotions and actions by faith-based willpower. The opposite of self-control is out-of-control, and out-of-control people are volatile, explosive and quick-tempered.

In the athletic arena, being out-of-control is synonymous with defeat. If we can't control our thoughts, emotions and behavior we won't be able to perform at higher levels. In other words, we are our own most fearsome competition, not the other team. This is true in life as well. To get the most out of ourselves we seek to master those obstacles that prevent us from achieving our full potential. The key is not what happens to us, but rather, how we *handle* what happens to us.

There are many things that prevent self-control — laziness, irresponsibility, self-gratification and ignorance to name a few. Once we overcome these obstacles, we are on the road to regaining self-control.

In order to regain self-control we must develop disciplines in our life. We must discipline our minds, emotions and bodies to those things that best help us grow in godliness. Disciplines are the voluntary actions that enable us to restrict our liberties and freedoms from behaviors that are detrimental to us while at the same time strengthening us in behaviors that are beneficial to us. When repeated on a regular basis, these disciplines set up virtues in us that empower us to be more self-controlled.

Most people don't discipline themselves because they don't want to put in the hard work it will take to build self-control.

To be disciplined we must first know the goal and payback we will receive from it. When we understand the payoffs, it then becomes well worth the cost.

To grow in self-control we must understand the following:

- Tests, suffering and pain are part of life.
- Trying to avoid suffering and pain is useless because they occur to everyone in life. We can't avoid them, but we can overcome them and we can minimize their effects.
- People who live to avoid pain and suffering are easily swayed and hold no strong convictions.
- People who don't fear pain and suffering are more stable and well-grounded.
- Strong people aren't controlled by fear, they control fear.

Self-control gives you the strength to do the right thing even if you don't really feel like it. You do what you should do, not what you feel like doing. Out-of-control people are slaves to their feelings, but in-control people are masters of their feelings.

Three Key Principles

To understand how our feelings deceive us must know three key principles. Seek out the "Truth Principle", reject the "Pleasure Principle" and live according to the "Righteous Principle."

1. *Know and Study Truth* — From the moment we get up in the morning, our emotions are ready to pounce on us and control our lives if they can. We must turn the tables and control them instead. We need to establish dominance over them by getting alone with God. We must make it a habit to rise early every day and spend time in Truth (prayer and meditation on the Word of God). Jesus did this as told in Mark 1:35 —

> "Very early in the morning, while it was still dark, Jesus got up, left the house, and went to a solitary place where he prayed."

Prayer and meditation on God's Word are crucial to controlling your emotions because you ground them in God and His truth. In Psalm 119, a Psalm written about the study of God's Word, eight different times it talks about meditating on the Word, commands, decrees and laws of God. Only by cultivating our relationship with God daily can we master ourselves rightly. When we get up early, we can take charge of our emotions and form them around holiness and righteousness. When we start the day right, it is easier to end the day right. However when we start the day wrong, we often end it wrong too.

God is truth. Once we have a truth base we can compare our "feelings" to the truth of God. When the truth doesn't match what our feelings seek to encourage, we can kick them out.

God won't remove wrong emotions for us. We must do it ourselves. They won't go easily; they will only go by grabbing them by the scruff of the neck and kicking them out. We can pray "God, take this 'feeling' away," but He often leaves it for us to do. We must do this by study and resisting wrong "feelings."

2. *The "Pleasure Principle"* — If we don't feel like doing something then we usually don't do it. We naturally seek out contentment and run from discontentment. We live by the pleasure principle: "if it feels good, do it."

Paul gives us this command concerning concupiscence and those desires that feed the "pleasure principle."

> "Put to death, therefore, whatever belongs to your earthly nature: sexual immorality, impurity, lust, evil desires and greed, which is idolatry."(Col 3:15)

When we put something to death, it has no power over us. We are not scared of a dead lion because it can't attack us. Paul tells us to put to death our sinful lusts so they have no power on us. He then goes on to tell us to replace them with godliness and virtue. Replace the "pleasure principle" with the "righteous principle."

3. *The "Righteous Principle"* — When we embrace the Righteous Principle, we do what is right regardless of how it comes out or how we feel about it. If it is the right thing to do then we just do it, we don't even consider anything else. We deny thoughts of, "I don't feel like it" and replace them with "I will do the right thing." We don't need to "feel like it" to do the

right thing, we just do it. The "Righteous Principle" stops out-of-control behaviors and denies the "Pleasure Principle."

In life we often take the path of least resistance. As a result, most people never even come close to their full potential. The Righteous Principle seeks to get more and more out of us, in spite of how hard it becomes. Here's what Jesus calls us to do:

> "Enter through the narrow gate. For wide is the gate and broad is the road that leads to destruction, and many enter through it." (Matt7:13)

The narrow gate is harder, more work and not at all easy. God never told us it would be easy. He did tell us the rewards for our efforts and the price He paid for us on the cross. Those who observe the Righteous Principle live life by God's rules and seek to bring His Kingdom into life on earth as it is in heaven. We seek to do what is right regardless of the cost. Few are able to do this; it is the road less traveled.

Simply put, the Righteous Principle is living our lives and making our choices based on doing the right things and avoiding the wrong things.

Lasting Treasure

The artificial happiness we get from the "Pleasure Principle" is only temporary relief. The lasting relief we get from the "Righteous Principle" leaves us satisfied and content. We have a joy and peace from it.

Jesus said:

> "Don't store up for yourselves treasure on earth where moth and rust will destroy and thieves will break in and steal. But rather store up for yourselves treasures in heaven where moth and rust can't destroy and thieves can't break in and steal. For where your treasure is, there your heart will be also." (Matt 6:19-21)

Great teaching is found in those words. Only heavenly treasure — that which Christ promises — will last forever. Treasures on earth are here and gone.

Just what are treasures on earth? They are our "trophies," our worldly achievements and material possessions. These are never safe on earth. Not even the safest bank can keep them. The stock market can crash, possessions can be destroyed, and valuables can be lost or stolen.

When we talk about athletic abilities and our job skills, these, too, dwindle with time. As we age, our sports skills diminish. We lose strength, flexibility and endurance. As we age, our memory and thinking skills deteriorate. Every day that passes seems to steal our ability to attain earthly pleasure, while bringing us one day closer to eternity. Only the righteous in Christ will attain an eternal reward, and the passing of time only brings this reality into closer perspective. The older we get the more precious time seems to be.

Jesus teaches us that when our happiness is in temporary things, our joy will eventually be lost or taken away as time marches on. Conversely, when our joy is in eternal things, things that can never be taken away from us, our peace and joy are eternal. Living righteously can bring us the joy of living for others …things like acts of love, gifts of charity, righteousness to other people, giving of our time to someone else, giving of your possessions to another less fortunate, and so on. The rewards of these acts can never be taken away. These will be remembered in the minds of others forever and are eternal (1 Sam 26:23).

As we make it our life's aim to hunger and thirst for the lasting riches of eternal rewards, we will seek out righteousness. We won't be deceived by feelings or desires. We have purpose to why we are here. Our desire is to be set apart, to be holy, to belong to the LORD. It is to this purpose we now turn.

The Will:

The Purpose behind our Actions

...for this was all thy care-
To stand approved in the sight of God, though worlds
judged thee perverse.

John Milton

Would you know who is the greatest saint in all the world? It is not he who prays the most or fasts the most; it is not he who gives most alms or is most eminent for temperance, chastity, or justice; but it is he who is always thankful to God, who wills everything that God will's, who receives everything as an instance of God's goodness and has a heart always ready to praise God for it.

William Law

Rick Warren starts off his best selling book, *The Purpose Driven Life*, this way, "It is not about you. The purpose of your life is far greater than your own personal fulfillment, your peace of mind or even your happiness. It is far greater than your family, your career or even your wildest dreams and ambitions. If you want to know why you were placed on this planet, you must begin with God. You were born by His purpose and for His purpose."[64] The one sentence summary of his book is this: that if we know our purpose in life we have reason to live and live passionately.

Our purpose defines our reason for existence. It is the goal behind our life here on earth. It gives us resolution and determination. To know your purpose is to know the meaning behind your life. *Purpose directs why you live while Truth directs how you live.*

In His book the *"Reflective Life"* author Ken Gire states:

> "For we have big things, know big things, yet our nights are filled with anxiety, our days with drudgery, and in the forest around us we see only trees …We are starved for a life that not only senses the sacred in the world around us but savors it. We're famished for experiences that are real, relationships that are deep, and work that is meaningful."[65]

Compare this with the fast pace of life today. In America we live each day at break-neck speeds. We want everything to be faster. Faster food, faster cars, faster computers and faster you-name-it. We get anxious just waiting for a stop light. Life today is getting faster and faster while at the same time getting shallower and more superficial. Back in the horse and buggy days, life was a lot slower (and also a lot less convenient), yet it was much deeper in spiritual purpose.

Our world has become fast-paced but we've lost the reason for speeding it up in the first place. We speed things up so we can have more time, and why do we want more time? So we can do more stuff, of course! So, we keep adding more things to do — at work, at home, at play — and before you know it, whoops! we're out of time again. So the cycle continues, and we keep speeding things up to have more time.

Technology has certainly made life faster, but the problem is that not all things done fast are done well. In many ways, technology has increased the quality and length of life. However it can't be ignored that it has also lessened the depth of life as well.

We don't read a book — we watch the movie. We don't walk — we drive. We don't write letters — we send greeting cards. We don't cook — we order carry-out, delivered. Each one of these takes away depth from the process.

At a movie we're swept along by the filmmaker, mindlessly munching away at someone else's interpretation of the story, no thought or imagination required. Books, on the other hand, allow us to stop, think, reason and reflect. Cars zip us along from place to place, but a walk lets us enjoy the scenery and have a long, satisfying conversation with our walking companion, too. When we send a card, we're just signing our name to other people's words in the hurried hope that our thoughts for the recipient will somehow come through. A handwritten letter is so much more meaningful because it is a little piece of ourselves, expressed in our own words, as one part of an on-going conversation that will be continued at a later date. It is a gift of ourselves, and a gift of our time. It has depth, and depth can't be hurried.

God called us to live life with purpose and to do so we must slow life down, not speed it up. When we do, depth will be added and meaning will be created.

Make More or Give More

Another step to adding purpose to our life is to stop making more money and start giving more of yourself. We all harbor desires to make more money, build bigger houses, drive bigger cars, and have bigger bank accounts, but in our rush to get what we want, we give less of everything else. We become misers with our money, tightwads with our time, and skinflints with ourselves. It seems the more we get, the less we give. If it is more blessed to give than receive (Acts 20:35), then our blessings will be few indeed.

We make a lot of money but spend even more. Consumer debt is one of the biggest burdens on Americans today. Financial consultant Larry Burkett says this about our growing debt:

> "Americans are literally consuming their asset base and transferring their wealth to the lenders ...since the early sixties, virtually all major assets have been purchased on credit. Since the mid-seventies, even consumer goods have been acquired on credit via the use of credit card and equity loans ...most American families, in spite of their outward appearance of affluence, live on the brink of economic disaster. They have little or no savings to fall back on in difficult times and now are borrowing against the equity in their homes to buy nonessential goods."[66]

Compare all of this spending to the giving of ourselves, which — according to Ernest Thompson Seton in his book, *The Gospel of the Redman* — is the most important thing in life:

"The culture and civilization of the Whiteman are essentially material. His measure of success is, 'How much property have I acquired for myself?' The culture of the Redman is fundamentally spiritual. His measure of success is, 'How much service have I rendered to my people?'"[67]

Jesus said, "Love your neighbor as yourself." (Matt 22:39) *If we truly do this we come to the understanding that nothing we possess is more valuable than what we give to others.* No house, no car, no job can even come close. If we truly love our neighbors as ourselves, then our lifestyle should reflect this. How? By sharing our time, our treasures and ourselves with others.

In the same book by Ernest Thompson Seton, he tells this story that illustrates the point quite well. It is entitled simply, "The Old Onion Seller."

In a shady corner of the great market at Mexico City was an old Indian named Pota-lamo. He had twenty strings of onions hanging in front of him. An American from Chicago came up and said:

"How much for a string of onions?"

"Ten cents," said Pota-lamo.

"How much for two strings?"

"Twenty cents," was the reply.

"How much for three strings?"

"Thirty cents," was the answer.

"Not much reduction in that," said the American. "Would you take twenty-five cents?"

"No" said the Indian.

"How much for your whole twenty strings?' said the American.

"I would not sell you my twenty strings." replied the Indian.

"Why not?" said the American. "Aren't you here to sell your onions?"

"No," replied the Indian. "I am here to live my life. I love this market place. I love the crowds and the red serapes. I love the sunlight and the waving palmettos. I love to have Pedro and Luis come by and say: 'Buenas dias'...and talk about the babies and the crops. I love to see my friends. That is my life. For that I sit here all day and sell my twenty strings of onions. But if I sell all my onions to one customer, then is my day ended. I have lost my life that I love—and that I will not do."[68]

Our Working Will

As we have already said, the will is the "command center" in our spirit. It is the area that houses what we "long for" in life, what we wish for in our life. It is the dwelling place for our existence, our purpose in living our life.

Our will as a spiritual being determines our power in the sense that we act in accordance with our will. Our ability to physically act in a material world is how we exist. Only by our physical behavior can we exert influence on other living creatures and things — simply sitting quietly by and thinking our thoughts to ourselves will not turn the trick. Therefore, by our conduct we exhibit power in the world around us. Our power is based on our actions, and our actions are based on our will.

Our will is called and formed to do good (Gen 1:26) because it was made in the image of God. It was meant to be under God's control and guidance. Since the fall of Adam and Eve in the Garden of Eden, our will has been formed in original sin to do what we want (Gen 2:16, 3:1-9). Most of the key Reformers of the mid-16th sixteenth century, such as Martin Luther and John Calvin, expressly taught the total depravity of man. This meant that man was born with a sinful nature and could only sin. Martin Luther in His book "Bondage of the Will" states his belief:

> "He (Luther) does not say that man through sin has ceased to be man ...but that man through sin has ceased to be good. He has no power to please God. He is unable to do anything but continue in sin. His salvation, therefore, must be wholly of Divine grace, for he himself can contribute nothing to it; and any formulation of the gospel which amounts to saying that God shows grace, not in saving man, but in making it possible for man to save himself, is to be rejected as a lie. The whole work of man's salvation, first to last, is God's"[69]

We are fallen creatures, dead in sin and because of this we put "us" on the throne of our will. We have made ourselves God instead of the Creator Himself. Only by rebirth can we be restored (Col 3:10, Eph 4:24) and re-install God on His rightful throne of our will. We must then become born anew to know and do as God has designed us to be. We are to be righteous and holy to Him (Eph 2:10).

It has been said, "Jesus never came to make bad people good. He came to make dead people live." This certainly rings true. We must have life from God before we can serve God righteously. When God gives us life, He gives us a new will, His will (Ezek 36:26). This new will in us gives us the ability to do good and serve God. We become alive to His Spirit in us. We are no longer dead to God but alive to Him and dead to the world (Gal 2:20, Rom 6:3-14). We serve God in righteousness, not Satan and self in sin.

Our old will, as we have said in Chapter 3, is formed to fulfill the desires of the body in pleasure. We do what makes us happy. In living to please our body, our will desires anything that will satisfy it. This is contrary to the will God has for us. We are to put others first (Matt 22:39), we are to deny the lust of our flesh (Rom 1:24-32) and need to understand we grow through suffering (Matt 5:10-12, James 1, Rom 5:3-5). When we submit our will to God's plan of righteous living and love for others, we grow in Him and through Him.

God blesses the righteous. The book of Proverbs gives many blessings to righteous living. Here are a few:

- The righteousness of the upright delivers them (Pro 11:6).
- He who sows righteousness reaps a sure reward (Pro 11:18).
- In the way of righteousness there is life, along that path is immortality (Pro 12:28).
- Righteousness guards the man of integrity (Pro 13:6).
- The LORD detests the way of the wicked but he loves those who pursue righteousness (Pro 15:9).
- He who pursues righteousness and love finds life, prosperity and honor (Pro 21:21).

Righteousness is virtue in morality, justice in government and love in our living. Righteousness and justice are the foundations of God's throne …the heavens proclaim His righteousness (Psalm 97:2, 6). God is a God of righteousness and He demands His people to be righteous as well. We must reestablish this, through life in Jesus Christ in our will. Then and only then can we start to live righteously. Choice is our ability to exercise our will and make decisions. Righteous choices reflect the power of Christ in our will and give us the power to be His instruments in a dying world marred by sin.

The blessings of God establish His desire for His children and the means to govern our choices. When our will is rooted in God's will, there is hunger for life and joy in our living. We live life in the full as Jesus promised to us.

<u>Living Life in the Full</u>

In the gospel of John, Jesus said, "I have come that you may have life and have it in the full." (John 10:10) What did he mean by this?

We need to consider what happens when we die. Is there a life after death? If there is not eternal life then as the Apostle Paul said, "Let us eat and drink for tomorrow we die." (1Cor 15:32) This view makes our choices easier. Why not live for self because when you die this is all there is.

If on the other hand there is an eternal life as the Bible teaches we, need to consider it in several different ways:

1. If this present life is miserable and eternal life is just an extension of it, then eternal life is one of the worst things that can happen to us.
2. If this present life is miserable and eternal life is a far better life than this present one, then it is a good thing. The sooner we get to it the better.
3. If this present life is awesome and eternal life is much worse than this one, then it becomes something to dread and is again a bad thing.
4. If this life is joyous and peaceful and eternal life is just an extension of it but far better ("No eye has seen, no ear has heard, no mind has conceived what God has planned for those who love Him." (1Cor 2:9)) then it is the greatest thing. We look forward to it and long for its coming. This present life is good but eternal life is the best.

Of these four scenarios, the first and the third are anything but desirable. If our after-life existence is miserable and this goes on infinitely, we certainly don't want this or desire it. In the first scenario where this present life is miserable, we just want it to end. An eternal life of misery just makes it worse for then there is no end to it.

In the third scenario where life is good now but life after death is bad, then eternal life is again not to be desired. If this is the case then we will live for the moment and seek to get all we can in this life. Death ushers in less than we have in this life, and the question is how much worse will it be? The Bible talks about hell as a place of "Weeping and gnashing of teeth" (Matt 13:42) and a place of eternal torment (Luke 16:23-24). A place we certainly don't want to go to.

In the second example death is a good thing. The sooner we get to it the better off we will be. The scenario is a miserable life now but a joyous life eternally. In fact, in this scenario we might bring it upon ourselves, as people who commit suicide do. Why go on when eternity awaits us with endless joy and all this life brings us is pain?

Contrast these three scenarios with the fourth example, the one I believe Jesus is talking about when He says life in the full. Here eternal life starts here on earth in this present existence. We grow more and more in His joy and His peace as we come to understand what living is all about. It isn't only about a physical existence or seeking pleasure in our lives, it is about hungering and thirsting for righteousness, being pure in heart, being merciful, being poor in spirit, and about meekness ... (Matt 5:3-12)

The fullness of life Jesus promised us as His children on this earth is not a life full of winning lottery tickets and moving up the corporate ladder. This never does and never will bring lasting happiness, either now or eternally. The fullness is spiritual and it is about living life, hungering to become more godly and holy. It is about knowing who God is as our Father and obedience to Him.

C.S. Lewis says this about joy:

> "God was to be obeyed simply because of who He was, God ...He had taught me how a thing can be revered not for what it can do for you but for what it is in itself...If you ask why we should obey God, in the last resort the answer is, 'I am.'...I think it is well, even now, sometimes to say to ourselves, 'God is such that if His power could vanish and His other attributes remain, so that supreme

right were forever robbed of supreme might, we would still owe Him precisely the same kind of allegiance as we do now'…lead us to the conclusion that union with that nature is bliss and separation from it horror."[70]

Union with the Creator, Sustainer and Giver of all life is union with God. *To know who He is and who He is not draws us closer to Him but never pushes us further from Him.* Knowing God as He is and becoming more like Him is life in the full. It is to be desired in this life and eternally as well.

When we look at God's attributes we see why this is so:

- God is love (1 John 4:16)
- God is holy (Ps 99:9, Isa 6:3)
- God is light (1 John 1:5)
- God is life (John 1:4)
- God is righteous (Dan 9:14)
- God is just (2 Thes 1:6)
- God is wisdom (Col 2:3, Rom 11:33, Isa 55:8-9, Job chapters 38 and 39)
- God is kind (Jer 9:24)

This list could go on and on. The point is to know God and to desire to be like Him. To know God is to hunger to be near Him. To know God is to love God and seek to serve Him. Thus serving Him in obedience gives us peace and joy…and brings fullness to our life.

Think of someone you love dearly. Is there no greater love than to be with them, to serve them, to please them and make them happy? The reason so many people don't love God is they don't know Him and who He is. G.K. Chesterton said, "The Christian ideal has not been tried and found wanting. It has been found difficult and left untried."[71] The reason so many people have never known joy in life is either because their understanding of God is wrong or they have never sought to truly know Him.

Saint Augustine said, "Our hearts were made for you O' Lord and they are restless until they find rest in you." This is the filled life. This alone is the only way to live life in the full.

__Going Deep__

Going deep in life is to get below the surface and really search the hidden areas. This search reveals things we can't see on the surface. This provides inner strength. Trees with shallow, surface root systems will be knocked down by strong winds. Trees with deep systems may bend in the wind, but they will not be uprooted and swept away. The deeper the root system, the stronger the tree will be and the better it will be able to withstand storms. Depth provides strength. Thus, the deeper our life the stronger we will be. Jesus likened this to building one's house on a solid rock (Matt 7:24-27).

Another characteristic of depth is that people whose lives go deep have lives full of meaning and vigor. Calvin Miller describes "deep" this way:

> "The world around us is the outer world of 'outer relationships.' In such outer places we make friends, achieve success — get on in the world. In this busy, worried world we have appointments, face disappointments, and force our ego-driven souls to stab at achieving power. On the surface of our lives, things frenzied and dyspeptic dominate us. But in our hearts it is quite another matter …Deep is the dwelling place of God. Deep is the character of the ocean …Deep is where the noisy, trashy surface of the sea gets quiet and serene. No sound breaks the awesome silence of the ocean's heart …Most Christians …spend their lives whipped tumultuously through the surface circumstances of their days."[72]

Deep lives are ones where people spend time searching for purpose and then living life based on that purpose. This takes a lot of work, time and discipline, but it is the only way to get depth. It is the difference between snorkeling and scuba diving. Both these swimmers are in the water, but the sights they see are vastly different. Much of the ocean can't be seen from the surface, it can only be explored by putting on diving gear and going deep. So too in life.

We spend much of our time describing things we barely know or understand, yet thinking we know them well. We are as Calvin Miller describes it:

> "non-peakers talking to non-peakers about peak experiences."[73]

Our life and our God are subjects we could spend our whole lives researching and still barely scratch the surface of either. Sadly, we think we have it all figured out because we read a book on it, or go to church weekly. We talk about God and life thinking we know most of the answers when the reality is we don't. In fact we don't even know the question, let alone the answer. The depth of God and of life is far, far deeper than we know.

The book of Job is the story of one such man. Job lost his home, kids and health all in a very short time. Imagine losing all of that in one lifetime. He lost everything! He contemplates all of this with his friends Eliphaz, Bildad and Zophar. They come on the scene to give their distraught friend a shoulder to cry on and eventually, some advice. Sadly, the advice is from non-peakers talking to non-peakers about peak experiences and does Job no good.

Eventually Job questions all his misfortunes. Even though encouraged to curse God and die, he never does and remains faithful (Job 2:9-10). He wonders, "Why me?" Then in chapter 38 of the book of Job God responds:

> "Who is this that darkens my counsel with words without knowledge? Brace yourself like a man and I will question you and you will answer me…Where were you when I laid the foundation of the earth?…Who shut up the sea behind doors?…When I made the clouds its garment?… Have you ever given orders to the morning?…Have the gates of death been shown to you? Have you…?" (Job 38:1-3, 4, 8, 9, 12, 17)

God continues this relentless questioning until chapter 42 begins. Job's only response is:

> "Surely I spoke of things I did not understand, things too wonderful for me to know …My ears had heard of you

but now my eyes have seen you. Therefore I despise myself and repent in dust and ashes." (Job 42:3,5-6)

God longs to know us and have us know Him, but we can never know the deep by snorkeling, we must put on our diving gear and go deep. We can never talk about peak experiences until we discover the deep things of God. Calvin Miller continues,

> "Spirituality …presumes that deeper living is possible because God is near. Not only is He near but He longs to empower us in a deeper way and lure us ever deeper …to do this you must empty yourself of your own fullness …it is as a professor who was serving a student a cup of tea. He filled the cup and he kept pouring until the tea spilled over the top. Finally the student said, 'Sir you're overfilling my cup!' The professor answered, 'Well if you would just empty it, I would fill it with better stuff than this.'"[74]

God longs for us to have cups that are filled with the most excellent things of life. To do this we must empty our cups of ourselves and our agenda and seek out God and His plan and His agenda (Jer 29:13). This then becomes our purpose, and our purpose becomes our life. Only then do we start to go deep into life and all it calls us to be. In the deep places of life, we meet with God.

Knowing Your Purpose gives you Passion to Live

When you know your purpose in life, you will become more passionate about how you live and what you live for. When you are passionate, your choices will become much clearer and easier to make. You will make more "best" choices because they are now centered on your purpose.

To be passionate is to have a strong conviction within us, a burning desire in our hearts. This ties our body to our spirit and convictions are the result. Convictions focus our vision and develop in us a single mindedness, a steadfast way of living.

Conviction is different than belief. Many people have beliefs about things. They *believe* the Chicago Cubs are going to win the baseball World Series. They *believe* Florida is a great place to retire. Convictions are much deeper than that. Convictions are so formed in us they become part of us. They are constantly in our thoughts, emotions and our will. They then become lived out in our actions by guiding our choices. They are so grounded in us we would be willing to die for these convictions.

Let me illustrate it this way. Let's say I told you I had just invented a bulletproof shirt. Let's assume I am quite capable of this, and that I spent the better part of two years working on this bulletproof shirt. Then I ask you, "Do you *believe* it is bulletproof?" You say, "Why yes I do." Not trusting your response, I say, "Great, then put it on while I aim my shotgun at you to test it." Your response will illustrate the difference between a belief and a conviction. Can a belief become a conviction? Sure, it just depends on how strongly you believe it. Ready, aim ...

When we tie our convictions into our job, we love our job. When we tie them into our sport, we love playing the game. When we tie them into our education, we love learning. When we tie them into our lives, we love living.

We need to reach a point in our life where every second of every day we are passionate about our convictions.

Many men and women have lived with a religious passion and have died a martyr's death because of it. They would rather die than give up on their conviction. Others have used this energy to lead a nation. Abe Lincoln did it in the 1860's to end slavery, and our nation is forever in his debt. He died for his belief. Winston Churchill rallied Great Britain in World War II, and because of him the tide in the war was turned. *These great men became great because of their convictions.* The situations in which they found themselves forced them to make a choice — either lead with their convictions, or run from them. Happily for all of us, they chose leadership.

We must tie into a cause greater than ourselves. Jesus said:

> "...Unless a kernel of wheat falls to the ground and dies, it remains only a single seed. But if it dies it produces many seeds. The man who loves his life will lose it, while the man who hates his life in this world will keep it for eternal life." (John 12:24-26)

And again He said:

> "For whoever wants to save his life will lose it, but whoever loses his life for me will find it. What good will it be

for a man to gain the whole world but forfeit his soul? Or what can a man give in exchange for his soul? (Matt 16:25-26)

Jesus is calling us to live a life greater than ourselves. A life where we commit all we are to Him and to righteous living. A life where we put others first and ourselves second. A life not based on "What is in it for me?" but rather, "What can I do to help others?" Life is much bigger than we are, and we must live it for a cause greater than our own selfishness. Life in the full is lived when we are passionate about growing Jesus' Kingdom here on earth.

The energy created by passion and purpose in giving our life to the Kingdom of God will grow us in love. This love will then cast out fear. John in His first epistle says this of the relationship between love and fear.

"There is no fear in love. But perfect love drives out fear, because fear has to do with punishment. The one who fears is not made perfect with love. We love because He first loved us." (1 John 4:18-19)

When perfect love works on a soul, its effect is to cast out fear. It works on the mind and takes away anxious thoughts. When we have perfect love of someone, we have nothing to fear from them; they won't harm us because they have our best interest at heart.

To be so in love with God and with other human beings and to have their best interest at heart gives us peace and joy. It removes fear in the process. It gives us purpose, which gives us passion in how we live.

<u>Rebels without a Clue</u>

As I close this chapter, I'd like to address one more curious thing: the modern intellectual. He is a person who disbelieves almost everything that has been taught in the past concerning religion. He believes the older an idea is, the worse it is. His is a life in which relativity and cynicism guide all that he does.

These intellectuals deny the God of our forefathers, they reject historical morality, and they refute the traditions of yesterday. Paul Johnson in his book "*Intellectuals*" writes this about this new kind of thinker:

"The rise of the secular intellectual has been a key in shaping the modern world …priests, scribes, and soothsayers have laid claim to guiding society from the very beginning …Their moral and ideological innovations were limited by the canons of external authority and by the inheritance of tradition. They would not and could not be free spirits. With the decline of clerical power in the 18th century a new kind of mentor emerged …The secular intellectual was deist, skeptic, or atheist. He was just as ready as any pontiff or presbyter to tell mankind how to conduct his affairs. He proclaimed from the start a special devotion to the interests of humanity and an evangelical duty to advance them by his teaching…He found himself bond by no corpus of revealed religion. The collective wisdom of the past, the legacy of tradition, and the prescriptive codes of ancestral experience existed to be selectively followed or wholly rejected entirely as his own good sense might decide. For the first time in human history and with growing confidence and audacity, men arose to assert that they could diagnose the ills of society and cure them with their own unaided intellects; more, that they could devise formulae whereby not merely the structure of society but the fundamental habits of human beings could be transformed for the better."[75]

He goes on to ask the question: what kind of life did these intellectuals lead? People like: Rousseau, Marx, Ibsen, Hemingway, Sartre and Russell. Knowing what they taught, what kind of lives did they lead? He shows quite candidly they lived very sadistic and immoral ones.

The modern intellectual throws out religion because he is the anointed of God and knows far more than all humanity and history. Sadly, his beliefs not only lead others astray but have shaken the very foundations of society over the past 200 years. The intellectuals have taken away God and replaced him with man. They have brought more and more evil in society and focused less and less on morality and human ethics. Their beliefs have uprooted and caused a major cultural shift in America; this shift denies God and prescribes self fulfillment and self aggrandizement.

The modern intellectual is a rebel. A rebel without a cause and without a clue, oblivious to the disastrous consequences of his professions. G.K. Chesterton said this of the new rebel:

> "The new rebel is a skeptic and will not entirely trust anything. He has no loyalty; therefore he can never be a revolutionist. And the very fact that he doubts everything really gets in his way when he wants to denounce anything. For all denunciation implies a moral doctrine of some kind; and the modern revolutionist doubts not only the institution he denounces, but the doctrine by which he denounces it …He curses the Sultan because Christian girls lose their virginity, and then curses Mrs. Grundy because they keep it. As a politician he will cry out that war is a waste of life and then as a philosopher that all life is a waste of time. A Russian pessimist will denounce a policeman for killing a peasant and then prove by the highest philosophical principles that the peasant should have killed himself …Therefore the modern man in revolt has become practically useless for all purposes of revolt. By rebelling against everything he has lost the right to rebel against anything."[76]

His point is that many people rebel against society just to be a rebel. They stand for nothing.

The modern intellectual rebel is a very dangerous person. One arrogant in his ignorance, and determined to spread it around. He is a person who doesn't know where he came from or where he is going. He has everything to gain in personal freedom for himself and nothing to lose. Society, on the other hand, has everything to lose and nothing to gain. We are constantly putting out the fires they start. Since he has nowhere to go, he never knows if he gets there. *By standing for nothing he will fall for anything.*

We must understand history; it has much to teach us. God has given us laws to protect us, not control us. When we come to understand that all life is a gift and must be lived by the commands of the Giver, we have purpose and passion. We live each day to the fullest. However, when we remove fences that have been put in place for our own protection, we open the gates to anarchy and rebellion. Modern intellectual rebels have torn down many fences put there by our forefathers for the protection of future generations, and we are paying the price of countless broken and shattered lives, adrift and rudderless in the aimless currents of intellectual and moral relativism.

We must understand we were made to live with a purpose. To know this purpose gives us passion. Purpose and passion then in turn enable us to do far greater things than many of us ever set out to achieve. It calls us to live for a cause greater than ourselves. It is to this cause we must give all of our life, and that by committing to this cause we can do anything because it is not us at work, but God at work in us (Phil 4:13). This is the cause that Jesus came and gave his life for.

To grow in love of His life is to grow in virtue, and to grow in virtue is to grow in power. It is to this, virtue, that we now turn.

The Life of Virtue:

The Fuel for our System

For the eyes of the LORD run to and fro throughout the whole earth, to show Himself strong on behalf of those whose heart is loyal to Him.

2 Chronicles 16:9

For the eyes of the Lord are on the righteous and His ears are attentive to their prayer, but the face of the Lord is against those who do evil.

1 Peter 3:12

One of the main themes throughout this book has been to link growth in virtue with growth in spiritual power. In earlier chapters, we spoke of Truth as our compass, and our Will as the command center of the Spirit, which drives our lives. And now we come to Virtue …

If our life were a high-performance aircraft, Truth would be our guidance system, Will would be our auto-pilot, Mind would be the flight controls, Emotions would be our co-pilot and Virtue would be the fuel. Acts of Virtue energize our Spirit, developing power in us. (Acts of Vice have the opposite effect. They're the bits of gunk and filth that clog up the gas line, sapping us of power.) The more we fill our tanks with Virtue and clear the Vice out of our system, the more powerful we become. We will then achieve our God-given potential and have a maximum impact on those around us.

To understand the importance of virtue in our spirit we first need to recognize who God really is. How well you understand and know God determines how well and how effectively you will live your life for Him.

God wants us to know Him. God reveals Himself in the Bible for this very reason, so that we *can* know Him. Read these verses; they are just three samples of many:

- Isaiah 1:1-5
- Exodus 33:18-23
- Revelation 1:9-18

Each reveals a similar yet distinct perspective on God's character: His holiness, His purity, and His perfection.

1. Holiness of God -

> "In the year that king Uzziah died, I saw the LORD seated on a throne, high and exalted, and the train of His robe filled the temple. Above Him were seraphs each with six wings: with two wings they covered their faces, with two they covered their feet, and with two they were flying. And they were calling to one another, "Holy, holy, holy is the LORD Almighty the whole earth is full of His glory." At the sound of their voices the doorposts and thresholds shook and the temple was filled with smoke. "Woe to me!" I cried, "I am ruined! For I am a man of unclean lips, and I live among a people of unclean lips, and my eyes have seen the King, the LORD Almighty." (Isaiah 6:1-5)

We must be holy because God is holy (1 Pet 1:16). Holiness is separateness or sanctity of an object or being. The holiness of God reveals His moral wholeness. God is separated from man because man is impure, sinful and morally imperfect. In verse 3 of Isaiah the repetition of the word holy represents a literary device found in Hebrew to emphasize the importance of something. We do this in English by putting a word in bold lettering or underlining it.[77]

Of all of God's qualities this is the only one that is repeated three times. The holiness of God is to be emphasized and how separate He is from man. The fear that this brought to Isaiah to be in the presence of the Ruler, Sustainer and Giver of all life is clearly seen. Awe overcame him as he viewed the throne of the King of kings and Lord of lords. The temple doorposts were shaking, filling Isaiah with complete reverence, worship and adoration for the Lord.

When Isaiah saw the living God, the reigning monarch of the universe displayed before his eyes in all of His holiness, he cried out, "Woe is me!" The word *woe* is a crucial Biblical word, one that we cannot afford to ignore. Isaiah's use of *woe* is extraordinary considering he was a man of such integrity. His contemporaries considered him as the most righteous man in the nation. Then he caught one sudden glimpse of a holy God. In that single moment all of his self-esteem was shattered. In a brief second he was exposed, made naked beneath the gaze of the absolute standard of holiness. As long as he was allowed to compare himself to other mortals, he was able to sustain a lofty opinion of his own character. The instant he measured himself by the ultimate standard he was destroyed, morally and spiritually annihilated. He was undone. He came apart.[78]

The pattern seen here is one seen throughout the Bible. God appears and people tremble. An angel appears the prophet trembles. This isn't like TV shows today. Shows today reveal a normal experience with angels, ones common amongst our fellow human beings. When angels appear on TV shows, there is no reverence or awe instilled in those around them.

In the Bible when an angel appeared or the Presence of God was near, men fell prostrate in worship or in fear before them, similar to Isaiah 6 (Matt 28:1-5, Dan 10:7-12, Acts 9:3-7, Rev 1:9-18, Rev 22:8-9). God is holy and we must know Him this way only in awe and fear (respect). God promises blessings to those who fear/revere Him. The fear of the Lord:

- Is the beginning of wisdom (Ps 111:10)
- Adds length to life (Pro 10:27)
- A man avoids evil (Pro 16:6)
- Bring wealth and honor to life (Pro 22:4)

To know God in this way alone leads you to worship as Isaiah and fall down on our knees for we too are men of unclean lips. God is holy and demands us to be holy as well. We must see Him in this holiness, anything less reveals a false god.

2. Perfection of God-

> "On the Lord's Day I was in the Spirit, and I heard behind me a loud voice like a trumpet...I turned to see the voice that was speaking to me. And when I turned I saw seven golden lampstands...and among the lampstands was someone "like a son of man" dressed in a robe that was down to his feet and with a golden sash that was around his chest. His head and hair were white like wool, as white as snow, and his eyes were like blazing fire. His feet were like bronze glowing in a furnace, and His voice was like the sound of rushing waters. In his right hand he held seven stars, and out of his mouth came a sharp double-edged sword. His face was like the sun shining in all of its brilliance. When I saw him I fell at his feet as though dead (Rev 1:10,12-17).

We are called to be perfect because God is perfect (Matt 5:48). This is the sum total of salvation in Jesus Christ, to be perfect. This is the great yearning of God for us. This is impossible to do by ourselves. We do this on God's abilities, not ours. Jesus says later, "With man this is impossible, but with God all things are possible" (Matt 19:26). This will never happen totally in this life but will come to fruition in heaven. Yet still we must strive to be all we can through God's power at work in us.[79]

Here we have the glorified Christ revealing Himself. The attributes of Christ as part of the trinity of God are revealed here in this image John has. God is perfect, He is complete in Himself, He lacks nothing, and He has no flaws. He is perfect in all the characteristics of His nature. He is the basis for and the standard by which all other perfection is measured.

The traits of Jesus that John noticed are: His robe, hair, face, eyes, mouth, voice and feet. Each one of these represents a part of Christ and who He is. Take a closer look at each one of these qualities; see what attributes of His they represent.

- *His long robe-* this robe describes the high priests robe of the Old Testament. Jesus is our great high priest (Heb 2:17-18).[80]

- *His head and hair were white-* this represents Christ chastening and purifying His church (2 Cor. 11:2). This also shows his holy knowledge, wisdom and truthfulness.[81]
- *His eyes were like blazing fire-* His searching, revealing, gaze penetrates the depths of the soul. He knows everything there is to know about us (Matt 10:26).[82]
- *His feet were bronze* - this is His judgment. He will judge every man by his deeds (Rom 2:5-10).[83]
- *Voice was like rushing waters-* this is the voice of sovereign power, the voice of supreme authority. This is the voice that will one-day command the dead to come out of their graves. When Christ speaks we must listen to Him (Matt 17:5).[84]
- *Sharp two-edged sword came out of His mouth* — Jesus Christ protects his church and here it is the sword of His Word that does this. The power of God's Word is seen here (Heb 4:12).[85]
- *Face was shining* – this reveals the glory of the LORD that shines through Jesus and that brings Him glory (2 Cor 4:6).[86]

God is perfect. There is nothing impure, incomplete or false in Him. In His perfection lies His great sovereign power. God is perfect in power and perfect in knowledge. God is ever-present as well, and this allows Him to exercise His power and authority outside of the realm of time. He uses it to His eternal glory. Once we understand God's complete and total perfection, we can then view some of His other attributes in light of His perfection. Some of these other attributes are His perfect love, mercy, justice, immutability and righteousness. It is for this perfection we give Him all honor, glory, dominion and praise, forever and ever.

3. Purity of God-

> "Then Moses said, 'Now show me your glory.' And the LORD said, 'I will cause my goodness to pass in front of you, and I will proclaim my name, the LORD, in your presence. I will have mercy on whom I will have mercy and I will have compassion on whom I will have compassion. But he said you can not see my face, for no one may

see me and live.' Then the LORD said, 'There is a place near me where you may stand on a rock. When my glory passes by I will put you in a cleft in the rock and cover you with my hand until I have passed by. Then I will remove my hand and you may see my back; but my face must not be seen.'" (Exodus 33:19-23)

The fact that God is totally pure prevents anything impure from viewing Him. Anything that is impure that views Him will die, and the impurity that separates us from God is sin. Purity has to do with cleanness, and cleanness has to do with persons and property. When something is unclean it has been defiled, corrupted, contaminated. When something is unclean, its life and health become endangered. In the Old Testament, people with diseases such as leprosy were considered unclean. People were commanded to stay away from them because of this uncleanness. Today we must stay away from conditions that develop illness like typhoid fever or other physical diseases. This is true spiritually as well. We must stay away from spiritual conditions or behaviors that may lead to unrighteous actions such as drunkenness, hatred or lust. We must realize there is a close connection between spiritual cleanliness and morality.

In the Bible the word defilement described a sinful or unfit condition. Because of our disobedience to God we are all unfit or defiled. Sin defiles us. The New Testament lists sins of morality that lead to defilement (Gal 5:19-21). Believers in Jesus Christ are called to holiness and cleanliness and they are not to yield themselves to unrighteous or immoral deeds.

The Old Testament distinguishes between what is clean and helpful and what is unclean and unacceptable to God (Lev 10:10-11). The priest was to teach the people the difference. The teaching on uncleanness has to deal with God's holiness and how we as God's children must avoid these behaviors.

God demands purity and cleanness from us (Titus 2:5). He commands us to be separated from defiled objects and deeds (Titus 2:11-14). God also tells us there are consequences for our sin (Rom 6:23) and that we will give an account at the end of our life for our behavior (Matt 25:41, Matt 22:13, Luke 12:5, 2 Pet 2: 4-10).

God is pure, and only as we see Him in this purity can we revere and serve Him as His purity warrants. Outside of this purity He is just another being whom we honor and serve. In this purity He is the Lord of the heavens and the earth, our God and Father.

Accounting for our Life

Jesus did not save us according to our good deeds but rather because of His grace and preordained purpose. This is the foundation of the saving gospel and the sustenance of those saved by Him. We are called to God's plan and purpose for our life. His commands are to be the guiding principles of how we live and for what we live for. In doing this we grow in Him and His life by becoming more like Christ.

We are called to live this life we have been given in purity, perfection and in holiness (1Pet 1:15-16). God has a master plan for the world and it involves us, not our plan for ourselves, but rather His plan for us. This plan is revealed through Jesus Christ who set these plans out before the beginning of the world. The apostle Paul states this in his second letter to Timothy:

> "…by the power of god, who has saved us and called us to a holy life, not because of anything we have done but because of His own purpose and grace. This grace was given us in Christ Jesus before the beginning of time…" (2 Tim 1:8(b)-9)

Jim Loehr and Tony Schwartz describe it this way,

> "When we live for something beyond ourselves, we grow in the fuel that drives us. This fuel then provides energy for our living. When we live solely to self and only for what we can get out of this life here and now, we grow in self-centeredness. This makes our existence shallower, drains our energy and impedes our performance. The more preoccupied we are with our own fears and concerns, the less energy we have available to take positive action."[87]

We must also have a clear understanding that we are called to live according to God's commands and dictates in this life. However we choose to live, we will give an account of how we spent our time and how we lived our life when we die. This will then determine what happens to us after we die (Rev 20:12). We will either go to heaven and be in God's presence in eternal joy or go to hell, a place of eternal torment and suffering.

We will give an account to God for what we did in this life. This is clearly seen in several parables Jesus taught about how men used money given to them (Matt 25:14-30). The two that invested and grew their gifts were commended and given more. The one who did nothing with it had it taken from him, and he was thrown out into a horrible place where there was weeping and gnashing of teeth. God demands of us to use the gifts and talents for His purpose not our selfish gain.

When we live life knowing we will give an account for it, we live differently. We live for the greater good of others and we learn selflessness. We grow in peace and joy in this life. We have our hearts set on pleasing God and serving Him only. We seek to please Him, not ourselves. The will of Jesus is the joy and desire of our life.

In an analogy consider your boss at work giving you $1000 to spend on your department to improve it. Compare this to wining $1,000 in a lottery to be used how you desire. We will spend the money given to us by our boss more conservatively and cautiously than we would the money we won in the lottery. The reason is the expectations our boss has for its use and that we are accountable to him for how we spend it. No such expectation or accounting is set for us on the lottery money.

The Biblical concept of stewardships is seen here. A steward is a person who is in charge of someone else's goods or household. We are to manage it with their best interest at heart. God commands us to do this with our talents and gifts for His ultimate good. We must prove faithful in the stewardship of our life for God's glory.

Our life was given to us as a gift and our salvation has been purchased at the greatest cost. Our life is not our own (1 Cor 6:19-20) and it must be lived this way. We have a choice how we live our life now, but we won't have a choice where we spend eternity.

Commitment to Excellence

God is holy, pure and perfect and demands this of us as well. John Wesley, one of the founders of the Methodist denomination, understood this well in his life. He had an unending commitment to holiness before God and this is seen in his life and some of his writings.

> "These convinced me, more than ever, of the absolute impossibility of being half a Christian; I determined,

> through his grace …to be all-devoted to God, to give him all my soul, my body and my substance."[88]

Wesley believed that being a "half-Christian" or a "lukewarm Christian" was the worst thing of all, worse than open sin. In fact Wesley stated that a man who does not engage himself entirely in the practice of religion is in greater fear of damnation than a notorious sinner.[89]

Again on this practice of holiness Wesley furthered stated,

> "I take religion to be, not the bare saying over so many prayers, morning and evening…not anything superadded now and then to a careless or worldly life; but a constant ruling habit of soul, a renewal of our minds in the image of God, a recovery of the divine likeness, a still-increasing conformity of heart and life to the pattern of our most holy Redeemer."[90]

A holy life is a virtuous life. Virtue is a habitual and firm disposition to do good. They are building blocks for moral living. They are also means to empower us. Virtue comes from the Latin word *virtus,* which signifies power, strength and ability. To build virtue in life is to build power and strength that enable us to overcome.

In their book about the transforming power of virtue Tim Gray and Curtis Martin say this about virtue:

> "Without virtues we will neither be godly nor manly."[91]

The Bible calls us to meditate on virtue (Phil 4:8) and that we must seek to become virtuous (2 Pet 2:2-4). We are given the calling to be virtuous and reap the many benefits and blessings that will be bestowed on us because of it.

The apostle Peter tells in his second book that we are to continue to add virtue to virtue until we have the highest love possible, *agape* love. This is a steady moral advance in our life. The apostle Peter bids us to use all our energy to grow thus in accord with God's plan for humanity.

We are called to have faith in God, but we are also called to obey Him and His commands for our life, "For unless we have faith that is lived out in our actions our faith is not really faith" (James 2:18-26). Faith is not only commitment to the promises of Christ but also to the demands of Christ. [92]

New Testament scholar William Barclay says this about growth in virtue:

> "...Happiness depends both on God's gift and our effort. We don't earn salvation but at the same time we have to bend every energy towards the Christian objective of a lovely life."[93]

In Greek the word for virtue is *arête*. This is excellence in its highest form. It demands the best from us to acquire it and so in turn we must give our best to acquire it. To acquire virtue we must commit to it, and to commit to virtue will demand complete consecration to Christ.

Virtue is Power

There is an instance in the Bible where the word virtue is used with regards to Jesus healing power. In some translations the word is power and in others it is virtue. We said earlier that in Latin virtue means power. So it makes sense that the word can be translated either power or virtue. To get a feel for this we need to take a look at the verse.

> "Now a certain woman had a flow of blood for 12 years and had suffered many things from physicians. She had spent all she had and was not better, but rather grew worse. When she heard about Jesus she came behind him in the crowd and touched his garment...Immediately the fountain of blood had dried up and she felt in her body that she was healed of the affliction. And Jesus immediately knowing in himself that *virtue* had gone out of him, turned him about in the press, and said, 'Who touched my clothes?'" (KJV Mark 5:25-30 italics mine)

Here the Greek word for virtue is *dunamis*, which is power from within — power residing in the nature of a thing. So the power here comes from inside. Jesus taught the rules of life and how to live. He knew where energy resided, in virtue, and since He was of perfect virtue he knew the virtue in Him could be used by others if they acted in virtuous ways. Was the virtue of the woman here, faith in Jesus to heal her, or courage to admit she touched Him? It is both.

When we exercise and grow in virtue, we apply power from Jesus to our lives. It gives us strength, and this is what we need when we are weak. In fact, in our weakness we can become strong. Paul said,

> "And he (Jesus) said unto me my grace is sufficient unto thee: for my strength (*dunamis*) is made perfect unto weakness...Therefore I will boast all the more gladly about my weaknesses, so that Christ's power (*dunamis*) may rest on me...When I am weak then I am strong." (2 Cor. 12:9-10)

The same word for the power that flowed from Jesus at the healing of the woman in the gospel of Luke is used here as well. Christ's power is available to us when, in our weakness, we seek His power. Christ's power is made perfect or complete in our weakness. It can only be used when we are weak. When we feel strong, we don't look for help. We then miss out on Jesus' power. Only when we are weak do we look for help and the power Christ can give to us as believers. It has been said "Calamity is the occasion for virtue" and this is a law of life we need to apply. Power in weakness.

We can get power in weakness but it won't be automatic. We must know where the power comes from, we must know how to access the power and we must apply the power to the task at hand. Only then can Jesus virtue rest on us. Here the concept of "rest" on us means to make a tent, or dwell. What Jesus is saying is His power will dwell on us (2 Cor 12:10) as we access it through virtue.

This is seen again in the experience of the author of Proverbs: "The name of the Lord is a strong tower; the righteous run into it and are safe" (Pro 18:10). God often doesn't take away our infirmity but rather imparts strength to us to endure it and we then grow stronger because of it. We want God to remove our pain or take away any obstacle that is in our way, but God has better plans for us using suffering or pain to grow us and make us stronger through it. By removing it we wouldn't grow stronger. We have to look at how the Lord will mature us in these tests. *His plan is to make us better, not make life easier.*

God is the author of life and therefore knows the laws of it. When we apply those laws to our life, we can conquer all things. We then don't ask for an easier life but more strength to make it through life. No matter what this world gives us we have the strength and power to overcome it, our strength is in the LORD (Eph 6:10). God then is present in virtue and absent in vice. Physical power is found in the foods we eat, and spiritual power is found in Christ by way of virtue.

Covenant — Taking God at His Word

Covenant in the Bible is a word with much depth and meaning to it. A covenant is a contract, an agreement, or a disposition. It is between two parties binding them mutually to an undertaking on each other's behalf. A covenant can't be broken except under the strictest and most dire of consequences. Both parties commit themselves to the obligations of the covenant by faith.

God is a covenant God. He wants to enter into covenant with His beloved people. He offers blessings for keeping of the compact and curses for breaking it (Deut. 28). This contract is based on God's character and is only established when His children ratify it. Most covenants in the Bible were signed in blood, because blood is life.

God's covenants in the Bible are unfailing and are therefore to be believed and embraced by His people. Today we need to better understand covenant. Contracts today are broken all the time. Participants would often rather suffer the consequences, or hope they can go to court and get off the hook. Contracts based on our word are no longer binding. With a good attorney, many written ones are no longer binding either.

This is far from what God wants. Jesus said:

> "…And do not swear by your head, for you can't make one hair on your head white or black. Simply let your 'Yes' be 'Yes" and your 'No be 'No'; anything else beyond this comes from the evil one." (Matt 5:33-37)

Jesus commands us when we commit to something, we commit! No further discussion is needed. When you understand this, you then understand His covenant with us signed in His own blood (Matt 26:26-28).

The word covenant in the Old Testament has its roots in the Hebrew word meaning "to cut." This explains the strange custom of two people passing between the cut pieces of slain animals after making an agreement with each other (Jer. 34:18). The two parties were thus saying if either of us should break this covenant, let what happened to these animals be done to us. They were saying if I break my end of the covenant I agree to death. This again shows the importance of blood in covenants in the Bible, it signifies life and death.

A covenant is only as good as the two parties agreeing to it. Both sides must keep their end. Some of God's numerous covenants are: covenant with Noah, covenant with Abraham, covenant with Israel, covenant with David, and most importantly the New Covenant in Jesus Christ.

Kay Arthur in her book *"Our Covenant God"* says this about God's covenants:

> "Covenant was a pledge to death. A pledge born of love. A pledge cut in blood. This is the root of covenant. Covenant does not allow for abandonment — at least not without horrible consequences."[94]

When we come to understand how God made these terms, we see what a just and righteous God He is. He makes promises to us and if we keep our end He will always keep His; He can't lie. The covenant formed in Jesus' death is ratified by faith, it is lived out by obedience and a holy life. Thus virtue becomes a requirement for us by God as a means He uses to solidify and testify to our terms of keeping the covenant. This covenant started in the Old Testament with the prophet Jeremiah. He told Jeremiah,

> "This is the covenant I will make with the house of Israel after that time," declares the LORD. "I will put my law in their minds and write it on their hearts. I will be their god and they will be my people…" (Jer. 31:33)

Jesus died and rose, and afterwards He promised His Holy Spirit would be given to those who entered into covenant with Him (John 14:16-18, John 16:7-11, John 20:21-23). His Spirit enables us and empowers us to live righteously. We were created to live in good works (Eph 2:10). When we build and grow virtue, we honor our part of the covenant. God for His part gives us life, truth and power to rise above this world.

Kay Arthur adds this,

> "The result of a covenant commitment is the establishment of a relationship in connection with, or between people …A covenant commits people to one another

...To make a covenant is to make a walk into death...The sovereign Lord of heaven and earth dictates the terms of his covenant ...Either you come to God on his terms or you don't come. It is that simple ...and it doesn't matter what man thinks."[95]

God is a covenant God. It is this covenant where God promises to never leave you or forsake you (Deut 31:6-8). It is this covenant that God promises to be with you always (Matt 28:20). It is this covenant that God tells us He is our rock and our strength (Matt 7:24-27). When we know God and that His covenant is based on His character, we then know how sure His covenants are.

God's covenants are made on the terms of love. The Hebrews had a word that incorporated God's love for His people and His kindness towards them as well. It is the Hebrew word *hesed*. This word is used over 240 times in the Old Testament. It means mercy, grace, steadfast love, goodness. The main ingredients of the word must have these three components: strength, steadfastness and love. Any understanding of the word without these three elements loses part of the meaning. The covenants of the Lord are made out of *hesed*.

When we come to understand covenant, we will grow in trust of God and love for Him as well. God loves us unconditionally and unfailingly, therefore entering into covenant with Him is the greatest opportunity we will ever have. We must also understand it is a lifetime commitment and unbreakable. We commit to righteousness and virtue no matter what happens to us in our life. Then God for His part will strengthen us in it and make us better because of it. God is love and to enter into covenant with Him by a virtuous life is to reciprocate this love (1 John 4:16).

<u>The Moral Law</u>

Morality is human ethics; morals are the guidelines for proper conduct in society. Morality seeks the welfare of the individual as well as society as a whole. When we allow all behavior, we have chaos and history will show that such permissive societies soon destroy themselves. They become cancerous and are destroyed from the inside out.

Morality serves as an ethical philosophy, and its function is to show how human life must be lived out to realize its ultimate purpose, which is for the ultimate good of humanity as a whole. It seeks to advance such causes as justice, goodness and honesty. Ethics therefore will be a reflection and a judgment on actions or conduct as to their rightness or wrongness as measured by a standard. It becomes the guidelines to acting in a right and proper manner to avoid the pitfalls of uncontrolled behavior.

Our right and good moral behavior then assumes man has a duty to society and is responsible for his actions. This behavior is the ideal to which man aspires, what he "ought" to become. The word "ought" is the obligation he owes to society with its best interest at heart.

For Christians, God and His laws have revealed the supreme good of man, and His commands will dictate our actions. God has predetermined our ultimate good for us (Jer. 29:11). Hence moral life can only be understood in reference to the Moral Law Giver, God. These then form our ethics and determine right from wrong for society. God not only gives us the moral law but gives us the power to implement it as well.

Ethics are directed at the heart, not at outward action. Actions alone often become cold and systematic. It is directed at the mind, emotions and the will. This then helps mankind not only know how to act, but to understand why and how to do it as well.

In the Old Testament, God was for the Jews the Supreme source and author of the moral law. God's commandments were the criterion and measurement of man's obedience. Today God's Law has for the most part been taken out of society and **man** is left to decide right from wrong. This has left much disagreement in society about moral choices. When we obey God's moral law, these decisions are made very clear.

When life is lived and dictated by God's Law and standards, several things happen:

- Right and wrong become clear.
- We enter into God's covenant with Him when we obey His commands.
- He gives us power to help us through the process.
- Eradication of sin begins.
- This then becomes our ethics or moral law.

Once we have defined our moral law, anything that helps us to grow in these behaviors becomes a benefit to the individual and society. Anything that prevents them becomes sin and is offensive to the individual and society. .

Susanna Wesley had this brilliant definition of sin that she gave to her sons:

> "Whatever weakens your reason, impairs the tenderness of your conscience, obscures your sense of God, or takes off your relish of spiritual things; in short, whatever increases the strength and authority of your body over your mind, that thing is sin to you, however innocent it may be in itself."[96]

These virtues, as we have said, become a source of fuel and ultimately power in life to live in obedience to the moral law as given by God. The control of our passions and the denial of physical pleasure become the barriers to living out this moral code. Our duties in this life are to God, fellow man and ourselves. Ethics lead us to act in the ways God has foreordained for us. Ethics become counselors for us and guides for our actions in this life. Obedience then steadily helps us endorse this in covenant with God.

There are many lists of virtues. Here are some of the basic Christian virtues: wisdom, temperance, justice, courage, patience, meekness, faith, hope, self-control, determination and love. I would now like to take a closer look at some of these and how they work in us.

The Core Virtues:

The Means to Achieve Maximum Impact

> *I still believe that all spiritual life consists of practicing God's presence and that anyone who practices it correctly will soon attain spiritual fulfillment. To accomplish this it is necessary for the heart to be emptied of everything that would offend God. He wants to possess our hearts completely. Before any work can be done in our souls, God must be totally in control.* [97]
>
> Brother Lawrence, The Practice of the Presence of God

To have maximum impact, to achieve your full potential in life is our ultimate goal. We must train for this all of our lives. We often look at top athletes as examples of individuals who achieved maximum impact in their sport. There are better examples of this outside the world of sports, individuals whose very lives are models of how to be at your very best when life seems to be at its very worst.

The best place to look for this is in the lives of those who have been martyred for their beliefs, specifically Christ-centered ones. These men and women died because of the ideas they espoused. They were persecuted for these beliefs they held, but they refused to give in to intimidation and threats. They faced torture and death in their fight of faith, willing to stand for their beliefs and the Word of God regardless of the price ... The courage and dedication of these men have inspired us to live for Christ today.[98]

Models of these strengths are seen in the life and deaths of the apostles of Jesus Christ. These men did much more than simply live for Jesus, they died horrific deaths for Him. In their deaths they proved their convictions about who He was. All except John are believed to have been killed for their faith in Jesus Christ. Here are the accounts of their deaths[99]:

- "James the holy apostle of Christ…was beheaded in A.D. 36"
- "Thomas…suffered in Calamina a city of India, being slain with a dart."
- "Simon who was brother to Jude and to James the younger…was crucified in a city of Egypt."
- "Mark the evangelist and first bishop of Alexandria…was burnt and afterwards buried."
- "Bartholomew…was beaten, then crucified; and after, being excoriated he was beheaded."
- "Andrew the apostle and brother to Peter…was crucified."
- "Matthew, otherwise named Levi… an apostle…was run through with a spear."
- "James the brother of the Lord…and they took him to smite him with stones…and a priest said, 'Leave off what do ye? The just man prayeth for you.' …and one of those who were present took an instrument and smote the just man on his head…they buried him in the same place."

The boldness and courage with which these men lived and died is inspirational to us. A man who is passionate, knows his purpose in life, is guided by truth, strengthened by obedience and fueled by virtue can rise above the worst man, nature or the devil can throw at him.

The words of a dying man are most revealing of who and what he lived for. These are the dying words of Andrew on his way to the cross to be crucified,

> "He (I) would not have preached the honor and glory of the cross, if he (I) had feared the death of the cross…O cross, most welcome and long looked for! With a willing mind, joyfully and desirously, I come to thee, being the scholar of Him which did hang on thee; because I

have always been thy lover, and have coveted to embrace thee."[100]

What qualities enabled men like this to live so powerfully when such frightful threats were made to them and carried out? From where did they get the power to overcome such tremendous circumstances? Why would they choose death in the most horrible means when many could have been set free by just renouncing their beliefs? The answer is found in this reply from Brother Lawrence:

> "My preference is to retire with Him to the deepest part of my soul as often as possible. When I am with Him there, nothing frightens me, but the slightest diversion away from Him is painful to me."[101]

The spiritual strength they had came from a source outside them, Jesus Christ, and was activated by their faith. They were able to physically endure whatever the world threw at them because spiritually it didn't touch them. They were grounded in an inner strength not manufactured but real, because of the relationship they had to the Living God. This is clearly seen in Hebrews 11.

> "Now faith is being sure of what we hope for and certain of what we do not see …and without faith it is impossible to please God, for who can come to Him wondering whether he exists and whether he rewards those who earnestly seek him …For time will fail me if I tell about Gideon, Barak, Samson, Jephthah, of David and Samuel and the prophets who by faith conquered kingdoms, performed acts of righteousness, obtained promises, shut the mouths of lions, quenched the power of fire, escaped the edge of the sword …Others experienced mockings, scourgings, yes, also chains and imprisonment …They were stoned, they were sawn in two …they were put to death with the sword …Men of whom the world was not worthy …Having gained approval through their faith… (Heb 11:1,6, 32-40)

The power of some men comes from their faith. The power of other men comes from their love. The power of still others comes from their patience. It is the power in the unseen world of God. This power is established in us when the Living God indwells His people by His virtues. To grow in these qualities is to grow in Christ-likeness and the strength that these saints of God exhibited.

I want to now look at these specific qualities, virtues, and how we are called to live them out — how they enable us to be strong in present trials as well as future ones.

__The Virtue of Faith__

Faith is a part of our everyday life. Most everything we do demands faith. For instance we exhibit faith when we:

- Get into our car. We have faith the brakes will stop us and the steering wheel will turn the car the way we want.
- Eat out in a restraint. We have faith in the food we eat that it hasn't been "ill prepared" and that it is OK to eat.
- In our bank. We have faith in the bank that the checks we deposit are worth the given dollar amounts tendered on them, and the bank will keep them safe for us.
- In our medical care providers. We have faith in our doctors that they are treating us with the best possible medicines and proper information that will help us and not harm us.

There are many more examples of faith we exhibit every day, but suffice it to say, making it through each day requires faith. This is also what God demands of us as we live for Him in this world. However, this is often where we fail. We simply lack the faith needed to accomplish the tasks before us.

Faith is, "Being sure of what we hope for and certain of what we can not see" (Heb 11:1). In this definition it assumes there is no physical sight. Where there is physical sight, then faith ceases. In the Christian life, "We walk by faith and not by sight" (2 Cor 5:7). Faith is our second set of spiritual eyes. It is clear from these two verses that God demands faith from us. We are saved by faith (Eph 2:8-9). It is evident then that faith requires three key things:

1. Faith becomes trusting in God and taking Him at His word. To do anything else would be to doubt who He is and His attributes. Doubt often will then lead to unbelief.
2. Faith is evidenced by our deeds or our actions. Faith is not just speaking about something, it is confirmed by our behavior.
3. Faith is a commitment to God's will or plan for our life. We enter into a covenant with Him and trust in Him and that He knows what is best for us.

Faith then binds us to God.

There are two types of trust described in the Bible. In the Old Testament it is faithfulness, fidelity or trustworthiness. This is total trust in God grounded in His character. He is worthy of our trust. It acts to treat the future promises He has given to those who love Him and obey His commands as if they were present. This is passive.

The other type of trust is faith, and this is found in the New Testament. It is the faith of belief and conviction. This is active and is hope in the unseen God and His love for us. It is built on the hope that no matter how bad the situation, God is in control of it. He is using it to grow us in godliness. He has our best interest at heart and will always be with us.

Let's take a closer look at these two.

1. *Faithfulness* –

God demands us to trust in Him, not only is He worthy of our trust but is faithful to His children and cannot lie (Heb 6:18). This becomes our response to Him. This type of faith becomes a resting place, a hoping in God, a cleaving to Him, a waiting for Him and making Him our shield and tower of refuge. This is where God's servants have an unwavering trust in their God to save them from their foes and to fulfill the promise to bless them.

The Old Testament is full of stories of faithfulness. God's prophet, king or servant is faced with an almost insurmountable task or obstacle, and their faithfulness in God empowers them over the impossible. They are blessed for their trust in Him and because of this they overcome great odds. Here are just a few men and women and how their faith conquered the impossible.

- **David and Goliath** is a classic story found in 1 Samuel 17. Little shepherd boy, David, goes up against a 9-foot-tall giant. He is laughed at but his trust in God is his strength. David says to Goliath, "You come against me with the sword and spear and javelin but I come against you in the name of the LORD God Almighty, the God of the armies of Israel whom you have defied. This day the LORD will hand you over to me and I'll strike you down …it is not by the sword or spear that the LORD saves; for the battle is the LORD'S… (1 Sam 17: 45-47). We all know how the story ended.
- **Daniel and the lions' den** is another classic story of faith in God (Daniel 6). Daniel was a faithful servant of God and he was called to worship and bow down to king Darius. Daniel refused knowing this would go against the commandments of God not to worship any god or person but Him. He was cast into the lions' den. The next day the lions had not harmed Daniel and he said this to the king, "My God sent his angel and he shut the mouths of the lions. They have not hurt me because I was found innocent in his sight" (Daniel 6: 22).
- **Shadrach, Meshach, and Abednego** are three other men whose faith was unwavering (Daniel 3). They too were called to worship an idol. This idol was 90 feet tall, shaped in the image of King Nebuchadnezzar. They, like Daniel, refused to bow down to an idol and trusted in God more than they feared death. They were brought before the king and asked if they refused to bow to the statue. They said yes and that they could not worship any false god. By this refusal they were to be thrown in to the fiery furnace and killed. Their testimony was this, "We do not need to defend ourselves before you in this matter. If we are thrown into the blazing furnace the God we serve is able to save us from it, and He will rescue us from your hand O king. But even if He does not, we want you to know, O king, that we will not serve your gods or worship the image of the gold you have set up" (Dan 3: 16-18). They were thrown in to the furnace and the flames never touched them. They were saved by their faith.

- Other accounts are of Moses before the Pharaoh and at the Red Sea (Exodus 14), Elijah confronting the prophets of Baal (1 King 18), Gideon (Judges 6-7), Noah and the flood (Gen 6:14-8:22) and many, many more (see Hebrews 11:8-40).

It is this faithfulness of God to His children that these servants of God counted on and relied upon to be their strength. God allows these tests to see if His children will trust in Him. The same loyalty we demand in human relationships of business colleagues or military soldiers is no less than what God demands in us.

This concept of faithfulness ties back to the concept we have already discussed, God's loving-kindness, His *hesed*. This *hesed* is likened to a marriage often in the Bible and faithfulness to your spouse. This covenant between God and man or a man and his wife is grown out of the *hesed* of mutual trust. Faithfulness becomes the only appropriate response back to God for His faith and love for us as His children. This faithfulness then strengthens us in the power of God working through the hearts of his people. We are able to do the impossible, the unimaginable and the unthinkable because God is with us.

God pledges a lasting relationship to us and invites us to enter into it with Him. When we do, we commit our lives to this covenant in faithfulness.

2. *Faith* –

We are called to have unqualified acceptance and dependence on God and in Jesus Christ. Faith signifies conviction. We must live by the truth we receive. Faith is living on the facts that we know to be true and trusting the outcome to God.

There is an intellectual assent to truth involved in faith (James 2:14-16, Gal 5:6). This requires the right belief about God. This rests on the fact of what God has revealed about Himself, grounded in His character and His purposes for mankind. In the New Testament faith is believing that Jesus Christ is the Messiah and the incarnate son of God. Denial of this is idolatry and puts you outside the salvation of Jesus' atoning death on the cross. Orthodoxy is crucial for salvation.

The "God-inspired" witnesses of the apostles of Christ are formed in faith. To believe is to certify God is true and to reject it is to make God out to be a liar. Christian faith rests on the recognition of apostolic and biblical testimony as God's own testimony to His Son. We believe what was spoken about Jesus and who He is. Therefore what He said about salvation through Him and Him alone becomes the cornerstone of our belief.

Faith and hope go together. The same object of our hope becomes the object of our faith, too. Faith becomes a living hope that is so real it gives absolute assurance. This is evidenced as we saw in faithfulness by the Old Testament saints. They took the promises of God and believed them and based their lives on them. All of the promises were related to the future. They claimed the promises in faith and acted upon them in the present. So faith is a present essence of a future reality.

Faith is the only way to please God, "And without faith it is impossible to please God, because anyone who comes to him must believe that he exists and that he rewards those who earnestly seek him" (Heb 11:6). This trust is not natural and only by God's grace does He give us the ability to have faith. It comes from God.

Faith implies a response. It is this hope which looks forward with conviction that what it believes in will come to pass. The Christian hope is such that it possesses a man and makes him do all he does. Moffat said there are three directions where hope operates:

- <u>Belief in God against the world</u> – this is staking all on God instead of the rewards of this world.
- <u>Belief in the spirit against the senses</u> – this says there is something beyond what we can just see, taste, hear and feel.
- <u>Belief in the future against the present</u> – no man can exile the truth, and on the hope of eternity, the truth of Christ, do we place our trust.[102]

To have hope is to grow faith. Let's take a closer look at how hope grows faith:

- When you have hope, you have safety and security.
- Hope is the expectation of future good. This hope then becomes a refuge or shelter in times of trial. It produces a confident expectancy of future actions or situations.

- Hope involves two things: that which is hoped for, and the actual act of hoping for it.
- Hope comes from and is grounded in God (Ps. 39:7). I must not hope only in what I can do but in God who can do all things and is infinitely more powerful than I.
- Hope by definition is the desire and search for a future good. We don't hope for what we already have.
- Hope empowers us in our times of trial, sustains us and compels us to go on. This hope then produces the ability to endure any trial that may come our way.
- The stronger the desire to have what we hope for, and the greater the belief in attaining it, the more powerful our hope becomes. As our hope becomes more and more powerful, we gain strength to sustain and overcome the most difficult of trials, people or situations.
- To be hopeless under trial means almost certain failure. To have hope is to triumph, no matter how great the test.
- The fullness of hope expresses the completeness of its activity in the soul. It is the anchor of the soul, and gives it staying power amidst the storms. It also purifies us.
- Faith strengthens us, and hope sustains us in the world of the seen. Faith grows our views of the unseen, and hope grows our desire of the unseen.
- Inherent in hope is waiting. Waiting for the thing we hope for and not demanding it right away. This implies patience.

In summary, faith and faithfulness empower us to hope in the unseen and that there is more to being at our best than just our physical existence. Faith takes a truth and takes ownership of it by living it out in our life. We know whom we trust in, God. The apostle Paul spoke about faith often:

> "That is why I am suffering yet as I am. Yet I am not ashamed because I know in whom I have believed and am convinced that he is able to guard what I have entrusted to him for that day." (2 Tim 1:12)

To live out your faith demands courage. Courage is our next empowering virtue. Let us now unpack courage and find some of its treasures.

The Virtue of Courage

Courage is the quality of mind or spirit that enables us to face tests or trials with firmness for good. Courage allows us to overcome the feeling of fear despite the outcome. Bill Bennett said in *The Book of Virtues*, "The brave person is not the one who is never afraid … courage is a settled disposition to feel appropriate degrees of fear and confidence in challenging situations …It is also a settled disposition to stand one's ground."[103]

So the question is, how do we become brave or courageous?

- First, it is in knowing what you believe by gaining knowledge and having wisdom to apply it.
- Second, by taking this knowledge and taking ownership of it, we must then apply it in all of our life. This requires making it more than a belief but making it a passion, in the case of courage the passion to do right. A passion that burns deep within you.
- Third, by the continual practice of courage we become brave. In other words, acting brave becomes a habit. Aristotle said,
    "We become brave by doing brave acts…by being habituated to despise things that are terrible and to stand our ground against them we become brave, and it is when we have become so that we shall be most able to stand our ground against them."[104]

If we can better understand the enemy of courage, which is fear, it will help us to better value and cultivate courage. Thus the key to developing courage is to understand its greatest enemy. Fear paralyzes us and often prevents action.

Fear comes from worry. Jesus tells us to not worry (Matt 6: 25-34). It is an action to stop what is already being done, worrying, and not start it again. It is a command.

Worry is usually extremely small compared to the size it forms in our minds and how much damage it does to our life. Yet worry unchecked grows into fear and fear then often prevents us from acting or doing the good we are commanded to do.

Worry is a thin stream of fear that trickles through the mind. If encouraged it will channel out so wide that all our other thoughts will be drained and only fear will be left inside us. Worry divides your thoughts and prevents you from being focused and single-minded. It is a major distraction. Once your mind is divided, it is incapable of giving all needed resources to the cause at hand. It weakens you and makes your determination and resolve weaker.

Tim Gray and Curtis Martin say this about fear and the power it has over you to control you:

> "Fear makes our will hesitant to follow reason because of the perceived difficulty. Consequently, we allow fear to determine our actions, rather than acting according to what is right according to God's will and law. Courage empowers us to have the firmness of mind and will to overcome our fear and do what is right and good, regardless of any difficulty. Thus Thomas Aquinas says, 'Fortitude of soul must be that which binds the will firmly to the good of reason in the face of the greatest evils' …fear creates cowards, men who give up the truth or some good for fear of suffering. It hinders us from being men of action …Courage empowers us to take on what is hard and persevere through the difficulties."[105]

Worry takes the joy from life. Worry often focuses on things we can't control or things that are unknown. Since we can't control them or can't know them, it is silly to focus on them or worry about them. Worry about the weather, worry about what other people will think of you or worry about the stock market are all useless. You can't control these things, and worry won't change them one bit. Focus on what you *do* know. Focus on what you *can* control. Now when this is our thrust, we have our center of attention on where we can have the most impact.

Worry provides us with no benefits, but leads to many problems. It just adds to the burdens we carry. These burdens weigh us down as we go through life. Remember, the biggest worries we face are the ones that usually never come to pass. Also keep in mind that worry is blind and refuses to learn from the past. Rid yourself of worry and put up a roadblock to fear.

We fear many things, one of the greatest is our fear of others and what they may think of us. The fear of others and the dread of their opinions are what make most of us cowards. We fear what they will say or think of us. It encourages us not to act as we should, but to act in whatever way will meet with their approval. What is at the root of most of this fear is our desire — sometimes natural, but often irrational — for the praise of man. This becomes most valuable in our minds.

Fear in the right place protects us; in the wrong place it opens us to disaster. We *should* fear driving 65 mph on an icy road. We *should* fear loaded guns. We *should* fear the effects of drugs, nicotine and alcohol. These fears are healthy and protective. The problem is, most fears are not based on proper apprehensions, but imagined ones. Such as: what will coworkers think of me if I do this or say that. This type of fear should seldom, if ever, be a factor in our actions. Rather, the question should be: "What would God have me do?" What is the righteous thing to do here? This will give direction on how to act.

When lightly held beliefs are in a man, he will often fear others' disapproval more than anything else. This often will prevent action. A man with deep convictions will most often act because courage is grounded in convictions.

To help overcome fear you must seek righteousness and goodness. Most people are apathetic about goodness. To be courageous we must be passionate and driven by it. Consider the following ways to help grow courage:

- Fall in love with goodness, and bad things lose their power over us.
- The more we do righteous deeds, the more we *want* to do them.
- Most people desire goodness in their heart, but when the moment of decision comes they are not prepared to make the effort or sacrifice which goodness demands. Prepare in advance to act righteously no matter the cost.
- Without righteousness in our lives, we have no meaning and without meaning we have no hope for courage. We must draw lines in the sand where we won't give in on our core beliefs, and then live them out.
- When passion meets righteousness, we get courage. Grow your passion for righteousness and you will grow your courage.

Courage is one of the foundations of the Christian life. It is talked about over and over again in the Bible. The phrase "be strong and courageous" is mentioned 22 items in the Old Testament. Most often it is God telling His people to act in spite of the danger or the odds. He often tells them to not be afraid. Don't be afraid because, "I will be with you." *God never commands us to do what He doesn't empower us to do.* Obedience becomes the highest degree of practical courage. We must trust God and act in spite of danger, terrible odds, or fear. We need to be willing to die for truth and right causes.

Courage is almost a contradiction in terms. It means a strong desire to live, yet at the same time being prepared to die. This paradox is the whole principle of courage. This is reflected in the life of soldiers engaged in battle. They must seek to live while not being scared of death at the same time. G.K. Chesterton talks about the soldier's courage in this way,

> "They can only get away from death by stepping within an inch of it. A soldier to escape death, when trapped behind enemy lines, must combine a strong desire to live and carelessness about dying. To cling to life is to be a coward, to wait for death is suicide. He must seek life with furious indifference; he must desire life like water and yet drink death like wine."[106]

This is the courage we must all seek to acquire in the cause for goodness and truth.

Courage is a day in and day out duty, not a one-time event. As we do more brave acts we will become a brave person. To grow in courage is to grow in freedom and to be released from fear. We must also be patient with ourselves in the process.

The Virtue of Patience

Patience is the endurance or constancy to accept trials with a calm and unruffled temper. Basically, it gives us staying power to hang in there and not give up. It helps us see we don't have to have success immediately. We are willing to wait for the thing hoped for and not demand it right away.

Motivational speaker Andy Andrews talks about life lessons learned from great people in history in his best selling book *The Travelers Gift*. In one chapter he talks about how people give up too quickly and because of this forego many great achievements. He talks about all the great things that could have been invented but weren't because of a lack of patience. He has this to say about giving up too soon,

> "Circumstances are rulers of the weak …but they are weapons of the wise …Are your emotions controlled by circumstances…Circumstances do not push or pull. They are daily lessons to be studied and gleaned for new knowledge and wisdom."[107]

The point is people quit because the situation discourages them or they don't feel like putting in the extra effort. They lack resolve to keep fighting. Once you give up, you are finished and will never succeed. To keep fighting no matter what others say or how tough the situation is requires patience. This is true in all aspects of life, from dealing with a child to solving a math problem. To grow in patience is to grow in your ability to keep at it and ultimately your ability to conquer.

Andrews also adds this:

> "I choose to persist without exception …I compare myself to my potential …I will claim a faith in the certainty of my future. Too much of my life has been spent doubting my beliefs and believing my doubts …For me, faith will always be a sounder guide than reason because reason can only go so far — faith has no limits."[108]

Patient people are not swayed by the ups and downs of daily life. Impatient people are impulsive and irritable. They act on emotion spontaneously. Patience has to do with long suffering. It is a calm willingness to accept situations that are irritating or painful. Patience suggests the following characteristics:

- That we become stronger in trial and grow *because* of trials.
- We don't expect everything to always be great or go our way.
- We learn in difficulties and can gain critical knowledge from them.

- Your ability to endure tough times produces perseverance.
- To become patient is to mature.

When we act on impulses or emotions we do things randomly, and this often produces harmful or wrongful actions. We have already talked about the problem of acting on our emotions in Chapter 7. Patience is controlling these emotions. Patience is slowness to anger. Patience is acting in deliberate and self-controlled ways. When we don't act on emotions, we exhibit patience and act consistently. When emotions rule, inconsistency reigns.

We must consider the great advantages patience can give to us in life. Think of the ability to be calm and peaceful in a traffic jam because you are patient. Imagine working on a project for a long time and being no closer to the solution but enjoying the process because of patience. The disadvantages of impatience are irritability, anger, frustration and discouragement.

Going through life being patient not only is more empowering, but it is more enjoyable as well. Patient people are happier people. The more patience you develop, the more it will bring you closer to your potential and help you make the best choices.

Irritability makes us more sensitive to our emotions, and patience makes us less sensitive to them. Irritability produces impulsiveness, and spontaneous behavior often leads to sin. Through patience we destroy our impulsiveness and many of the sins it produces. We replace evil with good and act in a controlled and thought-filled way.

Patience is determined in the mind as much as in the heart. It is deciding ahead of time you won't give in to emotions. Deciding in advance that you will respond with fortitude and tolerance. To be patient is to be persistent and this produces a steadfastness and constancy in us.

When we develop patience in our life we have resilience, and from this we become conquerors. The conquering power of patience turns trials into glory. No matter what people or situations throw at you, patience overcomes all.

Patience and long suffering are a very powerful team. Patience often deals with people while long suffering has to do with situations. Long suffering is fortitude that no situation can beat, while patience is staying power that people can't beat. No circumstance can defeat your strength and no human can defeat your love. Patience and long suffering combine to form endurance that never gives up and results in an indestructible character that maintains control, whatever life throws at us.

The Virtue of Encouragement

Encouragement is to inspire with hope, courage, or confidence; to lend support to people and hearten them in their endeavors. The purpose is to stimulate a person to do specific deeds or exhibit certain behavior. To discourage is to oppose, dampen and depress. When things are not going well, a little discouragement goes a long way toward destroying us. On the other hand, encouragement empowers us. It is from encouragement that we build support to cultivate more patience.

Encouragement is very crucial during times of trial. It is during these times that you are most likely to become unsure of yourself, down and depressed. Encouragement builds you up. It is a source of energy and fuel to power us up. Coaches use encouragement during games, parents use it to motivate their kids and bosses use it to inspire their employees. A good encourager can get people to do many things and be excited about it in the process.

The goal of encouragement is to get the person to not focus on the trial or situation no matter how difficult it is. It seeks to get them to keep fighting and to never surrender or quit. Encouragement is motivation, stimulation and inspiration.

Encouragement always focuses on the positive. Discouragement always focuses on the negative. Discouraged individuals can't see the good in situations and constantly find the bad. They will search and search until they find something bad to focus on. They become a self-fulfilling prophecy of defeat. When the inevitable happens, they say, "See I told you so." They almost hope something bad happens so they can say those favorite words, "I knew it wouldn't work." Negative people lack determination and creativity.

Encouragement says the best is yet to come. It inspires us. Encouragement produces hope that becomes a shelter in times of trial. It lets you to see the opportunity in the trial. To a positive person, problems are not threats, but rather, opportunities. They see the potential in the situation and want others to see it, too.

One of the keys to being a good encourager is this little rule:

"Give four positive comments to every one criticism we tell."

Encouragers grab the energy from the good and focus on it. To be an encourager you must have a short memory. You must determine to forget the bad of the past while focusing on the potential good in the future. Discouragers, on the other hand, deplete energy and focus on the bad. They key on this bad and the harm it has done or could do. Encouragers choose to focus on the good and learn from the bad.

We can be a good encourager of others but this doesn't make us a good encourager to ourselves. Good encouragers practice what they preach. We must be an encourager to ourselves as well as others.

Once we exhibit encouragement, others will soon follow suit. This world needs more encouragers. The power of encouragement can't be overestimated.

The Virtue of Love

Love is possibly the most powerful of virtues. The best writing ever produced on love is in 1 Corinthians 13. Here the apostle Paul tells much about love. He starts off by telling why love is so important:

"Love never fails. But where there are prophecies they will cease; where there are tongues they will be stilled; where there is knowledge it will pass away." (1 Cor 13: 8)

Other things will pass away, but love endures forever. The love of another person endures forever past their death and lives on and on. The love of a parent or special person in our life can motivate us and inspire us years after they have died. We still remember those gifts of love from them. Their physical body is gone but their teaching, their example and their behavior live on inside us.

Nothing can stop love. A person who has this love that Paul is talking about will do anything for the one he loves. Love is such a powerful motivator for good. Once it resides in the heart it becomes a burning fire within that can't be overcome. It says, "I will stop at nothing for the one I love. I will do anything for the one I love." The reason is simply because of what love is, which Paul then goes on to define:

"Love is patient, love is kind. It does not envy, it does not boast, it is not proud. It is not rude, it is not self-seeking. It is not easily angered, it keeps no record of wrongs. Love does not rejoice in evil but delights in truth. It always protects, always trusts, always hopes, always perseveres." (1 Cor 13: 4-7)

When this kind of love fills the heart, you begin to get a glimpse of the love God intended for mankind. This is the love that defines God, because God is love (1 John 4:8, 16). From God and through Him we can exhibit this love to others.

This is not love for a movie or love of pizza. It is *agape* love, as it is used in the Greek, the highest form of love. This *agape* love strengthens us and lives in us through our actions more so than our words. Love is not a feeling, it is far more a responsibility, a pledge, a promise, but most importantly it is a covenant. We talked about the depth of a covenant in the last chapter. It is from this understanding of *agape* love that Paul elaborates on these characteristics in 1 Corinthians 13. He gives these fifteen attributes:

1. <u>Love is patient</u> — Patient love is slow to anger. Think of how many relationships are harmed due to harsh words spoken out of anger. Once words are said, they cut like a knife and the relationship will never be the same. Words can be a dagger that destroys.
2. <u>Love is kind</u> — Love is nice to all. It honors the old wisdom, "If you can't say anything nice, don't say anything at all." It is sweet to everyone it meets. Love says there is no reason to be unkind to anyone.
3. <u>Love is not greedy or envious</u> — Unloving people covet what others have. We often do this for no other reason than we just don't want others to have something if we can't have it. Greed has been the spark to many conflicts simply because we want more and more. Simply being content with what we have would bring much joy and peace to this earth. *It would leave us satisfied with what we have, instead of being unsatisfied because of what we don't have.*

4. *Love does not boast* — This is humility. When we come to see ourselves as unworthy, as blessed by God instead of self-made men, we begin to grasp humility. Our talent and opportunities are provided by God, not us. We are the ones who train for them, but God decides the outcome of them. This is modesty.
5. *Love is not proud* — The Bible says God opposes the proud but gives grace to the humble (James 4:6). This says we are not inflated with our own importance. We need to think less of ourselves instead of more.
6. *Love is not rude* — This is being courteous, polite and well mannered. It is the person who lives by example, not by words. If people had to describe you by your behavior what would others say about you?
7. *Love is not self-seeking* — There are two types of people in this world, those who think that the world owes them and those who believe they owe the world. Love seeks to serve, not be served. The person who loves in this way does not insist on their own rights, but rather they see the other persons needs ahead of their own. William Barclay said, "The world would be a better place if men thought less of their rights and more of their duties."[109]
8. *Love is not easily angered* — This is the person who has a long fuse. William Barclay commented on this verse, "The man who is a master of his own temper can master anything…Kipling said the real test of a man is to keep his head when everyone else was losing theirs…even if you are hated don't give into hate."[110] This is being in control of your anger. When we lose our tempers, we lose control of ourselves.
9. *Love keeps no record of wrongs* — This is a person who keeps no ledger when they are wronged, like an accountant would keep records of accounts payable. We must learn that there are things in life we need to forget.
10. *Love does not delight in evil* — The Germans have a word for taking pleasure in the misfortunes of others — *Schadenfreude*. This is the joy we sometimes feel when we hear ill of someone else. It is one of the perversities of human nature that we often would rather hear of the mis-

fortunes of others than rejoice in their good fortune.[111] Love finds no joy in bad news to others.
11. <u>Love rejoices in truth</u> — Simply put, "always seek the truth no matter how much it may hurt." Love seeks out truth because it has nothing to hide.
12. <u>Love always protects</u> — Another translation of this is that love endures all things. This is loyalty to a person and not ever giving up on them, faithful to the core. Devotion to them in good times and in bad times. This is not being a "fair-weather friend" and leaving them in their times of trouble. Rather, it is sticking by their side through thick and thin.
13. <u>Love always trusts</u> — A loving person always believes in others. This means always believing the best about other people. We often make other people what we believe them to be. By believing the best in them we make them better people.[112]
14. <u>Love always hopes</u> — Love always encourages others and says their best is yet to come. By inspiring hope in others, you help bring the best out in them.
15. <u>Love always perseveres</u> — This is not only bearing with another but in the process transforming them. Love can bear all things because it has the best intent for others. This is the persevering love of a parent towards a child as they are growing up.

These are the qualities that Jesus modeled for us and by His transforming power can help us attain as well. If we can grow in love we can conquer all obstacles that get in the way and hinder our performance. Some of these obstacles are pride, greed, laziness, discouragement, doubt, fear and so on.

It is said love conquers all and according to the Apostle Paul, love is the greatest virtue of all (1 Cor. 13:13). According to Jesus, love is the key to the two greatest commandments, "Love your neighbor as yourself" and "Love the LORD your God with all your heart, soul and mind" (Matt 22:37-39). Love is central to life and critical to its vitality. It is the foundation that all other virtues build on. To live in love is to love in living.

The Virtue of Determination

Determination is a conviction about "why we do" that hardens us to grow firm in "what we do." With determination we become passionate and don't cave in, and we also become stronger with time. To be determined is to not give up but fight on. It is to be single-minded, resolute, and unwavering. A determined person is hard to stop. As we said earlier, many people don't accomplish things in life because they quit too soon. Once you give up, you will never overcome. If we can develop determination we can grow in strength and power because we are engaged in the battle. Once we give up, the battle is always lost.

In order for determination to be developed, we need passion about what we are doing. If we have no passion in life then determination must be manufactured. The self-production of determination drains much of our vital energy needed in day-to-day activities. Passion, on the other hand, creates energy in us.

Convictions focus our vision and develop in us a single mindedness, a steadfast way of living. When we are so convicted of a truth that we will stand by our conviction no matter what the situation or consequences may bring, the result is determination.

No amount of fear or any obstacle can stop a determined person. Jesus gives an example of this involving prayer in Luke 11:5-13. He tells of a persistent man who won't take no for an answer. As a result he gets what he wanted. He tells us to ask God in prayer and to keep on asking. Jesus says.

> "Ask and it will be given to you; seek and you will find; knock and the door will be opened to you" (Luke 11:9).

The verb for ask, seek, and knock is the verb meaning to keep on without stopping. Therefore we should knock and keep on knocking, ask and keep on asking, seek and keep on seeking. That is the persistence found in the friend in the previous verses Jesus spoke of (Luke 11:5-6). Jesus is encouraging us to not give up and to be persistent, be it in prayer or simply in righteous living.

This is similar to a child who keeps on asking for a cookie and won't stop. The persistence of the child is often why we give in. It must be noted that this is not a blank check to ask God for anything and He will give it to us. It is a teaching on constancy and persistence. It assumes the person strongly desires the object requested, and the object is in God's will.

As an example of determination, I would give the determination of a drowning man for air or a starving man for food. They will go to great lengths to get these life necessities. This determination in a godly man or woman is even more powerful because the Living God is in them.

In a nutshell, determination in a person gives them the power to keep going and to not give up. Developing this virtue gives us an unstoppable spirit. Determination will drive us to our fullest potential, and encourage those around us to achieve the same.

The Impact of Virtue

Virtue is as essential to a Christ follower as a gun is to a soldier. It is the advancement of Christ-likeness in our life. It breaks down the walls that sin builds up. It restores the vitality in us for life and the resources of life. The great men and women of the Bible were virtuous people, and God used them in mighty ways. They impacted the world, and we continue to study their lives today.

The absence of virtue is sin, the presence of it is holiness. Virtue has its essence in God and His Kingdom. Therefore anything outside of His will is a "missing of the mark" that He has set for us. Sin is to disobey God. Thus virtue becomes the power of a life well- lived, a life whose sole purpose for existence is to love and serve God for His Kingdom and Glory. *To love virtue is to love God and to respond in virtue is to obey God.*

To develop virtue is to grow in godliness and live as He commanded us. It is to help us make best choices and gives us power to overcome. If we can build our life around acquiring these core virtues in greater amounts, we will be much more effective in life and have a far greater impact on those around us.

I'll unpack a few more core virtues in the next chapter.

The Virtuous Life:
The Power to Live Right

"...virtue is the art of living rightly."
"No one can doubt that virtue makes the soul good."

St. Augustine

Once virtue is rightly understood and applied in every aspect of your life, it becomes more than just fuel and power for the spirit, it becomes the highest form of living a human being can achieve. You will have maximum impact on a maximum number of people. Most importantly, you will have dedicated your life to the perfection of ultimate goodness in your spirit; this is called godliness in the Bible.

Thomas Aquinas was a medieval scholar who devoted a lot of thought to the subject of virtue. He wrote extensively on it.

> "Human virtue is a habit for the purposes of acting well. Now in man there are two principles of human actions: the intellect or reasoning and the appetite: for these are the two principles of movement in man."[113]

Aquinas believed man acted because his actions were either drawn by reasoning or his appetites. Intellectual virtues help us to think correctly and perfect the ability to reason. Moral virtues perfect the appetites within us. These appetites then function to make the other powers in our body act.[114]

Man has many appetites or drives. He has the sexual drive, the hunger drive, the drive to be loved and so on. We have noted throughout this book that these drives most often control a man's behaviors. His inability to say no to these appetites is what leads him to wrong actions, called sin. Sin destroys virtue because contrary acts, or vices, annihilate and corrupt virtue. The proactive process in believers, whereby the Holy Spirit enables them to overcome these appetites is grounded in virtue. The perfection of goodness must be cultivated daily in a person. If not, these appetites will gain more and more control over you and form habits of vice.

Man's inability to control his own drives makes him a slave to them. This total depravity in man means he lacks the ability to be good on his own. Only God by grace can change this. He gives us new life through new birth in Him. The gospel of John talks about this new life from God:

> "Yet to all who received him, to those who believed in his name, he gave the right to become children of God — children born not of natural descent, nor of human decision or a husband's will, but born of God." (John 1:12-13)

Here the implication is clear that to be born of God is to have new life, a new existence. This new life of God in us gives us the ability to seek goodness and desire after it. This is because we are children of God, and children become like their parents. His Holy Spirit thus indwells Christians and enables them to live daily unto His Kingdom. We are alive to God. Our Christian response is holiness to Him through the means of virtue and repressing these drives of vice in us.

Only by establishing and cultivating these drives of virtue from the Holy Spirit can man live the good life of moral virtue demanded by God. Out of control appetites make man like an animal, in fact, lower than animals. Aquinas noted this:

> "Man is the most noble of animals if he be perfect in virtue, so he is the lowest of all if he be severed from law and justice. For man can use reason to satisfy lusts and evil passions which other animals can not do."[115]

Virtue then empowers us to quell our appetites and frees us to act in goodness. It is the perfection of power where the product of this power is a righteous act as defined by Jesus Christ. Christian virtue is knowledge of this ultimate goodness, and the power from God to carry it out. God's glory and His will become our core desires, not self-gratification. This new nature then gives us the ability and character to stimulate consistently righteous actions.

When we consistently act in virtue, we serve God's Kingdom here on earth in our daily lives. When we act again and again in the same way, we are said to have formed a habit. Good habits form a power base in us to stimulate action.

<u>The Power of a Habit</u>

Aquinas taught that the body moves for one of two reasons: reflex or premeditation. In reflexive action, the body moves automatically, by instinct, but in premeditated action, the soul moves the body.

Put your hand on a hot stove, and you jerk it away immediately. It's the body's natural reaction to recoil from pain. No need for conscious thought, no need to build a habit. The action is involuntary; there's only one thing to do, and we just do it.

On the other hand, voluntary actions aren't so cut-and-dried. Now we can choose our actions, and when there are numerous possibilities, some for good and some for bad, habits are needed to help direct the proper response.[116]

Over time, our choice of actions tend to build on themselves. If, when faced with a particular situation, we choose to act in a certain way — be it for good or for bad — then when similar situations come up in the future, we're likely to recall our earlier actions and respond in the same way again. As we repeat this cycle, we think less and less about *why* we're reacting the way we do, and pretty soon … we don't think at all, we act out of habit. We have formed dispositions in the soul to repeat the act.

Think in terms of how an athlete trains. He performs a specific skill over and over so he can repeat the same action in a game situation, when everything is on the line. He trains by repeating the same action over and over again and the result is a more consistent ability to perform the action. His desire is to make a habit out of his practice techniques.

This also applies to thinking. A student studying for a test will review the same information over and over for two reasons: to help him understand it, and to help him recall it later when he needs it. The more he understands it, the better he can use it. The more he uses it, the greater is the learning.

Good habits form powerful, positive actions. Bad habits form powerful, negative actions.

Aquinas noted several distinct qualities of habits and virtues:

- We must note it isn't the form alone that gives the person the power but rather participation by the person in the form that gives him power to increase action and form it into a habit.
- We must also note the intensity of the act must be in proportion to the intensity of the habit, or surpass it, to increase a good habit or decrease a bad habit.
- One habit is not made up of many habits.
- There is potency in our being and in our actions. The perfection of both of these is virtue.
- Virtue belongs to the soul, not the body. It is a suitable disposition to the soul as health is to the body.
- The power of the soul is the subject of virtue. The soul is the principle of being in a living creature.
- Virtue is that which makes its possessor good and likewise his work good.
- Virtue is a habit where it never happens that anything but good is done.
- For a man to do good, it is necessary not only that his reason be well disposed by means of habit of intellectual virtue, but also that his appetites be well disposed by means of moral virtue.
- Prudence is a virtue. It has three parts: memory of the past, understanding of the present, and foresight of the future.
- Moral virtue can't be without prudence because moral virtue is a habit of choosing and prudence makes us choose well. Therefore moral virtue perfects the appetites by directing them to the good of reason.

When we come to understand virtue, we will come to desire it. When we come to desire it, we will train in habits that create specific virtues in us. Jesus Christ has given us the ability to do this by His justification on the cross at Calvary, and His sanctification through His indwelling Spirit in us. We must not only acquire virtue, but we must seek to perfect it as well.

Virtue: the Measure and Mark of Goodness

Aquinas said that there are three categories of virtue: theological, intellectual and cardinal. The theological virtues are from God. They are faith, hope and love. There are intellectual virtues which are developed in the mind. These include prudence and wisdom. Then there are the cardinal virtues or the principle virtues. These are prudence, justice, temperance and courage.

All of these areas of virtue ultimately build goodness in humanity and make man more like God. They build his ability to know and relate to God for they are all grounded in God. He alone gives the theological virtues and facilitates the development of the other virtues in Christians. We must work with Him in this development and understand it is never a one-time act that helps us attain virtue but a lifetime process.

God is central in the process of virtue. Augustine said:

> "The soul needs to follow something in order to give birth to virtue. This something is God, and if we follow Him we shall live the good life."[117]

We must note then that the exemplar of human virtue is God. Virtue must pre-exist in God just as in Him all things come into being and exist.[118] Thus Jesus Christ came and lived a perfect life and is the model for all men. But also from Him and through Him do we develop a life of virtue. Jesus clearly pointed this out in John 14:13-14, John 15:16 and John 16:24.

> "And I will do whatever you ask in my name, so that the Son may bring glory to the Father. You may ask me for anything in my name and I will do it." (John 14:13-14)

> "You did not choose me but I choose and appointed you to go and bear fruit that will last. Then the Father will give you whatever you ask in my name." (John 15:16)

> "In that day you will no longer ask me anything. I tell you the truth my Father will give you whatever you ask in my

name. Until now you have asked for nothing in my name. Ask and you shall receiver and our joy will be complete." (John 16: 23-24)

At first blush, these verses look like "blank checks" to get whatever we want from God. He becomes a sort of genie and does magic for us whenever we want. Help me make more money, let me win this game, heal my disease and so on. But is this what Jesus is really saying? No, because you need to understand the purpose of our becoming Christians is to become like Christ. Physical things won't build God's Kingdom in us, only the development of "Christ-likeness" in virtue will.

God gives us new life, *zoe*, when we are redeemed. Once we have this new life, He calls us to bear fruit and show it to a watching world. This fruit is God's will formed in us by way of virtue and is called sanctification. Through sanctification, we begin to look more and more like Him. We must ask God to grow this in us more and more.

Virtue grows us in giving up our control of life and giving control of it over to God. He becomes Lord of our life and His will is our desire. The function of virtue is to make the appetites in us subordinate to the commands of God and His righteous and holy life. That is what it means to be a man of God.

The term man of God is used some 83 times in the NIV. It refers to men who were very close to God or spoke for God as prophets. Moses was a man of God, so was Elijah, Elisha, David and others. In the New Testament Paul uses it twice to refer to Timothy and in both instances commands him to grow in virtue.

Clearly the Christian life must be grounded by virtue. The problem is many people call Jesus Savior but not Lord. To be Lord He must control how we act. To be Lord we must be obedient to Him in all we say and do. A.W. Tozer notes this about separating the Savior from His Lordship.

> "The truth is that salvation apart from obedience is unknown in sacred scriptures...It seems most important to me that Peter speaks of his fellow Christians as "obedient children." He was not giving them a command or an exhortation to be obedient. In affect he was saying 'Assuming that you are believers, I therefore gather that you are also obedient. So now, as obedient children, do so and so ...*Apart from obedience there can be no salvation, for salva-*

tion without obedience is a self-contradictory impossibility.'" [119] (Italics mine)

Virtue then becomes the measure and mark of goodness and therefore the measure and mark of a man of God. When we grow in virtue, we bring all of our being under ultimate control of God and holiness is our passion. When we are passionate for holiness and practice it day in and day out, the result is virtue by way of habit. Virtue then brings the appetitive drives under the obedience of Jesus and grows in us the mind of Christ (1 Cor 2:16).

I want to finish this chapter by looking at more virtues and some of the specific qualities of each virtue.

The Virtue of Forgiveness

I have heard forgiveness defined as taking the offender off your hook and putting them on God's hook. In other words, you no longer hold their sins against them; God may, but that is between them and God — you have made your peace. The word forgives comes from the Greek word *aphiemi* which means to send away or to let go. Corrie ten Boom, survivor of the Nazi concentration camps in Auschwitz, described it this way: "When we forgive someone we take their offence and cast it into a bottomless lake and post a sign 'no fishing.'"

Jesus speaks very candidly about forgiveness. I believe He does so for several reasons. The first is that our sins against Him are by far greater than any human could commit against us and far more numerous. Yet in spite of this fact, we are still forgiven in Christ Jesus. We must never lose sight of our sin and its stench to God, how we have rebelled against Him and committed cosmic treason, for which there is only one punishment, death. Yet by His grace, His endless grace, God the Father has poured His wrath out on Jesus Christ on the cross. The price paid was Jesus' death for us. The most costly price was paid so God could forgive us. God has taken our sin and cast it far, far away and so we must do likewise towards our fellow man.

Second, if we don't forgive those whose offense is by far less severe than is ours against God, how can we then expect God to forgive us? This is seen clearly in the parable of the unforgiving servant in Matthew 18:21-35. The servant begged forgiveness from the king and had a debt of *millions of dollars*. This was a debt he could never repay. The king forgave this debt totally.

Then later this servant saw one of his own servants who owed him *several dollars* and demanded his money. The servant couldn't repay so the one who had just been forgiven millions of dollars of debt had the other servant thrown in jail because he couldn't repay the few dollars owed to him.

Here is what the Bible says when the king found out:

> "Then the master called the servant in. 'You wicked servant,' he said, 'I canceled all that debt of yours because you begged me to. Shouldn't you have had mercy on your fellow servant just as I had on you?' In anger his master turned him over to the jailers to be tortured, until he should pay back all he owed." (Matt 18:32-34)

Remember he would never be able to pay back the millions of dollars he owed the king. He was to be tortured until he could pay back his debt. The words "until he should pay back all he owed" are the equivalent of saying "forever," because he could never repay his debts to the king. The servant is condemned forever because of his inability to pay back his debt. Likewise we can't repay our debts of sin to Jesus, but He still forgives us.

Then Jesus adds these words,

> "This is how my heavenly Father will treat each of you unless you forgive your brother from your heart." (Matt 18:35)

The key to this verse is "from your heart." To forgive in words is one thing but to forgive from the heart is totally different. This means to feel and act towards him as if he had never offended you.[120] The offense is never to be brought up again. We no longer carry the grudge. This person no longer owes us anything because the debt has been canceled.

To show how critical forgiveness is to God, Jesus made this statement:

> "For if you forgive men when they sin against you, your heavenly Father will also forgive you. But if you do not forgive men their sins, your Father will not forgive your sins." (Matt 6:14-15)

That is a very drastic statement that we must forgive all sins of our fellow man, or God won't forgive us. I want to further the point we have already made. The debt we have against God is un-payable. We have no way to atone for our sin. Our sin is ever before us and the wages of sin is death (Rom 6:23). We are forever in God's debt unless someone pays this debt for us. This is precisely what Jesus did for us on the cross. He paid our debt and ransomed our lives from hell.

William Barclay does a masterful job describing the debt of the servant in Matthew 18. Here is how he describes it:

> "The debt of the fellow servant was a trifling thing…it was approximately one five-hundred-thousandth of his own debt. A.R.S. Kennedy drew this vivid picture to contrast the debts. Suppose they were paid in sixpences. The hundred denarii debt could be carried in one pocket. The ten thousand talent debt would take to carry it an army of 8600 carriers, each carrying a sack of sixpence weighing sixty pounds in weight; and they would form, at a distance of a yard apart, a line five miles long! The contrast between the debts is staggering. The point is nothing men can do to us can in anyway compare to what we have done to God; and if God has forgiven us the debt we owe him, we must forgive our fellow men the debts they owe us. Nothing that we have to forgive can even faintly or remotely compare with what we have been forgiven…our debt is beyond all paying"[121]

We must see our offenses against God, and how appalling they are to Him. Only then will we beg Him for mercy. Unless God extends us mercy and grace, we remain un-forgiven. When our fellow man comes to us with their sin and demands mercy, we must give it to them as well. The forgiveness extended to others gives us the ability to see our sins as God sees them. We have to see transgressions with God's eyes, not our own, or forgiveness is inconceivable.

When we forgive, we not only extend mercy but we extend compassion and kindness as well (Eph 4:23). The forgiveness we give aims at the command of Jesus to be a peacemaker (Matt 5:9) and to not carry a grudge based on past actions. This stems from a "Christ-centered" command to love all (Mark 12:31) and to forgive one another (Col 3:13). This as we have said comes only from *agape* love. When we love this way, forgiveness is the gift we give to others, but also we give to ourselves. Think of the hatred and anger that is caused by a refusal to forgive. This grudge — this lack of forgiveness — seethes inside us until it boils over into our hearts and we act on it. This is seen all over the world in racism and "ethnic cleansing." People can't forgive so they continue to hate and get revenge. Forgiveness stops the hate and replaces it with grace and love.

The Virtue of Contentment

When we are content, we are satisfied. It is satisfaction with what we have. This self-sufficiency is a state of mind that is completely independent of all outward things. This then carries the secret to happiness within itself. Contentment never comes from the possession of external things. It is an inward attitude to life.[122]

The world of today continues to tell us we need more things. It says in effect that only by getting more will we be happy. The problem is once we acquire more, there is still something we don't have and we won't be happy until we get it as well.

Greed says to desire more than what you need. Contrast this with contentment which says I am happy with what I have and more won't add anymore joy to my life. Only when we learn to be content will we learn the worthlessness of material things and the pricelessness of spiritual treasures. The apostle Paul spoke about this in his first letter to Timothy. He said this,

> "But godliness with contentment is great gain. For we brought nothing into the world, and we can take nothing out of it. But if we have food and clothing, we will be content with that. People who want to get rich fall into temptation and a trap and into many foolish and harmful desires that plunge men into ruin and destruction. For the love of money is a root of all kinds of evil. Some people eager for money have wandered from the faith and pierced themselves with many griefs." (1 Tim 6:6-10)

I will use these verses for the proper understanding of contentment. There are several key ideas we must note from these verses.

1. *We brought nothing into the world.* We came into this world with nothing, yet God has provided for us. All we have is a gift from God and it must be appreciated as the gift that it is, not as something we deserve because of our great work ethic. We must use our time, talent and treasure for the glory of God, not the fulfillment of our desires.
2. *When we die, we take nothing with us materially.* We will all die, a fate no man can avoid. The question is can we take any of our possessions with us into the next life? No! We must also understand that the more we have, the more we care for it and seek to protect it. It adds worry to our life that those with little don't have. People with expensive cars often park them far away (or take up two parking spaces!) so no one will dent it or scratch it. Folks with more modest modes of transport know that dings and dents are just part of life, and so go on their way, unworried.
3. *The basic needs for food and shelter will be provided for by God.* We often mistake "greeds" for "needs." A need is for the basic essentials to keep us alive such as food, water and clothing. This is all we *need* to sustain our existence. Everything else can be viewed as greed. Don't get me wrong, having a nicer house, newer car, and fancy dinner china are not bad things in and of themselves. Only when they become greedy passions are they wrong. The accumulation of money and possessions must never be the all-consuming, ultimate purpose behind what we do.
4. *People who want to get rich fall into temptation and a trap.* As I just said, the extras in life are not all bad unless they become the ruling disposition in us. Wealth is not bad in and of itself, but when the accumulation of wealth becomes our driving force, we become poor and bankrupt in spirit. When we work to get wealth instead of work to serve God, we fall into a trap. What money we have is a gift from God. We can use it humbly and graciously, to further God's purpose, or we can let it make us prideful and unwilling to part with it. It must not be hoarded and "kept for a rainy day," but used for God's Kingdom. Jesus

also talked about how difficult it was for a rich man to go to heaven (Mark 10:25). I believe this is true because for many wealthy people, money becomes all-consuming.
5. *The love of money is the root of all kinds of evil.* Money is not good or bad in and of itself. It is like a gun — it can be used for good or bad. It is the attitude towards it that makes the difference. John MacArthur gives these signs as a love of money:
   a. Those who love money are more concerned with making it than honesty or giving a quality effort.
   b. Those who love money never have enough.
   c. Those who have money tend to flaunt it.
   d. Those who love money resent giving it.
   e. Those who love money will often sin to get it.[123]

Much evil is brought about by money and the love of it. We must make sure we control it rather than letting it control us.

Paul teaches us so very much in these verses (1 Tim 6:6-10), and we must each search our own heart and ask God to reveal our true attitude towards money and all it can buy. As spiritual beings in Christ, we must understand we are not of the world and are merely travelers in it. This is not our home; our home is eternity with Christ in heaven (John 17:11-19).

William Barclay makes some brilliant observations about these verses that I want to share with you:

> "Contentment comes from an inner attitude to life. Shakespeare draws a picture of a king wandering in the countryside, in places unknown. He meets two gamekeepers and tells them he is a king. One of them asks him, 'But if thou be a king where is thy crown?' The king answered, 'My crown is in my heart, not on my head. Not decked with diamonds and Indian stones, nor to be seen; my crown is called content. A crown it is that seldom kings enjoy.' Epicurus said of himself, 'To whom little is not enough nothing will be enough.' Great men have always been content with little. So who then is rich? He that is contented with his lot."[124]

He sums this up as he talks about eternal treasure and how we can learn, and become content. He notes this about our present life,

> "The mind that has learned to appreciate the moral beauty of life, both as regards God and men, can scarcely be greatly moved by any outward reverse of fortune, and what our age wants most is the sight of a man who, who possess everything, but yet willingly contented with little…Two things alone a man can take to God. He can and must take himself; and therefore he must build up a self he can take without shame to God. He can and must take that relationship with God into which he has entered in the days of his life …contentment comes when we escape the servitude of things and when we find our wealth in love of men and when our most precious possession is our relationship with God made possible through Jesus Christ."[125]

The Virtue of Hope

We have noted that faith and hope go together in chapter 10. *Faith is related to past and present, while hope relates to the future.* Hope is the confident expectation of a future good. This hope is fixed on Christ and relates to salvation. It produces the moral fruit of confidence in God, unashamed patience in tribulation, and perseverance in prayer. It stabilizes the soul like an anchor by grounding it to God's steadfastness and His faithfulness. [126]

This hope is based on the good news declared by the angel in Luke 2. The gospel is the good news of Jesus' birth and salvation for mankind. This is stated over and over in the New Testament. Through Jesus' death and resurrection, we can be redeemed by faith in Him. Paul notes this about hope:

> "… (we) groan inwardly as we wait eagerly for our adoption as sons, the redemption of our bodies. For in this hope we were saved. But hope that is seen in not hope at all. Who hopes for what he already has?" (Rom 8:23(b)-24)

"For everything that was written in the past was written to teach us, so that through endurance and the encouragement of the Scriptures we might have hope." (Rom 15: 4)

"May the God of hope fill you with all joy and peace as you trust in him, so that you may overflow with hope by the power of the Holy Spirit." (Rom 15: 13)

"Therefore since we have such a hope we are very bold." (2 Cor 3:12)

"Dear friends, now we are children of God, and what we will be has not yet been made known. But we know that when He appears, we shall be like Him, for we shall see Him as He is. Everyone who has this hope purifies himself, just as he is pure." (1 John3: 2-3)

In these verses the power, or virtue, in hope is in Jesus Christ and in spending eternity with Him. We have this hope because:

- Christ has suffered and died for our sin on the cross. His atonement for sin, once and for all, is for us. We have hope in this salvation.   (Heb 5: 9-10, Heb 7:27-28, Heb 9:12-14)
- His resurrection is our resurrection in eternal life. The power of sin and the sting of death has been overcome in Christ. We have been redeemed from death and have hope that death is not the end (Hos 13:14, 1 Cor 15: 54-58).
- The Scriptures have been written as a witness for us to testify about Christ. The prophets of old and the apostles have written and testified about this to us. In their testimony we have hope (Luke 1:1-4, John 20:30-31).
- We are adopted sons of God and His gift of the Holy Spirit who lives in us and testifies to us, gives us joy and peace. We trust in this promise of God and by this our hope overflows by the power of the Holy Spirit.

- The power of God at work in us to bring about righteousness in us gives us a boldness to live and speak for the glory of Christ. This power of God in us is our hope.
- When we die and are with Christ in eternity, we shall see Him face to face and we shall see Him as He is. We shall also be like Him. This hope of eternity in His glorious presence with Jesus purifies us.
- In the New Jerusalem there will be no more sin, sadness or death. There will be a new order and we will see the glory of the Lord. What a joyous hope this gives Christians for all eternity (Rev 21:1-5, Rev 21:22-22:5).

We are redeemed and children of God. William Barclay comments that we have the privilege to be God's sons and daughters. We must understand the standard we are called to live up to. Just as bearing the name of a great school or church inspires us to new heights, so must our title "child of God" motivate us to greatness.[127]

This hope we have is so profound and inspiring that it is difficult to even consider it, let alone understand it. The promises of 1 John 3:2-3 are that we shall one day see Christ and that one day we shall be like Him. These produce infinite hope in us to endure all things while we are still in this physical body. That we shall one day bear the redeemed image and likeness of God as it was originally in the Garden. Sin will be no more in us, and we shall be reflections of Christ who is the sinless and spotless Lamb of God.

William Barclay noted this about seeing God:

> "The goal of all great souls has been the vision of seeing God. The end of all devotion is to see God."[128]

Some privileged men have seen the glory of God. No one can see the face of God and live because God is holy and pure, and we are sinful and impure. One day though, it will not be this way. In our glorified bodies we shall see Him and be like Him. When we look at those who saw the glory of God, we can get a glimpse of how majestic this will be. As the apostle Paul said,

"No eye has seen, no ear has heard, no mind conceived what God has prepared for those who love Him." (1 Cor 2:9)

Here is just a glimpse of what those who saw His glory said:

- The glory of God revealed how sinful Isaiah was. He then longed to be holy. Just the train of the robe of God filled His holy temple with His glory. Isaiah said, "Woe to me!" I cried "I am ruined! For I am a man of unclean lips and I live among a people of unclean lips and my eyes have seen the King the LORD Almighty." (Isaiah 6:5)
- When Peter, James and John saw Christ in His transfigured body, they didn't want to go down the mountain but wanted to stay in this glorious place. Luke says this, "Now they woke up and saw Jesus covered with brightness and glory ...Peter, all confused and not even knowing what he was saying, blurted out, 'Master this is wonderful! We will put up three shelters ...'" (Luke 9:33 TLB)
- When Moses saw the glory of the LORD pass before him, his face shown of this glory of God. The people made comments about it. It says this in Exodus, "But whenever Moses entered the LORD'S presence ...and when he came out and told the Israelites what he had been commanded, they saw that his face was radiant." (Exodus 34:34-35)

Words can't reveal what these men saw, but they never forgot it. How much more glorious will it be for us, children of God, to see Him as He is seated on His throne in Glory. So too, words cannot describe the glorious scene we will one day see of Jesus seated on His Throne of Glory at the right hand of God. We can only imagine what it will be like. It is this hope of being in the eternal presence of Christ and His glory that we as Christians call upon to help us endure whatever this life sends our way.

The book of Revelation describes the glorious place called the New Jerusalem.

"And I heard a loud voice from the throne saying, 'Now the dwelling of God is with men, and He will live with them. They will be his people and God himself will be with them and be their God. He will wipe every tear from their eyes. There will be no more death, or mourning, or crying, or pain, for the old order of things has passed away.' He who was seated on the throne said, 'I am making everything new!'" (Rev 21: 3-5)

What a glorious hope we have in Christ! Amen.

The Virtue of Gratitude

To be grateful is to be thankful for what you do have because you realize how much you have been given. Gratitude is similar to contentment but differs in the respect that in contentment you desire nothing more; whereas in gratitude you are thankful for what is given you. There is a difference. Gratitude is being thankful for being content.

One who is at peace with God is thankful because He knows who he is in relation to who God is. This sense of humility and meekness leads to a spirit of thankfulness. This spirit calls us to keep on being thankful and is a continuous obligation. This is seen in Paul's writings:

> "Let the peace of Christ rule in your hearts, since as members of one body you were called to peace. And be thankful. (Col 3:15)

Paul speaks about thankfulness some forty-one times in his writings. It was a constant theme to be thankful. The reason is that many blessings flow from thankfulness. Here is a list of some:

It honors God — To give thanks is to show understanding that what you have is a gift, a gift from God. James tells us that all good gifts are from God. (James 1:17) When we give thanks, we understand this and bring honor to the Giver of our blessing. We also understand that what God gives He can also take away, so we don't hold on too tightly. We are thankful for what we have for as long as we have it, but we honor God forever for giving it to us in the first place.

It makes us more dependent on God — Gratitude is an attitude that recognizes all we have and receive comes from the Creator and Sustainer of life. All we have is given to us from God (1 Cor 4:7). Therefore, thankfulness brings an understanding that only from God can we receive, and only for God can we properly use His gifts. We must seek His will, and use what He gives us for His glory. This creates a sense of dependence on God, and dissuades us from reliance on our own inadequate abilities.

It reveals the grace of God — God continues to give us blessing after blessing, even though we have done nothing, can do nothing, to deserve them. So many of these blessings we take for granted. He has given us salvation, the knowledge of this salvation, the ability to live a holy life, the ability and opportunity to witness to others, His desire for us to know Him ... all these and more are His blessings. The knowledge of the boundless grace of God towards us makes us see how much He loves us and is so merciful to us. We are rich beyond compare, and all because of the fullness of His grace. (John 1:16)

A thankful heart is a worshipful heart — Once we come to know the grace of God towards us, we long to praise Him for His mercy anew each day. We want to give Him back what is rightfully His, which is praise and honor and glory, and power forever and ever. We sing his praise because we have come to know of His agape love for us. We have come to see how He delivers us from danger. (Ps 86: 12-13)

God blesses us to cultivate more thanksgiving in our hearts — God gives to us so that we can give to others as a way to show our thanks. Our blessings from God will make us generous to others out of a thankful heart, and we will desire to give to them more and more. Out of this attitude, we will need less and be able to give more. These blessings of God are not for our own luxury but to be used generously in giving and love to others.

Our giving then causes others to be thankful to God — Our giving will cause the receivers to thank God as well and He will then be seen more and more as the giver and source of all wealth. Through the gifts that we pass on to others, God receives more honor and praise. (2 Cor 9:11-15)

A thankful heart is a submissive heart — When we are grateful to God it reveals a level of trust in Him. This trust says, "Thy will be done in me." We then submit joyfully to the will of God because we know He is faithful and worthy of our trust. William Barclay notes this about thankfulness to God, "It is only when we are fully convinced that God is working all things together for good that ...the perfect gratitude is formed of which believing prayer demands."[129]

We receive the peace of God — Thanksgiving leads to trust and trust to peace. When we are focused constantly on God, this trust in Him then will guard our hearts and minds (Phil 4:6-7) as a military watchman guards over the camp. This peace is a peace that is not agitated by trials in life. It is a perfect peace because our mind is steadfast and in total trust in God. (Isa 26:3)

There are many benefits of a grateful heart. This is just a short list but the thankful man is a godly man who understands all he has been given and Who has given it. It is a way of life and an attitude that says he who has received much therefore gives much as well.

Actions, Habits and Virtue

We have talked about how we are to act in this life and specifically how virtue is formed in us. We have seen how goodness is perfected as well. The better we know who Jesus is and how He demands us to live, the more fully can we come into communion with Him and bear fruit for Him. Many Christians understand salvation but don't understand the Lordship of Christ. His Lordship demands obedience, just as any lord or master would. Obedience seems too hard for many people because they don't understand how we can live as Jesus commands. Jesus as Lord loves us and desires the best for us. We must give Him our service.

Jesus said,

> "Come to me all you who are weary and burdened and I will give you rest. Take my yoke upon you and learn from me, for I am gentle and humble in heart, and you will find rest for your souls. For my yoke is easy and my burden is light." (Matt 11: 28-30)

In this verse the yoke of Jesus is servitude to Him. Paul often talked about being a servant of Christ (Rom 1:1, Gal 1:10) and called himself such. We too are called to be servants of Christ as this verse says. We should also take heart that the yoke is easy and the burden light.

The life of virtue is a life of servitude to Christ. Jesus demands no less than any other master. The only difference is our work is not just for Him, it also conforms us and makes us like our Master, righteous and holy. His Spirit then is in us and forms us. We then desire to be near Him, we desire to be like Him and we desire His glory more and more. It is to His glory that we now turn …

The Glory:

The Passion of God for His Glory

God desired to keep saints for Himself until the end of the world. These saints would pay Him respect worthy of His grandeur and majesty and would be models of virtue because of the holy example they set.[130]

Joseph de Beaufort

"The longer I live, the more clearly I see my dependence on those who have gone before. The more I know of what others have thought, the less original my thinking appears."[131] John Piper states this in his recent book, *God's Passion for His Glory*. By familiarizing ourselves with the best theological thinkers and writers of the past, we can then better understand the theological thoughts and ideas about God in the Bible. One of these thinkers is Jonathan Edwards, and one of these concepts is God's glory.

Edwards studied Scripture as few have, resolving, "to study the Scriptures so steadily, constantly, and frequently, as that I may find, and plainly perceive, myself to grow in the knowledge of the same."[132] Edwards studied the Word of God diligently and pursued it with a passion.

In his writings, Edwards exposes the God who created this universe and the deepest thoughts about God's glory. One of his best-known works is "The End for Which God Created the World." In this essay he simplifies what is meant by God's glory and in the process helps answer the question of why God created the world in the first place.

Many writers have tried to reveal the answer to the questions "Why am I here?" and "What is my purpose in life?" No writer does a better job of explaining this than Edwards. In this particular essay, he discusses man's ultimate purpose in life is to glorify God. John Piper, who reprinted Edward's masterpiece and included some thoughts of his own in his own book, states this:

> "The further you go in the revealed thoughts of God, the clearer you see that God's aim in creating the world was to display the value of His own glory, and that this aim is no other than the endless, ever-increasing joy of his people in that glory."[133]

The better we understand God's glory, the better we will know the God we worship and serve, and the better we will reflect God's glory as believers because it radiates from within us. We will then be consumed with the knowledge.

The Bible speaks much about God's glory but yet so little is understood about it. His glory is the central theme to the creation of mankind. This theme can be summed up as follows:

> "The end of the creation is that the creation might glorify (God). Now what is glorifying God, but a rejoicing at that glory he has displayed? The happiness of the creature consists in rejoicing in God, by which also God is magnified and exalted."[134]

The ultimate end for man is therefore to know God's glory. Edwards elaborates:

> "God in seeking his glory seeks the good of his creatures, because the emanation of his glory …implies the …happiness of his creatures. And in communicating his fullness for them, he does it for himself, because their good, which he seeks, is so much in union and communion with himself. God is their good."

> "Thus it is easy to conceive how God should seek the good of the creature …even his happiness, from a supreme re-

gard to *himself*; as his happiness arises from …the creatures exercising a supreme regard to God …in beholding God's glory, in esteeming and loving it, and rejoicing in it."[135]

God reveals His nature in His glory. He longs for us to know Him in this glory, and when we do, God is thus glorified in us. When we long for His glory and become consumed with it, we are fulfilling the reason for God creating us. Piper puts this as well as anyone:

"God is most glorified in us when we are most satisfied in him. My paraphrase is: 'The chief end of man is to glorify God by enjoying him forever.'"[136]

God's glory reveals His attributes to all, and when we come to know those attributes, we better know God's glory. We come to understand His justice is pure. His goodness is wrapped up in His righteousness. His sovereignty is seen in His grace. His love is revealed in His Word come to earth in Jesus Christ. The best man can ever hope to be is defined in the glory of God.

This glory of God, as seen in His character and His ultimate goodness in all He is, is revealed in many ways in the Bible. This glory is seen in the brilliant and blinding light Paul saw on the Damascus road (Acts 22:1-11). It is seen in the pillar of cloud and fire that went before the Israelites (Ex. 13:21-22). It is seen as a powerful and intense fire that consumed the offerings of the Israelite people (Lev 9:15-24). There are many other instances where God's glory is seen in visible ways for man to witness. Where God's glory is seen, His awe and wonder are felt and known.

We are called to exhibit His glory. We as believers are to be transformed into God's glorious image (2 Cor 3:18). The main way we do this is to live a life of virtue because true virtue is found only in God. Without God there would be no virtue.

The Nature of True Virtue

Much of what is called virtue today is not. It is simply desirable qualities in people that are labeled virtue. What is the difference then between virtue and "niceties" of those around us? The answer is simple. Virtue is tied into God. Unless God is in it, it can't be virtue.

Edwards goes on to discuss the nature of true virtue in his essay entitled "The Nature of True Virtue." He writes:

> "Virtue is the beauty of those qualities and acts of the mind that are of a moral nature …it is generally agreed …these belong to the disposition and will …virtue is the beauty of the qualities and exercises of the heart, or those actions that proceed from them."[137]

Here he determines virtue is of a moral nature. He says it is of the spirit and comes from our innermost drives and desires of the will. It can be noted from this that I can do a good act, say clean my room, begrudgingly, and this act of kindness is not a virtuous act. Our will is central to the act, and if our disposition is contrary to our outward actions, then the act is insincere. "Good deeds" are not virtue because many of them are done for selfish reasons and future benefits for ourselves. A kindness for pay is no kindness at all, it's just a business deal.

To be virtuous, the thing that appears, namely the act, must truly be beautiful in regard to all its tendencies and with everything to which it stands related.[138] The mind, the emotions and the will must desire God's good and perfect will in them for the act to be virtuous. It also must seek the very best toward the person and society as a whole which grounds the act in love. These two essentials, the will of God and the benevolence of man, are labeled "being" by Edwards.

Only the actions that have the ultimate best intentions towards "being" can be virtuous acts. Everything else, whether good deeds or bad, often have selfish motives behind them, and therefore can't be virtuous. Another example would be acts of charity where we give to receive the tax write-off instead of to help those in need. The intention is towards getting money off year-end taxes with little concern for the less fortunate. The money may be useful for the recipients, but as a virtuous act it is useless to us and shows no great honor unto God.

Edwards describes it this way:

> "True virtue is only that where the heart of an intelligent being consists in benevolence to being in general.[139]

Edwards talks much about "being." His focus on true virtue is that the general being of humanity must be universally good. We are all inter-connected to all other intelligent beings in some way. This makes us part of the universal system of existence, and so all we do stands connected to the whole.[140] Edwards elaborates and says:

> "The general and true beauty …is its union and consent with the great whole."[141]

Love is key to the nature of true virtue. Any act without this benevolence "is but a small part of this whole" and therefore selfish and self-centered. On the other hand, when the disposition of the heart is benevolent to "being," then its union and consent to the whole is attached. Thus virtuous benevolence has union to "being" as its ultimate object, and this ultimate propensity then becomes the highest good of "being" in general.

When actions conflict with the general well being and its ultimate good, the actions can't be virtuous. By using this definition, we see that what goes on inside of us is critical to the formation of true virtue. The sum of all of this is that virtue must chiefly consist in God, specifically in love to God. Edwards elaborates:

> "…true virtue must chiefly consist in love to God, the being of beings, infinitely the greatest and best …God has infinitely the greatest share of existence. So that all other being, even the whole universe, is as nothing in comparison to the Divine Being."

> "For as God is infinitely the greatest Being, so he is allowed to be infinitely the most beautiful and excellent; and all the beauty to be found throughout the whole creation, is but the reflection of the diffused beams of the Being who has an infinite fullness of brightness and glory. Therefore, he that has true virtue, consisting in benevolence to *being* in general, and in benevolence to *virtuous* being in general, must necessarily have a supreme love to God."[142]

The foundation and fountain of true virtue according to Edwards is God. It starts with Him and ends with Him as the ultimate response of the creature to the character of his Creator, His glory. God is the ultimate good in "being." Unless He is the supreme end of our desires, in our will, virtue is not the result.

Not only is God worthy of all of our desires and actions, but it is He who puts these desires in us to start. He does this once we become His children when we are born again in Christ. We have a new nature that comes from God. We desire to become more like Him. God is the definition of love, justice, mercy, righteousness, grace and all that is good. If He is the definition of these then He must also be the source. We must love Him above all else, with all of our being (Matt 22:37). Edwards once noted that, "Love to God is the most essential to true virtue."[143]

The result of true virtue in us is God-likeness. This is the end for which God created us. He made us for a purpose, and that purpose is His glory revealed and reflected in us. We not only become more like Christ, but we hunger for Him to be formed in us. This is our passion, our desire, and our consuming obsession.

We bear fruit for God as true virtue is grown more in us (John 15). This highest excellency of creatures and their true goodness must be grounded in the design of their Creator, the agreeableness to their ends as determined by God. I again use the words of Edwards to bring this point out:

> "For the true virtue of created beings is doubtless their highest excellency, and their true goodness, and that by which they are especially agreeable to the mind of their Creator. But the true goodness of a thing, must be its agreeableness to its end, or its fitness to answer the design for which it was made. Therefore, they are good moral agents, whose temper of mind, or propensity of heart, is agreeable to the end for which God made moral agents."

> "…a truly virtuous mind, being as it were under the sovereign dominion of love to God, above all things, seeks the glory of God, and makes this his supreme, governing and ultimate end."[144]

As creatures of the Creator, we not only seek Him above all else, but this becomes our greatest joy. God's greatest end for us is to seek Him and become like Him. In the process He is our greatest desire and joy. This then unites us to God. The exercise of all of this is true virtue. In the Bible this is also called holiness. We become holy because as believers we have His Holy Spirit indwelling us and aiding us in its development.

Our Relationship with the Holy Spirit

C.H. Spurgeon said of the Holy Spirit:

> "The Holy Spirit is to be to us all what Jesus was to His disciples. Jesus was such a strength to His disciples when He was with them."[145]

In John 14:16 Jesus tells us He will send us the Holy Spirit. The word used in the Greek for Holy Spirit here *Paraclete*, is very rich in meaning, and no one English word can suffice to represent it. It means Comforter, Helper, Advocate, and Counselor. The Holy Spirit is given each of these names in different translations. This word is all of this and so much more. That is why Mr. Spurgeon says quite confidently that the Holy Spirit is to be to us all that Jesus was to the disciples.

Jesus was guide, friend, teacher…and so is the Spirit of God. Let's look at roles that Jesus played in the lives of others.

1. *Jesus as Comforter* — When Jesus was present, He brought comfort to all those around Him. The Story of Lazarus in John 11:1-44 tells of Jesus raising Lazarus from the dead. What is central to our discussion here is how the sadness of losing a brother is turned to expectant hope when Jesus arrives. Jesus had a presence about Him that gave comfort to others no matter how terrible the "storm" was that they were in.

2. *Jesus as Helper* — Another word for helper is friend. When Peter had denied Jesus three times, Jesus came to Him and restored him in their relationship (John 21:15-19). Many people have friends who are there in good times and leave in bad. A friend is one who is there in good times as well as in bad times. Jesus was such a friend to Peter. That is why when we next see Peter in the book of Acts he is such a powerful proclaimer of Jesus as Savior. That is why Peter refused to be crucified as Jesus but rather he said crucify

me upside down because I am not worthy to die as my Lord. Jesus said to the disciples, "I no longer call you servants…Instead I have called you friends…" (John 5:15)

3. *Jesus as Advocate* — An advocate is one who supports and believes in another. Jesus in His prayer to the Father in John 17 is seen as our Advocate, and He is also our Mediator in heaven with God the Father (1 Tim 2:5). Jesus prayed in John 17 that we be strengthened, protected, sanctified, unified, be with Him in heaven, that we love and live as Jesus did. Jesus wants nothing but the best for us and has only the best plans for us, but it isn't in this world that we will receive it. It will be when we see Him face to face as He is in heaven. Jesus so loves us and nothing can separate us from His love for us (Rom 8:37-39). His *agape* love for us means He will never leave us or forsake us (Heb 13:5).

4. *Jesus as Counselor* — Jesus was constantly giving the disciples wise counsel. This is seen Luke 5:1-10. Peter is fishing, for he is a fisherman by trade, and Jesus tells him where to catch more fish. Peter reluctantly gives in, and then he catches many, many fish. Jesus taught about life and how God wanted them to live. He opened up the Word of God to the disciples, tells them about salvation, and tells of future events (Luke 24:44-49). Jesus is the Master Teacher.

Just as Jesus performed these roles for the disciples, so too does the Holy Spirit perform these roles in our lives today. He shapes us and conforms us into the image of Jesus in holiness and virtue. To do this the Holy Spirit is Comforter, Helper, Counselor and Advocate.

The key to serving God is to know His will and understand his teaching. The way we must do this is to listen to His voice. We speak to God often but seldom listen. In fact, we really don't expect to hear His voice. We spend much time in prayer but seldom listen to the voice of God in reply. We are so busy with life that we seldom are able to hear His voice in our daily affairs. He speaks softly and quietly; He doesn't raise his voice to be heard above the raucous din of our daily lives, nor should He. He expects us to be listening.

When we read the Bible, we need to ask the Spirit of the Living God in us to open the words, as Jesus did for the disciples in Luke 24:45. The Holy Spirit will teach us and give us understanding (John 14:26). When this is done, these words are no longer just words, they are the power of the Living God in us to act and fulfill God's eternal purpose in us. Then we can know and utilize the power in them.

The Holy Spirit makes the Word of God visible in us. This truth must enter into us and become part of our being. We must ingest it as we do food through study and prayer. As food becomes part of us to nourish our body, so too will the Word of God nourish our soul by the resident Teacher or Helper, opening it to give us understanding and how to apply it in our life. This truth of God must be so interwoven in us that it is in every fiber of our actions. The Word becomes our teacher. Our resident Counselor, the Holy Spirit, will then direct us and guide us into God's will by applying it in our lives. Then we know truth because we live it, we experience it and manifest the power in it.

Jesus tells us to go out into the world, a world where we will be foreigners. A world that will be cruel to us, despise us and will persecute us because of the name of Jesus whom we proclaim (John 15:18-21). However, He won't leave us as orphans (John 14:18). So He is sending us out into a difficult world, but He is giving us the resident Comforter who will support us and encourage us. He will also enable us to do God's will as the resident Advocate (*Paraclete*) goes before the Father pleading our case. He strengthens us, protects us, sanctifies us and unites us to the Father in all we are becoming.

Through all of life as believers, we are given God's Holy Spirit to continue to perfect us. This will happen infinitely because for all eternity God is making us like His Son, and we will one day see His glory face to face. Until then we walk with the eyes of faith in our Risen Savior and the Spirit of the Father dwelling and living in us.

The Power of the Spirit

The Holy Spirit brings power, God's power to our lives. There are several verses that speak of this power.

> "I am going to send you what my Father has promised you; but stay in the city until you have been clothed with power from on high.   (Luke 24:49)

> "But you will receive power when the Holy Spirit comes on you…"   (Acts 1:8)

> "For God did not give us a spirit of timidity but a spirit of power…"   (2 Tim 1:7)

> "…by the power of signs and miracles, through the power of the Holy Spirit (Rom 15:19)

These verses speak of the power of God that works in us by His Spirit. The word here for power is the Greek word *dunamis* that we have talked about before, but it is force or ability as well as power. We must be careful that we don't think we are Superman because we have the Holy Spirit in us. This power comes from God and is only for His Kingdom's advancement. It is not for our own agenda or to glorify ourselves.

He works in us that we bring glory to Jesus, and in this His will is done as it is in heaven. By living in fellowship with the Spirit of God He will reveal His plans for our lives. C. H. Spurgeon said,

> "All life any believer has comes from Jesus, for we have no life of our own."

We become unified with Jesus and His will. That is why in the Lord's Prayer Jesus says to pray "your will be done on earth as it is in heaven" (Matt 6:10). We can accomplish nothing outside of God's will and sovereign plans. He is in full and total control, and He does not give us power for our own pleasure, to do as we see fit.

Jesus said,

> "I am the vine and you are the branches; he who abides in me and I in him he bears much fruit, apart from me you can do nothing."   (John 15:5)

"If ye abide in me and my words abide in you, ask whatsoever you will and it shall be done unto you."(ASV John 15:7)

In these verses we see how attached we must be to Jesus to manifest the power of the Spirit. A vine grows branches, and these branches have no plans of their own. The branches do only what the purpose of the vine requires. So too we must only seek out Jesus' glory by asking Him through the Spirit what it is He wants done. When we pray this way, He reveals it to us. He will then give us the power to accomplish it. The task may be tough or the enemy strong but God will accomplish His plan. *He does this by giving us the power of His will from the knowledge of His will by the Spirit of His will.* We must then carry it out or we sin.

In difficult times this power is available to us to strengthen us. God never gives us more than we can handle. Through these times, He provides us with the *Comforter* to empower us. He won't take away the pain, but rather He will strengthen us to get through it. Then when we come out of these "storms" we will have a deeper reliance on God and a stronger relationship with Him because of it.

We have power when the Holy Spirit as *Counselor* brings remembrance of God's truth or promises to our life. He doesn't give us new truth but just makes old truth available to us. We can know it is the Word of God and apply it to the given situation. We can use it for counsel on how to act as well. Often our memory fails us and we lose things when we need them, but the Spirit within us helps us to remember God's Word.

We have power when the Spirit as *Helper* reveals sin in our life. It is this unconfessed sin that hampers us from knowing God's will. Sin keeps us from God. By confessing sin and repenting of it, we know that God will forgive us and thus restore our relationship to Him. Sin gets in the way and blocks God's ability to work in us. Confession of sin and repentance of sin gives us power to remove that stumbling block in us. Through guilt or shame, God can cause our conscience to reveal sin in our lives.

We have power when the Spirit as *Advocate* enables us to overcome temptation as well. The Bible says this about temptation,

"No temptation has seized you except what is common to man, and God is faithful he will not let you be tempted beyond what you can bear. But when you are tempted, he

will provide a way out so that you can stand up under it."
(1 Cor 10:13)

God knows us and knows the temptations we face. He allows these temptations — tests, actually — to come into our lives knowing they will do two things for us. First, these tests will reveal our heart and who we really are. Talk is cheap as the saying goes, and action tells what we really believe. This is similar to how God tested the Israelites in the wilderness (Deut 8:2) to see what was in their hearts. He wanted to see if they would follow His commands. Thus, we test steel or wood to see how strong it is. So too God allows tests and we are strengthened as we pass them.

Second, testing can strengthen an object. *It is strengthened because it is tested.* Had the object not been tested, it wouldn't have grown as strong. This is how we strengthen a muscle. We test it through difficulties; such as lifting weights at the gym. We test the muscle with the weights and then let it rest. Then we test it again, this time with heavier weights. Likewise we become stronger as we resist and overcome temptations as well.

We have power when the Spirit as *Helper* encourages us along the way. The Bible says this of Jesus:

> "For we do not have a high priest who is unable to sympathize with our weaknesses, but we have one who was tempted in every way, just as we are –yet was without sin. Let us then approach the throne of grace with confidence, so that we may receive mercy and receive grace to help us in our time of need." (Heb 5:15-16)

Jesus knows what it is like to suffer and go through life on earth with its many difficulties. But we must remember Jesus lived here thirty-three years. He understands our needs, troubles, worries and doubts. He took on flesh and had the same struggles we face every day and overcame them. He understands what it is like to face trials and be persecuted. He also is our Helper to enable us to get through them because of His role as our Mediator.

Knowing we can and will overcome in the power and strength of the Holy Spirit, as our fellow brothers and sisters have in past centuries, must be the bedrock of our commitment to love and serve Christ. God gives us the power in the Holy Spirit and the many roles He plays. It is our job to use this power to grow virtue.

The Life we are called to Live

God has called us to a life far above mediocrity. In fact, He has called us to a life of perfection (Matt 5:48). He has called us to live a life worthy of His glory. Jesus in His prayer to the Father prays this:

> "I have given them the glory that you gave me, that they may be one as we are one: I in them and you in me. May they be brought to complete unity to let the world know that you sent me and have loved them even as you have loved me." (John 17:22-23)

If Jesus dwells or abides in us He therefore must make His abode in our body, physically and spiritually. He must be given total control to do as He wants in our home. He cleans up what is dirty, throws away what is unneeded and restores what is broken. He makes the home suitable for Him to live in. You can be sure He will deal and get rid of all the dirt and sin in our home. No one wants to live in a dirty home.

When we buy a home, we don't keep it as the previous owners had it. We make changes so that it will reflect us and what is important to us. We hang up pictures we like, put in furniture we like and paint the walls colors we like. We make it ours so that it reflects us. God does the same when He takes up residency in our body, making our home suitable for Him to live in. He renovates it and the home takes on a new look. It no longer looks like the old owner, nor should it, but rather reveals what the new owner desires.

To let someone fully renovate your home means you totally trust them and what they will do. It means we believe it may take a lot of work, and may be costly, but we have confidence they will make our home much better than it once was. If this is true for our homes it is also true of our body. If Jesus renovates our body here on earth He will renovate in such a way that it will be by far the greatest display of us. It will be the best representation of us the world will ever see. This is true because God knows why He created us, how He created us and possesses all the materials to carry out His plan.

We must let the Master Builder redesign our home. As believers we know His Spirit indwells us, but we often don't let Him redecorate the house. To do this we must die to our flesh, the old house, and live for the new home that is being built. It won't be finished in this life but will be carried on in eternity. We have this hope in Him.

This hope in Him then is the hope we hold for the resurrection of our bodies on the last day. Jesus said, "I am the resurrection and the life. He who believes in me will live even though he dies…" (John 11:25) We then come to understand that this life is not all there is. We know we will die. We must trust in Jesus to resurrect us from the dead. He was resurrected on the third day and will do the same for us. The home He is building is not meant just for earth but for so much more. It is meant ultimately for eternity in heaven with Him. Our resurrection in Christ eternally is why the house was built in the first place. *We must believe as much in our death in this life as we believe in our life in Christ in the next life.*

When we come to fully grasp this concept, we come to the understanding that God calls us to believe in Him to give us life after we die. This life is not all there is. There is so much more when we die and he has purchased our souls from damnation. He has given us so much evidence of how we have life in Jesus, both now and eternally when we die. For the unsaved, death is scary and they must go it alone. God has conquered death (Heb 2:14, 1 Cor 15:54-56, 2 Tim 1:10). He calls us out of love to trust Him in this.

This belief is founded on the commitment and unqualified acceptance of who God is and how He has called us to live. He has given us the terms for salvation and has ransomed His own Son as a payment for our life. Our life is not our own but rather, was bought by God. The apostle Paul said,

> "Do you not know that your body is a temple of the Holy Spirit, who is in you, whom you have received from God? You are not your own; you were bought at a price. Therefore honor God with your body." (1 Corinthians 6:19-20)

God is preparing us a home to live in. It is a mansion in the clouds. "It is beautiful beyond description, too marvelous for words. Like nothing ever seen or heard." These song lyrics describe God's glory. When we know God this way we can be sure the home He is preparing for us in heaven will be glorious as well. Jesus said,

> "In my Father's house are many rooms; if it were not so I would have told you. I am going there to prepare a place

for you. And if I go and prepare a place for you, I will come back and take you to be with me, that you also may be where I am." (John 14:2-3)

The problem is that we often don't like His design or His plans, and thus we have asked for a new one, plans we design and then give to God. Sadly, our home is a sandcastle by the beach. It is nothing compared to what we could have. Unless God builds our home, the home is built in vain (Ps 127:1).

The Life of Worship

What does a life filled with God's Holy Spirit look like? It is a life of worship. Worship is "worth-ship" giving back to a being what is rightfully deserved. It is the giving of honor and reverence from an inferior being to a superior being. This is the glory and honor that is deserved or owed to a deity.

Worship is not a one-time act on a Sunday morning, but rather it is a lifestyle, an attitude we have in how we live. It is living our life in fear and trembling before a holy God, knowing He could snuff out our life because of our sin in an instant. It is living a life of love, knowing our salvation cost God the life of His Son as a ransom. It is living a life that is worthy to give as an offering to the God we serve. It is living in understanding of the power, wisdom, eternal existence, total authority, glory, purity, mercy, grace, wrath, and love for our LORD and God.

Worship knows that there is nowhere we can't go where we are out of God's sight. He is present throughout the whole universe. We don't need to go to a temple or church to worship Him. In worship we come to understand that God is spirit. He can manifest Himself in a Physical entity if He so chooses, but He must be worshiped in spirit, because that is who He is (John 4:24). We don't need to go to a church or temple to worship God as the Old Testament Jews did. Our body is now the temple of the Holy Spirit; this is the New Covenant in Jesus Christ.

We think of our body as a home made by God, but it is also a temple whereby we must worship God every minute of the day. Our body is a temple of the Holy Spirit who is in us (1 Cor 6:19-20). When we view our body as a temple, that goes with us wherever we go, we will come to see it as sacred ground, never to be defiled.

When we go to church on Sunday we seek to be on our best behavior because we are "in" church. We talk quieter, we are more polite and we are more reverent. Since our body is the temple we must do the same with it. The only difference is we are never "out" of church. We are always "in" church since this temple goes with us everywhere.

If I were to go to your church and you had the rule that all people who enter must take off their shoes before entering the sanctuary, you would be greatly offended if I refused to take off my shoes. So is God offended when we don't honor Him with the rules He has laid out for us in His temple that we call our body. We must be consumed with abiding by His rules, not ours. David said this about God's house:

> "I love the house where you live, O LORD, the place where your glory dwells" (Ps 26:8).

There are temple rules God has for us. We are to worship Him only in the way He has determined. Our worship must be worthy and acceptable to Him. God must be worshipped as He declares and nothing else will be accepted. We can offer Him anything but He won't accept just any type of worship. True worship, worship that God accepts, must be:

- To the One True and Living God
- To the One True and Living God in a way acceptable to Him
- To the One True and Living God in a way acceptable to Him with a right and pure heart

Anything else will not be accepted by Him (Mal 1:9-14, Jer 6:20, Amos 5:21-24). God is holy and demands to be worshipped as holy with nothing but the best we have to offer. God demands the best we have and we must give Him our best, as anything else isn't worthy of His name. He is King of kings and Lord of lords. His name is above all names on the earth and our worship must reflect this.

When God indwells our body by His Holy Spirit, we must understand it is His temple not ours. He sets the rules for it. We just live by His decrees in His temple, our body. God saved us to make true worshippers out of us. This must be the primary goal of our salvation. When we do this, we unite with the angels and saints in heaven. *We were saved to give God the glory He deserves as His true worshippers.* The cost of our salvation was very high and worship is the proper response to give back to the God who saved us.

Worship is what we will do in heaven, and we will join in with the angels in praise to the Lamb who is worthy. The worship we offer there will be in the most perfect way. This is the scene we get of heaven in Revelation 5:11-14:

> "Worthy is the Lamb, who was slain to receive power, and wealth, and wisdom, and strength, and honor and glory and praise …To Him who sits on the throne and to the Lamb, be praise and honor and glory and power forever and ever…Amen."

Until we get to heaven, this life is just a recital for the one day when we will see Him as He is. Then our worship to Him will be perfect, as it is now offered to God by the angels before His throne.

Saints of Old

Over the centuries, God has revealed His saints to be representations of who He is. These men and women have been consumed with the love, worship, and modeling the life of Him alone who is worthy. They have not only been fashioned in Christ's likeness, but they have made it their life-long pursuit as well.

Such a man was Brother Lawrence. His dear friend Joseph de Beaufort published an account of his life shortly after he died. He said this about Brother Lawrence[146]:

- "God has shown them the nothingness of the pleasures of the world and touched him with a love of heavenly things."
- "He made a firm resolution to accept the teachings of the Gospel and walk in the footprints of Jesus Christ."
- "The humility of the cross became more desirable to him than all the glory the world had to offer."
- "From the very beginning prayer was of particular importance to him."
- "This same faith gave him a profound respect and love for the Word of God."

- "Brother Lawrence called the practice of the presence of God the easiest and shortest way to attain Christian perfection and to be protected from sin."

The lives of those godly men and women we call saints who have gone before us offer models for us, models in ways to grow in holiness and give glory to God by being passionate about His glory. They were consumed with knowing His glory and living a life worthy of it. They then sought to reflect His glory in their lives. If we know some of the disciplines they developed to draw them closer to God, we can grow in virtue as well by acquiring them in our life. The question is how do we train in virtue? It is to the answer that we now turn …

The Training:

The Process of Maximum Impact

"We think that we are in the land of the living going to the land of the dying when in reality we are in the land of the dying headed for the land of the living." [147]

Paul Azinger quoting the PGA Tour Chaplin

We have talked throughout this book about how we are called to live powerful productive lives. Lives where we achieve the potential God intended for us when He created us. Lives where we are accomplishing maximum impact for Christ. Lives where we make best choices regularly, and where we are at our best when the situation is at its worst. Our existence is marked by purpose in our actions and passion in our hearts. Our spirit rules over our body with truth as our guide. We then present each day to God as an act of worship to Him whereby He cultivates true virtue in us because His Spirit indwells us. The result is we are passionate for His glory to be made manifest more and more in us.

This is the person who lives with an eternal perspective. They live with one foot barely touching the earth and the other firmly planted in heaven. Peggy Noonan says this about eternity:

> "I think we have lost the old knowledge that happiness is overrated…Our ancestors believed in two worlds, and understood this to be the solitary, poor, nasty, brutish and short one. We are the first generation of man that actually

> expected to find happiness here on earth and our search for it has caused such unhappiness…"[148]

What she is saying is very profound. Today we seek happiness in all we do. If something does not produce it we seek change. Happiness, pleasure and joy are the primary objectives of life today. We put all of our stock in this world and make little preparations for the next. We desperately want to be happy at all costs.

We assume God has the same perspective on happiness as we do. All He wants for us is to be happy. He must want this for us if He is really a loving God. So we pray to God mainly to accomplish things for us that will make us happy. When He answers our prayer and gives us happiness, He is a good God, and when He doesn't we feel He doesn't love us.

This often assumes that what will make us happy is material things. More stuff, more promotions, more money and more power. God isn't interested in making us happy He is interested in making us more righteous and holy to Himself. God will use any means He can to accomplish this and often trials and difficulties are his best means. C. S. Lewis said, "God speaks to us in pleasure but pain is His megaphone."

Life isn't about happiness, it's about growth. It's about becoming all He has created and planned for us to be. Once we understand this, we realize life is our training ground to prepare ourselves for this. We are called to be prepared daily and make the most of each day. We must not waste any of them for they are all precious in His sight. We know not when our life will end (James 4:13-17), and we must be prepared each day for Jesus to come back (Matt 25:1-14). It is living each day as if it would be our last which gives us an eternal perspective. I heard it said once and believe it is true, "Most people spend much more time planning their vacations than they do where they will spend eternity."

It is this planning which enables us to live more effectively and powerfully in this current life. It is this training that we must establish as a pattern for our lives, and it is training that enables us to reach our full potential. When life is viewed as a training mission for the next world, eternity, then all that we do must make us more righteous, holy and godly. In other words, we must train to cultivate true virtue and anything that hampers its progress in us must be totally eradicated. If not it will eradicate virtue in us.

Training to be Your Best

We were made to be at our very best, all the time, and accepting nothing less. We have been given all the tools necessary to accomplish this task. We are called to make this world a better place and to prepare for what lies beyond this world when we die. We each have a potential we were designed to attain. This will take a lifetime commitment. And demand 100% dedication.

The majority of people don't reach their potential, in fact they don't even come close to it. Why? Here are three scenarios to explain this:

1. They try to do it on their own, without God. People are so caught up in living life as they see fit that spiritual issues have little effect on them. They're in life for the here-and-now and are hardened to the Word of God because of sin.

2. When life doesn't go their way, they blame God. As long as God is "working" for them, they stay with Him, but when life turns sour they change course and pursue other ways to live a "happy" life. These people only follow Christ for the ease and benefits they can get in this world.

3. The worry of this world and the riches of this world choke out their abilities to live for Christ. Often, to live for God demands many sacrifices of which money is just one. Many will not give up the desire for money to serve Christ. Jesus said, "No one can serve two masters. Either he will hate the one and love the other or he will be devoted to the one and despise the other. You can't serve both God and money." (Matt 6:24)

All these scenarios are played out in the parable of the sower in Matthew 13. This is the story of seed being planted. The seed is God's Word and the soil is man's heart. Some fell along the way and birds ate it up (our first scenario). Some fell on rocky soil and got scorched by the sun and died (the second scenario). Some fell among the thorns and got choked by them (our third scenario). However, some fell on good soil and produced a great crop (Matt 13:1-23).

The odds from this parable are not that good. To those that hear the Word of God only one out of four become believers in Christ. Satan, the world and our fleshly lusts make it very difficult to cross over from spiritual death to spiritual life. However, all life comes from God and "if God is for us who can be against us" (Rom 8:31). We must also trust in the power of Jesus. He said:

> "I give them eternal life, and they shall never perish; no one can snatch them out of my hand. My Father who has given them to me, is greater than all; no one can snatch them out of my Father's hand."(John 10:28-29)

Our training must be by God and for His Kingdom purposes. Our life is not our own but His. When we serve Him, we can do all things because He gives us the strength with which to do it (Phil 4:13). Our job is to train for His Kingdom to come in us.

The following diagram illustrates what it looks like when God's Kingdom lives and reigns in us.

Maximum Impact to Perform

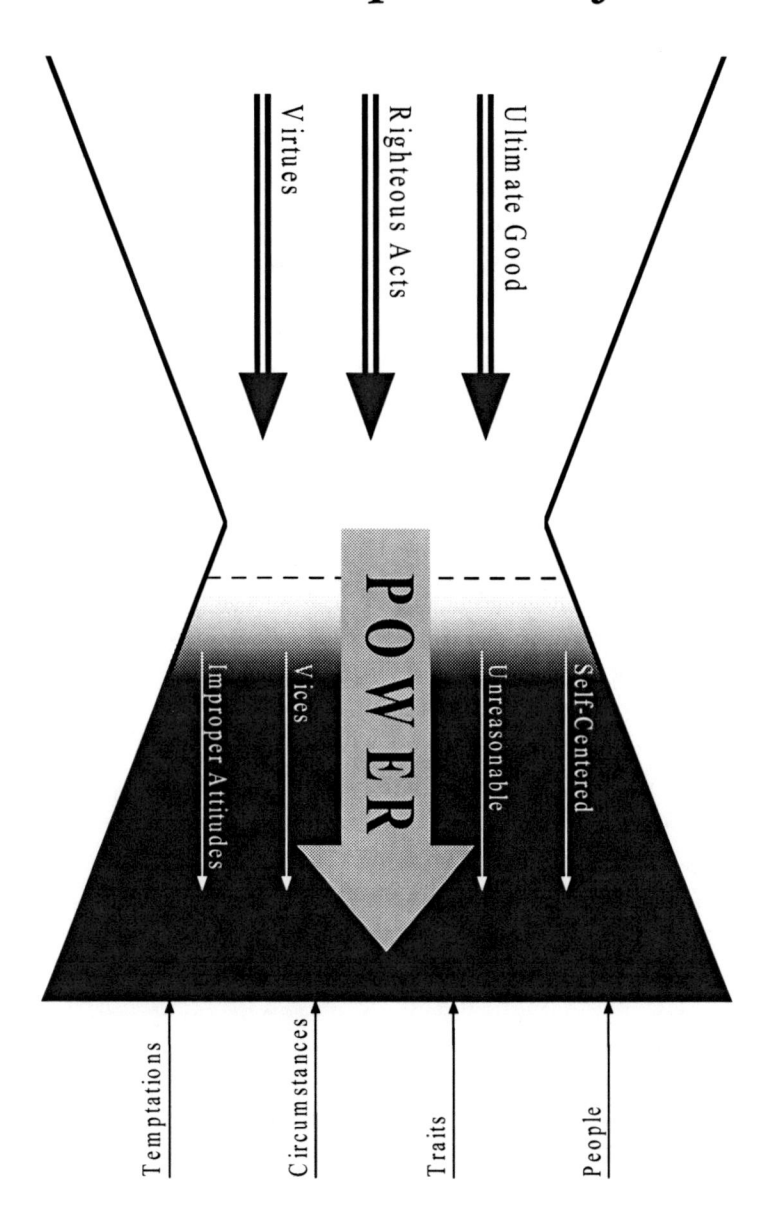

In this diagram life is lived from the top down where God's power flows in and through us into the world. He enables us to cultivate virtue and thus righteousness and ultimate good are done. This is seen by the open end at the top revealing God's unlimited power available to us.

The bottom of the diagram reveals where the storms of life cause us to react in vice, unreasonable thinking, self-centeredness and we then form improper attitudes. The good news for those in Christ is the power we have from Him to overcome this destructiveness and to let His power flow into our will, our mind, our emotions and ultimately, our behaviors is much greater.

The grey area marks the battle for control in us where the "storms" pop into our life. It is for this purpose we train, to be our very best in the worst of situations. It is weathering these "storms" that we develop the ability to be our best; even when we are at our weakest, we are still able to become strong because of Christ in us (2 Cor 12:10). As we said in Chapter 4 this is not our natural response, but it is what we must train for. It is how we are sanctified through Christ as our strength when we seek His will and His power in our trials. In the diagram we seek to rid our lives of the black color (sin) and replace it with the white color (virtue).

The Soldiers Armor

Our training is not to do battle in this visible world but rather in the invisible world, the spiritual world. This is clearly seen in Ephesians 6:10-13(a) which says:

> "Finally, be strong in the Lord and in His mighty powers. Put on the full armor of God so that you can take your stand against the devil's schemes. For our struggle is not against flesh and blood, but against the rulers, against the authorities, and against the powers of this dark world and against the spiritual forces of evil in the heavenly realms. Therefore put on the full armor of God, so that when the day of evil comes, you may be able to stand your ground, and after you have done everything, to stand."

These verses clearly state our enemy is spiritual, and so is our training. Our strength is in the power of God, not in ourselves. To fight, we must be armed and equipped spiritually. Just like a soldier fighting in battle must be armed, so too must we be armed for Christ's army. Our armor, or rather the weapons we fight and defend with, are named in Eph 6:14-17:

- Belt of truth

- Breast plate of righteousness
- Feet fitted firmly with the readiness that comes from the gospel of peace
- Shield of faith
- Helmet of salvation
- Sword of the Spirit of God

Equipped with this armor, we can do battle with our enemy; without it we are in trouble. This assumes that we will fight. We must engage our enemy offensively, and defend against his attacks. To fight, we must have weapons, to win we must use them, and to use them well we must have training.

Let's take a closer look at each piece of equipment. Bible scholar John MacArthur does a marvelous job of describing these articles of clothing and how Roman soldiers used them[149]. I will use his expertise to discuss each part of the armor briefly.

1. *The Belt of Truth* — This is the part of the soldiers clothing that girded it all together and demonstrates the readiness to engage in hand to hand combat (most warfare was done that way). The content of God's truth is of absolute necessity to battle Satan who is the father of all lies. Without knowledge of Biblical teaching, we are subject to being carried away.
2. *The Breastplate of Righteousness* —To put on the breastplate of righteousness, we act obediently, day by day in submission to our heavenly Father. This is holy living and obedience to God's commands for our lives. Most of the emotional and relational problems in believer's lives start with unrighteous living. Sin is the name the Bible uses for this action.
3. *Feet shod with the Gospel* — The gospel of peace is the marvelous truth that in Christ we are at peace with God and at one with Him. Therefore, we stand with our feet shod in that peace with God, His love for us, His union with us and His commitment to fight for us. The believer who stands in the Lord's power need not fear any enemy, even Satan himself. God is our defender.

4. _The Shield of Faith_ — The faith spoken of here is the trust in God for salvation and daily provision. This is faith that God exists, that Jesus died for our sins, that Scripture is the infallible authoritative Word of God and that Jesus will come back again. Faith is only as reliable and helpful as the trustworthiness of its object.
5. _The Helmet of Salvation_ — This helmet can only be worn by persons saved by Christ. Once you are saved, you are an enemy of Satan. As long as you are unsaved you are on his side whether you know it or not. So it is in the "hope of salvation" that we don our helmet.
6. _The Sword of the Spirit_ — This is the only offensive weapon Paul mentions for the battle. This refers to the Holy Spirit who indwells us and is our resident truth teacher. This sword is the Word of God. We must be trained in the knowledge and wisdom of the Bible. It is our most potent weapon; we must be proficient in its use.

To be able to fight we need armor and weapons. To win the fight we need training. We must train our spirit to guide the body. This is not to say that we neglect training our body, it is simply saying training the body is not all there is. The training is spiritual first and foremost, then we must train the body.

Training the Body

Since we live this life in our body, we must first train our body. There are many aspects we must keep in mind to keeping our body in good working condition. Imagine trying to run your best marathon with no sleep in the last 48 hours, no food in the last 48 hours and no physical conditioning in the last year. How well would you do? Just as preparing for the marathon, we must enable our body to be at its very best, and do it every day. To do this we need sleep, proper food, enough water and exercise.

Let's take a closer look at the best way to nurture each of these key areas in our bodies so it can function at its best each day:

1. _Sleep_ — To perform at our best we must have a well-rested body. Most experts say at least 7-8 hours of sleep each day. Yet how often do we neglect sleep and get less

than this? Lack of sleep will greatly hinder performance because your body isn't fully recouped from the previous day's exertion. Sleep is one of the body's means to recovering and restoring vital ingredients it needs to function. We can't ignore sleep but rather must make it a priority in each day's agenda. To be at our best we must be well rested.

2. *Eating* — The old saying that you are what you eat is very true. Most people put better fuel into their car than they do into their body. Eating is done on the run, with whatever is quick and easy. Unfortunately, what we eat is the fuel to give us energy and make us go, and filling up in the fast food lane doesn't do much but clog up our engine. Most of the food we eat is only filler food, not performance food. Many studies say breakfast is the most important meal of the day, yet many skip it. We must eat food for nutritional value, not just for taste or convenience. Food is your main source of physical fuel and must be chosen wisely, not as an afterthought.

3. *Drinking* — We must not use thirst as an indicator of our water needs because thirst is not always an accurate gauge. We need to drink at least six 8-ounce glasses of water each day. It seems tough to drink this much water, but when you take a large 32-ounce container with you throughout the day and sip away, it isn't that difficult. This is what many people do with coffee or soft drinks at work, so just substitute water. (Do you get tired at work? The major cause of workday fatigue is lack of water.) Drinks with caffeine in them are diuretics and flush out much of the water in your system. By drinking less alcohol, pop and caffeine and replacing them with more water, you will keep your body hydrated and more efficient.

4. *Exercise* — It seems there isn't a day that goes by without some new study telling of a new benefit of exercise. Exercise helps us burn more calories, helps our muscles become stronger, gives us emotional benefits that help fight depression, helps us release stress and keeps us in good cardiovascular condition. Many experts say as little as a 20-to-30 minute walk is all you need to get these benefits.

Exercise also helps you sleep better at night. It can also help you wake up in the morning. If you feel tired in the day, try taking a 10-minute walk. You most certainly will feel rejuvenated and have more energy.

This list is by no means exhaustive. The point is that if you want your body to be at its best you must give it the best. Training our body requires areas of commission and omission. There are things we need to commit to doing such as the four just mentioned and there are other areas that we must train our bodies to avoid, omit.

In spiritual terms the areas we refrain from periodically are called fasting. To fast is to deny your body certain things it desires and thus the control it exerts over us. Fasting is not giving in to our body's urges as it wants things. It is where our spirit says "no" to our body and makes it submit to the spirit's control. This is simply saying to the body, "You will do without for the amount of time I decide." The Bible talks much about fasting. Fasting from certain foods, fasting completely with all foods for periods of time, and fasting for certain lengths of time, from one day up to 40 days as Jesus did in the desert.

Fasting is training we undertake to help our spirit gain better control of our body. I believe there are four types of fasting we must train our bodies in: food, material goods, sexual desires and words. I want to take a closer look at each of these:

1. <u>Foods</u> — One of our most basic needs and desires is for food. In America,

when we are hungry we eat something. When we are done, we usually walk away from the table filled. Most of us rarely pass up an opportunity to eat, whether it be a light snack or a full meal. The major exceptions to this might be those on a diet, or those so poor they cannot afford food, but for most of us, when we want food, we eat food, it's that simple. To deny our body this yearning for food is very hard but at the same time is a discipline we need to help us master our bodies. If we can master our desire for food we have started down the path to restraint.

There are several types of food fasts. One is where you simply deny yourself certain foods for a time, this could be deserts, alcohol, fast food and the like. The second is to totally skip a meal in a day. The only exception would be water for this type of meal fast. The third and most difficult is the total fast, where all food for a day, week or several weeks is given up.

This is of course very serious and dangerous to your health so must be done with proper medical advice.

The purpose of these fasts is when your body says "I want food now!" you simply reply "No." One of the best ways to help yourself do this is to replace eating with prayer, meditation on Scripture, or study of God's Word. You can reduce your hunger pains and build spiritual strength at the same time. The more you do this, the better you will get at saying "No" to things your body says it wants. You will also learn to cultivate the power of the LORD at the same time by focusing on Him in the process.

2. *Material Goods* — The Bible has much to say about wealth and money.

Here are a few samples:

- "…Watch out! Be on guard against all kinds of greed; a man's life does not consist of the abundance of his possessions." (Luke 12:15)
- "But godliness with contentment is great gain. For we brought nothing into this world and it is certain we can carry nothing out." (1 Tim 6:6-7)
- "For the love of money is the root of all evil." (1 Tim 6:10 (a))

We talked about money in a previous chapter so I won't go into detail here. Suffice it to say, money is a very difficult thing to handle. To deny ourselves material goods can help you gain control of money, rather that it gain control over you. To deny material goods, is to grow in temperance. When we deny ourselves material things, we assert power over these lusts we have for the comforts of life. Many of these comforts we can easily do without anyway. Just because we want it does not mean we should have it. The more we refuse life's material comforts, the more we learn to live without and thus learn to live within. We learn to say no to the pleasures of this world.

3. *Sexual Desires* — Today we live in an "over-sexed" society. We greatly desire the joy of this physical act, and it is believed to be one of our "rights." This is largely based on physical attraction and pleasure gratification. God calls us to higher standards than mere animals that can't control their breeding instinct. We have a conscience and the inborn understanding of right and wrong. In our hearts we know extra-martial relationships are wrong, yet our society seldom admits this fact.

The only arena where God allows this physical intimacy to occur is in the marriage covenant. This is where one man and one woman for one life become one in the covenant of marriage (Gen 2:24). The covenant is between themselves and God. This is the way it has always been from the creation of the world and was always meant to be. This is the greatest intimacy between two individuals.

Sadly, this union has become everything but this, and the joy of sexual union is made to be a right for all mankind. From this uncontrolled passion man has lost his ability to control his sexual drive. We have become products of our own lusts. God has given many deprived men and women up to their own lusts (Rom 1:24-27).

When we say no to the act of sexual intercourse outside of marriage, we agree with God on the depravity of this sinful act **outside** of the marriage covenant, and we grow more in control of our bodies. In the context of marriage, we can do the same. Married couples use many oral birth control methods that allow for intercourse as often as they want but without the consequences of children. When we do this, we lose this opportunity to regain more physical control of our body in the marriage context as well. Family planning methods such as NFP (Natural Family Planning) emphasize the intimacy of the union between man and woman while at the same time accepting the gift of children as a possibility. It also requires abstinence during the woman's fertile part of her cycle.

When we say no to our sexual desires, we say no to our body through our spirit. This is an area where great men have fallen and their inability to control themselves sexually has cost them so very much. We must be in control of our sex drives and not allow them to control us.

4. <u>Words</u> — The hurt caused from the power of words is immeasurable. We cause wounds to others by the many hurtful words we say to them. We must remember that we don't have to say everything we think. Many times wisdom for us would be silence. Instead we speak about things that are of no concern to us, speak without full knowledge of situations or speak with the main intent to hurt the other person. We show little restraint with our mouths.

Nowhere is this more rampant than in gossip. We pass along information about others without even seeking to find out if it is true. We pass information along knowing we would never say this if that person were standing with us. We pass along information acting as if we care about them when we really are just gossiping.

James says this about words and our inability to control our tongues:

"Likewise the tongue is a small part of the body, but it makes great boasts. Consider what a great forest is set on fire by a small spark. The tongue is also a fire, a world of evil among the parts of the body. It corrupts the whole person, sets the whole course of his life on fire, and is itself set on fire by hell." (James 3:5-6)

The analogy to fire is very important. The power of the tongue to destroy is great. It can do this at a distance, it ranges over the whole earth and can't be deflected. You can ward off a blow from an assailant but you can't ward off their words. Once a rumor is started, it spreads with great speed. We must all remember that once a word is spoken it can't be withdrawn. Once it is spoken, it can do great damage. We must also remember that we will answer to God for all of our spoken words.

Some final thoughts on our words;

- Words used to lift up are better spent than those used to bring down.
- When we aren't sure whether or not to speak, most times we shouldn't.
- Finally, we should learn to be better listeners than talkers. We speak far more often than we listen and as a result miss many opportunities . God has given us two ears and one mouth and we should use them in that ratio.

The Discipline of the Mind

We live and become as we think (Pro 23:7). Therefore what we think and how well we think leads us to become who we are. Our worldview is shaped from this. The Apostle Paul said:

"…we take captive every thought and make it obedient to Christ." (2 Cor 10:5(b))

To have a disciplined mind means to put up fences around our mind and severely limit what we see and hear. Jesus said:

"The eye is the lamp of the body and if our eyes are good your whole body will be full of light. But if our eyes are bad your whole body will be full of darkness. If then the light within you is darkness, how great is that darkness." (Matt 6:22)

This is true with pornography and how the sexual instinct is driven so often by the visual. We must be like Job: "Make a covenant with our eyes not to look at a woman lustfully." (Job 31:1) We must not look at material that will seduce us and stimulate our baser instincts. We must monitor what we allow our eyes to see because what we see affects how we think and what we think affects what we do. We must work very hard at this discipline to control the eye-gate or it will control and destroy us.

We must put up fences about what we hear. This is in the form of music, gossip, TV and movies. The music industry is a great example of how we must monitor what we listen to. There is a horrific impact on kids today in the words of heavy metal music, gangster rap, and countless other types of music. So much of what kids listen to today subtly works on how they process ideas. Compare this to the great hymns of the past such as "Amazing Grace" or "Ode to Joy" and how these exalt God and who He is. How powerfully music conditions us to worship God or destroys us through the idols in the world around us. We must guard our ears as well.

We must seek out the wisdom of great men of the past and great thinkers in years past. When we grow in the art of reading great books, we grow in our ability to learn. Today reading classic books is no longer in vogue. Compare this to what C.S. Lewis says about classic books:

> "There is a strange idea abroad that in every subject the ancient books should be read only by professionals, and that the amateur should content himself with the modern books...Now this seems to me topsy-turvy. But if he must read only the new or only the old, I would advise him to read the old ...it is a good rule, after reading a new book, never to allow yourself another new one till you have read an old one in between."[150]

Mortimer Adler includes these thoughts on the significance of reading:

> "...the books that enlarge our grasp of truth and make us wiser must feel, at first, beyond us. They must make de-

mands on you. They must seem to you to be beyond your capacity. If a book is easy and fits nicely into all your language conventions and thought forms, then you probably will not grow much from reading it. It may be entertaining, but not enlarging to your understanding. It's the hard books that count. Raking is easy but all you get is leaves; digging is hard, but you might find diamonds."[151]

Reading encourages thinking. We must be able to discern truth from lies and right thinking from wrong thinking. As Paul said, "…casting down arguments and everything that exalts itself against the knowledge of God." (2 Cor 10:5 (a)) Today countless people exalt themselves and their ideas against the knowledge of God. God had words for these people. He called them point blank "fools." Fools are unwise people who ruin their lives by their bad choices.

In the Bible in the book of Proverbs the word "fool" in used forty five times. God uses it to depict behavior that is unintelligent. It is used in references such as:

- The way of a fool seems right to him but a wise man listens to advice. (Prov 12:15)
- The tongue of the wise commends knowledge but the mouth of the fool gushes folly. (Prov 15:2)
- A fool finds no pleasure in understanding but delights in airing his own opinions. (Prov 18:2)
- Wisdom is too high for a fool; in the assembly at the gate he has nothing to say. (Prov 24:7)
- As a dog returns to its vomit so a fool repeats his folly. (Prov 26:11)

Finally, in Psalm 14:1 it says this, "The fool says in his heart there is no God." Clearly the life of a fool is to be shunned and avoided at all costs. To the foolish they think themselves wise but they are deceived by themselves and their own stupidity and folly. So the task for us becomes to avoid the life of a fool and become wise. This starts by training our mind and disciplining how we think, priding ourselves in the hunger for knowledge and the truth of God. Seeking the advice from wise counsel, searching out history's greatest minds and reading their ideas, and most of all, applying God's truth in our lives. When our mind is cultivated in truth, it is a great weapon for our spirit. When it is not, it is a great tragedy and tool for the enemy. The mind is a terrible thing to waste.

__The Discipline of the Emotions__

We have talked about how deceitful emotions are and how domineering they are toward our actions. Advertisers target our emotions and through them gain access to our desires so we will buy their products. When we gain control of our emotions we can respond to situations or people with much more discrimination and clarity. But how do we discipline our emotions?

The Psalmist David said this concerning his emotions:

> "Create in me a pure heart, O God, and renew a steadfast spirit within me." (Psalm 51:10)

The first thought this verse indicates is the view that our emotions are wired for vice. The desire for a clean or pure heart, emotions that grow us in virtue and holiness, must replace the ones that draw us towards vice and sin. God desires emotions and feelings that are right in us. Ones that are correct and accurate with the way God calls us to be.

Once God creates in us a right or correct set of emotions, the next step is for us to be steadfast in applying these emotions. To be steadfast is to be fixed and firm, not easily swayed or moved. So the prayer is for a heart that would be fixed towards virtue and righteousness, to stay the course. This unwavering commitment to emotional purity seeks a heart that won't give in to temptation easily and one that is guided by God's will and law. To be steadfast and in complete control of our emotions must be our daily desire.

To be disciplined in seeking out godliness means we must first agree with God about wrong emotions and what they are. Here are some vices that God calls us to remove: pride, greed, gossip, slander, coveting, fornication, lying, stealing, love of money and anger.

Emotions are on the frontline of our life and are usually the first response we have to trials. By training in right emotions and ridding ourselves of the wrong ones we enable our mind to think clearly, rationally and logically.

The Disciplined Life

When we train, we need to prepare for the worst that situations or people can throw at us. It is in these times that we must be at our very best. We can't expect life to be easy. Our training must resemble the example used by the military. It trains its soldiers for the worst situations combat can throw at them. The soldiers don't train by heavy doses of lounging and loafing but through strenuous and difficult exertion. They know to be at their best when the situation is at its worst, they must train under those same conditions. We must use their example and train just as hard spiritually.

The goal of training is to make us better. We seek to reform our human system and make it better, to be able to perform tasks we couldn't have done before, to be better than we were yesterday. To do this requires exertion and hard work, so obviously training needs to be designed to be tough and rigorous. It must prepare us for the worst conditions we may encounter in our life. Few people are really ready for the worst life has to offer. Jesus said:

> "Therefore everyone who hears these words of mine and puts them into practice is like the wise man who built his house on the rock. The rain came down, the streams rose, the winds blew and beat against the house, yet it did not fall ..." (Matt 7:24-25)

Notice here Jesus didn't say the rains may come, or could come, but *will* come. He calls us to be prepared for life's worst times. To do this we are called to be strong spiritually in the life. We must do this daily, by seeking to be better today than we were yesterday. We seek out training that will empower us to weather the storms in life. When the storms come, we will be ready for them and be at our very best.

Yet most people don't want to go through the pain or discomfort this requires. In fact they do the opposite, they avoid this type of preparation. So when times get tough and the storms come, they don't do as well. *Training is not supposed to be fun, it is supposed to improve your performance!*

Training is designed to get more out of you: physically, emotionally, mentally and in your will. You must be at your very best in each of these areas in times of trial or you will be at greater risk to sin. How you train will enable, *or disable*, your body to perform in easy or demanding situations. For many people their training does not enable them to become better, in fact it disables them and their future actions. They do this by practicing bad habits in the four areas of the human system. The problem is they don't even know they are doing this. When situations come they now have acquired bad habits from their past. They repeatedly respond in sin and can't break this cycle. They have not been trained to enable themselves to respond the right way, in righteousness.

Training needs to focus on spiritual issues. The greatest growth occurs when we exercise the *internal self* to improve *external performance*. The body can't rise to the challenge alone. The body needs power from the spirit through courage, focus, determination, hope and patience that enable it to rise up to new levels of performance. To meet the tough demands of our daily battle with sin and evil, one must reach deep into one's spiritual resources. The resources we call on are the virtues, which give us power.

Just like the physical training athletes undergo, spiritual training requires a regimen of daily exercise routines. Some of these spiritual routines are prayer, Bible study, meditation on the Word of God, righteous living, godliness, confession of sin and repentance of sin. For top athletes, their exercise routines become daily habits, and top spiritual athletes must make daily habits of their spiritual routines. When this doesn't happen, we just fall back into our same old sinful habits.

Lack of internal training will also lead to confusion on how to "dig deep" in our human system. This is true because there is a lack of understanding on how we function as a person. Internal training seeks internal growth so we can be at our very best in the worst of situations. If we only train our physical body the resources then are just physical and are limited at best. When we unite both body and spirit, we are most effective. Practice and preparation must seek to bond these two elements of the human system.

The spiritual side of us needs to be trained. We must understand how to access our inner strength. We must understand the power that can be unleashed from inside. Finally, we must understand how to train the spiritual side, in tests and trials, not in comfort and calm.

Training is supposed to be hard because tough times will demand you to perform at your best in the toughest situations. If training is easy, you will enjoy it more, but not get much out of it.

Conclusion

Jesus Most Precious

"But what about you?" he asked "Who do you say I am?" Simon Peter answered, "You are the Christ the Son of the Living God." (Matt 16:15-16)

"Therefore, to you who believe, He is precious ..." (1 Peter 2:7(a) NKJV)

Jesus came to earth with one purpose, to redeem humanity (Hebrews 2:14-18). He became man, suffered, died, and rose from the dead so man would no longer be held in bondage to sin. He became the Mediator of a New Covenant to set man free from sin (Hebrews 9:15). To those that believe on His name we are children of God (John 1:12). Children called to live in this newness of life from God unto godliness and virtue (2 Peter 1:3-9). We are called to fill our minds with thoughts of virtue and godliness and to think on these things always (Phil 4:8). We are chosen and called to show forth holiness and virtue to the glory of Jesus Christ who called us to salvation (1 Peter 2:9).

Virtue is the power that flowed out of Jesus in healing the sick, lame, those with evil spirits and even the dead. This virtue that flowed out of Him was seen and known by all the multitudes, and they sought after Him for this life giving power (Luke 6:19). This power that He possessed was to give more than just physical healing, but spiritual healing as well. This virtue is what made Him so precious to the men and women of His day.

The question is, is He precious to you? To be precious to you He must be real. The book you are now reading and the chair you are sitting on are all real to you. Is Jesus that real? Until He is, He won't be precious to you.

C. H. Spurgeon said this about this preciousness of Jesus in the believer's life:

> "Since no sparkling gems or precious metals, no royal regalia, or caskets of rare jewels can ever equal the value of Jesus, the comparison is vain. We therefore place him by himself alone, and say that he is absolutely precious to believers. The diamond is precious; but give a man a bagful of diamonds instead of water and put him in the desert ... he would give all of his diamonds for a draught of pure water to drink or crust of bread to eat; so that, in certain cases, even the excellent crystal would lose its value. In fact mineral substances are merely arbitrary signs of value; they have but little worth in themselves ... But Christ is absolutely precious ... nothing can ever match Him, much less excel Him; and He is precious under all circumstances. Oh my soul, dost thou esteem Him so? My heart art thou sure of this, that unto thee he is precious beyond compare ... Is He to thee essential preciousness, the very standard of all value?"[152]

When we put Jesus' worth, value and esteem at the highest level in our life, when He becomes to us the very reason for our getting out of bed, His virtue flows through us. We will want to serve Him and bring Him glory and praise every minute of each day. He becomes our all in all.

Another way to look at His preciousness to us is to ask, "Who is Jesus in your life?" If He is your Lord and Savior you will do anything for Him. Jesus asked Peter, "Who do you say I am?" (Matt 16:15) Peter answered, "You are the Christ, the Son of the Living God." (Matt 16:16) Jesus responded to him, "Blessed are you Simon son of Jonah, for this was not revealed to you by man, but by my Father in heaven." (Matt 15:17) How we answer this same question determines not only how we live but also what we live for. The life we have lived will be a witness for or against us.

Spurgeon says again:

> "...Christ to be precious; for he 'hath raised us up together, and made us to sit together in heavenly places.'

> (Eph 2:6) 'Our conversation is in heaven; from whence we also look for the Savior, the Lord Jesus Christ' (Phil 3:20) whose Second Advent is to be the perfection of our spiritual life, the unveiling of the hidden beauties and manifestations of the sons of God. Just in proportion as you enter into your royal heritage, and live in it, and believe in it, in this proportion will be Jesus Christ will be precious to you."[153]

The very air we breathe must be the living Christ. The food we eat must be the living bread of Christ (John 6:51). The water we drink must be the living water of Christ (John 4:10). The very faith we have for our salvation must be in the living Christ. Our greatest desire must be oneness to Him in all we say and do. Then we long to be in the presence of the living Christ for all eternity. When He is thus, He is precious to us and His virtue flows in us.

We have maximum impact when we are most delighted in God by knowing, loving and serving Jesus; He is then most precious to us. I close with John Piper's words:

> "God is most glorified in us when we are most satisfied in him."[154]

Bibliography

Andrews, Andy, *The Travelers Gift*, Nashville TN: Thomas *Nelson*, 2002

Aquinas, Thomas, *Basic writings of Saint Thomas Aquinas, Volume Two*, New York: Random House, 1945

Arthur, Kay, *Our Covenant God*, Colorado Springs, CO: Waterbrook Press, 1999

Beckwith, Francis J. and Koukl, Gregory, *Relativism*, Grand Rapids, MI: Baker Books, 1998

Beckwith, Francis, *Politically Correct Death*, Grand Rapids, MI: Baker Books, 1993

Bennett, William J., *The Book of Virtues*, New York: Simon and Schuster, 1993

Bloom, Alan, *The Closing of the American Mind*, New York: Touchstone, 1987

Brother Lawrence, *The Practice of the Presence of God*, New Kensington, PA: Whitaker House, 1982

Bubeck, Mark I., *The Adversary*, Chicago, IL: Moody Press, 1975

Burkett, Larry, *The Coming Economic Earthquake*, Chicago IL: Moody Press, 1994

Carty, Jay and Wooden, John, *Coach Wooden One-on-One*, Ventura, CA: Regal Books, 2003

Chambers, Oswald, My *Utmost for His Highest daily devotions, Volume 2*, Grand Rapids, MI: Discovery House Publishers, 1991

Chesterton, G.K., *Orthodoxy*, Colorado Springs, CO: Shaw Books, 1994, 2001

Collins, Kenneth J., *John Wesley: A Theological Journey*, Nashville, TN: Abingdon Press, 2003

Edwards, Jonathan, *The Nature of True Virtue*, Eugene, OR: Wipf and Stock Publishers, 2003

Foxe, John, *Foxe's Book of Martyrs*, Springdale, PA: Whitaker House, 1981

Gire, Ken, *The Reflective Life*, Colorado Springs, CO: Chariot Victor Publishing, 1998

Guinness, Os, *Fit Bodies Fat Minds*, Grand Rapids, MI: Baker Books, 1994

Hanegraaff, Hank, *Resurrection*, Nashville, TN: Word Publishing, 2000

Henegraaff, Hank, *The FACE that Demonstrates the Farce of Evolution*, Nashville, TN: Word Publishing, 1998

Johnson, Paul, *Intellectuals*, New York: HarperPerennial, 1988

Johnson, Spencer, *Who Moved my Cheese*, New York: G. P. Putnam Sons, 1998

Lewis, C. S., *Mere Christianity*, New York: HarperSanFrancisco, 1952

Lewis, C.S., *Surprised by Joy*, San Diego, CA: A Harvest Book, 1955

Loehr, Jim and Schwartz, Tony, *The Power of Full Engagement*, New York: Free Press, 2003

Luther, Martin, *Bondage of the Will*, translated by J.I. Packer and O.R. Johnston, Grand Rapids, MI: Fleming H. Revell, 1957

Martin, Curtis and Gray, Tim, *Boys to Men*, Steubenville, OH, Emmaus Road Publishing, 2001

Miller, Calvin, *Into the Depths of God* Minneapolis, MN: Bethany House, 2000

Moreland, J. P., *Love God with all Your Mind*, Colorado Springs, CO: Navpress, 1997

Muggeridge, Malcolm, *Christ and the Media*, Vancouver, British Columbia: Regent College Publishing, 1977

Owen, John, *The Works of John Owen Vols 3 &4 edited by W.H. Goold*, Edinburgh: 1850-53

Piper, John, *God's Passion for His Glory*, Wheaton IL: Crossway Books, 1998

Robison, James, *The Absolutes*, Wheaton, IL: Tyndale House Publishers, 2002

Sproul, R.C., *The Holiness of God*, Wheaton IL: Tyndale House Publishers, 1985, 1988

Stanley, Charles, *Walking Wisely*, Nashville, TN: Thomas Nelson Publishers, 2002

Stowell, Joseph M., *Eternity*, Chicago, IL: Moody Press, 1995

Tozer A. W. (Compiled by Warren W. Wiersbe), *The Best of A. W. Tozer, Book One*, Camp Hill, PA: Christian Publications Inc, 1980

Tozer, A. W. (Compiled by Warren W. Wiersbe), *The Best of A. W. Tozer, Book Two*, Camp Hill, PA: Christian Publications Inc., 1980

Warren, Rick, *The Purpose Driven Life*, Grand Rapids, MI: Zondervan, 2002

Willard, Dallas, *Renovation of the Heart*, Colorado Springs, CO: Navpress, 2002

Willard, Dallas, *The Spirit of the Disciplines*, New York: HarperSanFrancisco, 1988

Zacharias, Ravi, *I, Isaac, take Thee, Rebekah*, Nashville, TN: W Publishing Group, 2004

Zacharias, Ravi, *Recapture the Wonder*, Nashville, TN: Integrity Publishers, 2003

Computer References

Barnes, Albert, *Barnes Notes,* Seattle, WA: P C Study Bible (Version 4.3B), Biblesoft Inc, 1988 – 2005

Barclay, William, *Barclay's Daily Bible Study,* Las Vegas, NV: The Bible Library (Version 4.0, DXee, Deluxe Edition) Ellis Enterprises, Inc, 2000

MacArthur, John, *The MacArthur New Testament Commentary,* Seattle, WA: P C Study Bible (Version 4.3B), Biblesoft Inc, 1988 – 2005

Spurgeon, C. H., *Spurgeon's Encyclopedia of Sermons,* Seattle, WA: P C Study Bible (Version 4.3B), Biblesoft Inc, 1988 – 2005

Elwell's Evangelical Dictionary of Theology, Las Vegas, NV: The Bible Library (Version 4.0, DXee, Deluxe Edition) Ellis Enterprises, Inc, 2000

Endnotes

[1] A. W. Tozer, *The Best of A.W. Tozer* Book 2, p155-156

[2] Ibid p 156

[3] Thomas Aquinas, *The Summa Theologica* Volume 2, p 422

[4] Dallas Willard, *Renovation of the Heart*, p 18

[5] Jim Loehr and Tony Schwartz, *The Power of Full Engagement*, p 9

[6] Spencer Johnson, *Who Moved My Cheese?"* p 42

[7] Ravi Zacharias, <u>*I, Isaac take Thee Rebekah*</u> p 122-123

[8] Ibid p123

[9] Barna Research Group survey February 24, 2003

[10] Hank Hanegraff, *The Face that Demonstrates the Farce of Evolution*, p12-13

[11] Dallas Willard, *The Spirit of the Disciplines*, p 3-4

[12] Jim Loehr and Tony Schwartz, *The Power of Full Engagement*, p72

[13] Ibid p110

[14] Ibid p 96

[15] J.P. Moreland, *"Love God with all of Your Mind"*, p 65

[16] Neil Postman, *"Amusing ourselves to Death"*, p vii-viii

[17] Malcolm Muggeridge, *Christ and the Media*, p23

[18] Ibid p30

[19] Neil Postman, *"Amusing ourselves to Death"*, p 31

[20] Ibid p 155-156

[21] Ibid p 155-156

[22] Ibid p 163

[23] Alan Bloom, *"The Closing of the American Mind"* p51

[24] J.P. Moreland, *"Love God with all of Your Mind"* p.88

[25] Jim Loehr and Tony Schwartz, *The Power of Full Engagement*, p. 8

[26] Rick Warren, *The Purpose Driven Life*, p 127

[27] John Wooden and Jay Carty, *One on One* p 21

[28] Jim Loehr and Tony Schwartz, *The Power of Full Engagement*, p. 4-5

[29] These verses talk about entering new life in Christ. It is referred to by Jesus as becoming born again because we receive a new life in Christ.

[30] C.S. Lewis *Mere Christianity* p 158-159

[31] Ibid p 159

[32] Jim Loehr and Tony Schwartz, *The Power of Full Engagement* p 197-199

[33] Ibid p 199

[34] Thomas Aquinas, *The Summa Theologica*, p 426

[35] By eating of the forbidden fruit Adam, and all mankind after him through inheritance, were separated from God. They forfeited and lost their communion with God as once experienced by Adam and Eve.

[36] A.W. Tozer, *The Best of A.W. Tozer*, Book 2, p174-175

[37] Mark Bubeck, *The Adversary*, p. 28

[38] Ibid p 47-48

[39] Neil Postman, *"Amusing Ourselves to Death"* p58-61

[40] Ravi Zacharias, *Recapture the Wonder*, p xv

[41] Ibid p 46-47

[42] Ravi Zacharias, *Recapture the Wonder*, p 5

[43] Ravi Zacharias, Commencement address at Taylor University in 2003

[44] Alan Bloom, *"The Closing of the American Mind"*, p 25-27

[45] Frank Beckwith and Greg Koukl, *"Relativism"* p19-20

[46] Ibid p 20-21

[47] Charles Stanley, *"Walking Wisely"* p.viii

[48] James Robison, *"The Absolutes"* p 75-76

[49] Elwell's Evangelical Dictionary definition on truth (computer)

[50] The law of God is also used this way by Paul in Romans. In Romans chapter 7 the law is the standard whereby man is able to know right from wrong. It is this law that God uses to condemn mankind of sins.

[51] A.W. Tozer, *The Best of A. W. Tozer Book One*, p 43-44

[52] Ibid p 77

[53] Oswald Chambers, *My Utmost for His Highest* daily devotionals Volume 2, April 27

[54] J.P. Moreland, *Love God with all of your Mind* p21

[55] Os Guinness, *Fit Bodies Fat Minds*, p 9

[56] Ibid p 9-10

[57] Ibid p 10

[58] Francis J. Beckwith, *Politically Correct Death*, p21

[59] Ibid p 21-22

[60] Ibid p 25

[61] Ibid p 26

[62] J.P. Moreland *Love God with all of your Mind*, p128

[63] John Owen, *The Works of John Owen,* ed. W.H. Goold, Vols 3 and 4, p 11.347

[64] Rick Warren, T*he Purpose Driven Life, p 17*

[65] Ken Gire, *The Reflective Life,* p. 11

[66] Larry Burkett, T*he Coming Economic Earthquake* p74-75

[67] Ken Gire, *The Reflective Life,* p 19

[68] Ibid p19-20

[69] Martin Luther (Translated by J.I. Packer and O. R. Johnston), *The Bondage of the Will,* p 48

[70] C.S. Lewis, *Surprised by Joy,* p231-232

[71] G.K. Chesterton *Orthodoxy*

[72] Calvin Miller, *Into the Depths of God,* p 16-17

[73] Ibid p16

[74] Ibid p18

[75] Paul Johnson, *Intellectuals,* p 1-2

[76] G.K. Chesterton, *Orthodoxy,* p 53-54

[77] R.C. Sproul, *The Holiness of God,* p 24-25

[78] Ibid p28-29

[79] John MacArthur, *Commentary on the Gospel of Matthew 19:26* (computer)

[80] John MacArthur, *Commentary on Revelation 1:10-17* (computer)

[81] Ibid

[82] Ibid

[83] Ibid

[84] Ibid

[85] Ibid

[86] Ibid

[87] Jim Loehr and Tony Schwartz, *The Power of Full Engagement,* p, 117

[88] Kenneth J. Collins, *"John Wesley, A Theological Journey",* p 41

[89] Ibid p 48

[90] Ibid p 49

[91] Tim Gray and Curtis Martin, *The Transforming Power of Virtue* p 17

[92] William Barclay *Commentary on 2 Peter 2:3-7* (computer)

[93] Ibid (computer)

[94] Kay Arthur, *Our Covenant God,* p 50-51

[95] Ibid p 54-55

[96] Kenneth J. Collins, *John Wesley A Theological Journey,* p 32

[97] Brother Lawrence, *The Practice of the Presence of God* p33

[98] John Foxe, *Foxes Book of Martyrs,* taken from the back cover

[99] Ibid p6

[100] Ibid p8-9

[101] Brother Lawrence, *The Practice of the Presence of God,* p 35

[102] William Barclay commentary on Hebrews 11:1-3 (computer)

[103] Bill Bennett, *The Book of Virtues,* p441-442

[104] Ibid p441

[105] Tim Gray and Curtis Martin, *Boys to men, the Transforming Power of Virtue,* p 52-53

[106] G.K. Chesterton, *Orthodoxy,* p136-137

[107] Andy Andrews, *The Travelers Gift,* p155

[108] Ibid p167

[109] William Barclay, Commentary on 1 Corinthians 13; 4-7 (computer)

[110] Ibid

[111] Ibid

[112] Ibid

[113] Thomas Aquinas, *The Summa Theologica*, p 444

[114] Ibid p 509-510

[115] Ibid p 783

[116] Ibid p 375-377

[117] Ibid p 473

[118] Ibid p 473

[119] A.W. Tozer, *The Best of A.W. Tozer* Book 2, p 180-181

[120] Barnes Commentary on Matt 18:35 (computer)

[121] William Barclay Commentary on Matthew 18: 21-35 (computer)

[122] William Barclay Commentary on 1 Timothy 6:6-8 (computer)

[123] John MacArthur Commentary on 1 Timothy 6:6 (computer)

[124] William Barclay Commentary on 1 Timothy 6:6-10 (computer)

[125] Ibid

[126] Elwell's Evangelical Dictionary on hope (computer)

[127] William Barclay Commentary on 1 John 3:1-2 (computer)

[128] Ibid

[129] William Barclay commentary on Philippians 4:6-7 (computer)

[130] Brother Lawrence, *The Practice of the Presence of God* p 75

[131] John Piper, *"God's Passion for His Glory"* p xi

[132] Ibid p xii

[133] Ibid p 32

[134] Ibid p 32

[135] Ibid p 33

[136] Ibid p 80

[137] Jonathan Edwards, *"The Nature of True Virtue"* p 1

[138] Ibid p 1

[139] Ibid p 2

[140] Ibid p 2

[141] Ibid p 2

[142] Ibid p 5

[143] Ibid p 6

[144] Ibid p 7

[145] C. H. Spurgeon sermon on John 14:16 (computer)

[146] Brother Lawrence, *The Practice of the Presence of God* p 77

[147] Joseph M. Stowell, *Eternity,* p

[148] Ibid p 23-24

[149] John MacArthur Commentary on Ephesians 6:14-17 (computer)

[150] John Piper, *"God's Passion for His Glory"* p 28

[151] Ibid p 29

[152] C.H. Spurgeon Sermon on 1 Peter 2:7 entitled "A sermon from a Sick Preacher"

[153] Ibid

[154] John Piper, *"God's Passion for His Glory"* p 80

About the Author

Steve Beier is married and has 4 children. He has a BA degree from Bowling Green State University and has been the director of tennis at the Fort Wayne Country Club for over 20 years. He has written and spoken regionally and nationally on the topic of Maximum Impact. Steve has studied Biblical principles and sought a deeper understanding of them and how they apply to the world of sports and life. Steve has devoted himself to understanding how physical creatures can have a relationship with a spiritual God. The results have lead him to a deeper life in Christ and a greater passion for God's glory embodied in Christians.

Printed in the United States
66669LVS00005B/1-99